D1554394

Mike Brown

Enjoy

THE DREAM BOWL

Where Goodman, Ellington, and the Grateful Dead Convene

With Profiles on: John Coltrane, Johnny Cash, Sonny Rollins, and Bob Wills

Michael Amen

Ideas into Books: Westview®
Kingston Springs, Tennessee

Ideas into Books®
W E S T V I E W
P.O. Box 605
Kingston Springs, TN 37082
www.publishedbywestview.com

Copyright © 2019 Michael Amen

All rights reserved, including the right to reproduction, storage, transmittal, or retrieval, in whole or in part in any form.

ISBN 978-1-62880-124-8

First edition, July 2019

The author gratefully acknowledges permission to reprint quotations and lyrics as listed beginning on page 281.

Front cover photo of The Dream Bowl by Rick Allen Rice. Used by permission.

Good faith efforts have been made to trace copyrights on materials included in this publication. If any copyrighted material has been included without permission and due acknowledgment, proper credit will be inserted in future printings after notice has been received.

Printed in the United States of America on acid free paper.

THE
DREAM
BOWL

Contents

The Dream Bowl

It was hard to miss the Dream Bowl if you were a kid in a car on the highway between Napa and Vallejo, California, during the mid-fifties. Having the open mind of a child, I was free to take in the surroundings as we went down the road, driving past it often on trips to visit my maternal grandparents, who lived in Vallejo.

I have fond memories of those delightful excursions: stoic grandfather, sweet grandmother, a toy box whose contents didn't add up to much but because it was in someone else's house amounted to more than it was, like the food that tastes better at a sleep-over. In the small front yard was an arbor with clinging honeysuckle whose nectar in each trumpet bloom was irresistible and which, miraculously, I learned from my sister Paula, still survives. Then there was the nearby malt-shop where I annoyed employees by repeatedly playing Little Richard's *Jenny Jenny* on the juke box, railroad-tracks close by where a passing train was still an exciting thing, and the adjacent Callen little-league field (still in use) which seemed bigger-than-life to me, all of which contributed generously to my imagination.

On return trips home from this stimulating change of scene, I'd see the Dream Bowl again, this time more closely from the side of the road nearest its location. The questions stirred from seeing it initially were restored and reinforced. There the dance hall stood—lonely, I thought at the time—in a large field by itself where only weeds beyond its expansive and unused parking lot competed for attention. I noticed its stark white paint, its marquee, its arched roof, and most of all its great size. What was that building for, I wondered? What had happened within its walls? The passage of time would eventually demonstrate to me, in emphatic manner, that a great deal had happened and more would happen beyond those mid-fifties sightings.

The Dream Bowl was the idea of Gene Traverso and John Zanardi, and its builder was a man named Walter Polley. The property on which it was constructed was purchased from the Greenwood family whose name can still be seen on the Greenwood Road street sign which intersects South Kelly Road near Hwy 12. Traverso and Zanardi were boyhood friends, a friendship that continued into adult life, and they went on to become successful business partners. With family help, they pooled their resources, took a risk, and the construction of the Dream Bowl began. It was scheduled to open in December of 1941—on December 7th as it turned out—but because of the bombing on Pearl Harbor, its opening was delayed. When shortly thereafter it did open, there followed an incredible run of top acts until the Big Band era began to lose steam. As the years passed, the expense of maintaining a large traveling band became prohibitive, and general interest steadily declined with the increase and popularity of home entertainment systems, especially television.

Following these developments, Country and Western music came in to fill the void, and a second chapter of the Dream Bowl story began in the mid-fifties that lasted until 1968 when it suffered a similar fate of changing interests. The shortest and final chapter lasted less than two months, when Bay Area and local Rock bands performed early in 1969. This time, in more accelerated fashion, the difficulty of running a music venue demonstrated itself yet again.

It is the efforts of the musicians that bring vitality and history to any venue, so a good deal of the focus of this book is on the musicians themselves, their highlights and their life stories which accompany them wherever they perform. I wanted to use as a subtitle the phrase "A Celebration of Music," but it would have cluttered the front cover. The idea of that subtitle, however, remains a central one in the construction of this book.

In February of 1969, I was lucky enough to see, on separate nights, both the Grateful Dead and Santana, and in doing so personally experienced several memorable hours from the great compilation of performance time that accumulated over the twenty-eight years of the Dream Bowl's existence as a music hall. In the world of entertainment and performance, this venue—this building—has to be seen as hallowed ground where some of the great names in music left their mark and sent out songs and melodies that rubbed off on all those who came through its doors. Those sounds were also absorbed into the materials of its creation. Here then is our cave of modern ritual, without the etchings and other life expressions found in ancestral counterparts. What we do have, however, are memories scattered everywhere, layered over by the passage of time, hoping to be given voice. In the opening line of the February 24, 1973 *Napa Register* article, *Memories of the Dream Bowl,* by Pam Hunter, she quotes Gene Traverso who said, "Oh, if that building could only talk." Well, I think it *is* talking, but you have to put your ear intimately close, and undertake patiently, as in archaeology, the tedious but rewarding work of bringing those voices to the surface.

The building itself still stands where echoes and traces of its livelier past are buffered and concealed by sensible renovation. Cordoned off by current office-space uses, it now houses a company, Caltest, which according to its web page profile "...is a specialized commercial environmental analytical chemistry lab focusing on analyses of regulated pollutants at low levels in water." I was graciously allowed a walk-through of the building and sadly only a fraction of its impressive overhead arches still remain visible above what is now the maintenance section, which formerly was the stage area where bands assembled. The fact that the building is still alive and standing allows me the absurd notion that like the Uptown Theater and Opera House in Napa, and the Empress Theater in Vallejo, it too could be beautifully restored. Purposeful workers could remove the tacked-on flooring that covers the original maple. They could get rid of the office cubicles and lowered ceilings so that the arches might be seen again in their fullness, inviting beautiful sounds to rise again to be absorbed by crossbeams already rich in their historic intake and anxious to function once again, naturally, within the intention of their original design. In the meantime however, we can amuse ourselves by going back to its real design-fulfilling heyday of music and dance.

The field in which the Dream Bowl stood was off Highway 29 near the Napa Airport, roughly mid-way between Napa and Vallejo. With an eye toward quality presentations, the roof was arched so that pillars, which would have been an obstruction of one's view and would also have been an obstacle on the dance floor, would not be required. The size of its maple hardwood floor (70 feet wide by 140 feet long) made the nightclub, when it opened, the largest in Northern California. It was described at the time as a "cavernous" ballroom, in keeping with the expansive measure of the dream its creators entertained and saw to completion. For comparison, college and professional basketball court dimensions are 50 by 94 feet; so as one can see, the dance floor had plenty of room for interested parties. Photographs show occasions when every square foot of that great expanse was covered with dancers.

In Pam Hunter's account of the Dream Bowl in her 1973 article in the *Napa Register*, she reports: "From 1941 to 1954, big band members…arrived for one-nighters at the stage entrance of the Dream Bowl. They came by limousine, bus, train and plane for a four-hour show in their journey through hotels, ballrooms, restaurants and nightclubs all across the nation." When I read this, I was intrigued by the fact that she included "plane," as a means of transport; at first glance, it struck me as an extravagant option for a traveling band from that time period, but then again the Napa Airport was very close by (only one mile away), and it might have been a cost-effective move during these very successful years.

When I first saw the impressive run of performances cited in Midge Lund's and Kiki Chiotti's book, *The Musicians: A Chronicle of*

Vallejo Bands 1920-1949, where they recount the names of some of the bands that played the Dream Bowl between 1941 and 1949, I could scarcely believe it. In chronological order, these were: Cab Calloway, Gene Krupa, Alvino Rey, Tommy Dorsey, Jack Teagarden, Count Basie, Freddie Slack, Stan Kenton, Jimmy Dorsey, Erskine Hawkins, Louis Armstrong, Jimmie Lunceford, Duke Ellington, Jan Savitt, Bob Crosby, Les Brown, Henry Busse, Harry Owens, Harry James, Joe Richman, Woody Herman, Freddy Martin, Dude Martin, Xavier Cugat, Russ Morgan, Benny Goodman, Charlie Ventura, Lionel Hampton, and Lawrence Welk.

Pam Hunter went on to say in her *Register* article that, "In '63 after the lull that followed the fading of the big bands, Country/Western moved into the Dream Bowl under the management of Black Jack Wayne. Names like Merle Haggard, Johnny Cash, and Tex Beneke dominated the marquee for a few years before the Dream Bowl heaved her final breaths." For the most part that is true, but it leaves out that final brief chapter, and there is a great deal more to talk about before we come up the years to the hall's final period.

As the Dream Bowl was set to open in autumn of 1941, World War II was uppermost on the minds of Americans. Hitler's invasions began in March of 1939. No one knew what the outcome of the war would be, and there was little cause for optimism, either for individuals or for the nation as a whole. A reluctance to involve ourselves in the war after the tremendous loss of life in World War I, was changed after the attack on Pearl Harbor. Several people I talked to for help with this book recalled, without prompting, blackouts during World War II when everywhere, lights would be turned off. My mother, among the people remembering these events, told me about the eerie silence that befell San Francisco when the entire city gradually wound down to utter quiet and darkness. Can you imagine?

The urgency of the war years brought people together in a mix of suppressed fear, a desire to keep hope alive, and a real need to courageously hold one another up. Couples were looking for something romantic to do with their time because a loved one might be shipped out the next day, and it might be the last time ever for them to be together. So the initial irony—an uncomfortable one—that a night-club built for entertainment and pleasure opened after bombs fell on Pearl Harbor, is adjusted in our minds because, as time went on, the value—we could say the necessity—of such an establishment became more clearly realized and appreciated. To have a place, an outlet where one could come to hear music, to dance, to congregate with friends, and to have one's mind, if just for a few hours, taken off the war and its consequences, and let's just say it: *dream*, was of great value. For providing a venue in which that important diversion might happen, a debt of gratitude is owed to Gene Traverso and John Zanardi.

While it goes without saying that the partners intended to make money, it's important also to recognize that this was bargain entertainment at its best. *The Musicians: A Chronicle of Vallejo Bands 1920-1949* tells us that "Admission was $1.10, with ladies and servicemen admitted for 55 cents...." Along with going to movies in which popular big bands often appeared, a night of dancing and music at a ballroom continued to be a viable option for entertainment—helped by the still-vibrant influence of radio where many of the big bands could be heard. Live broadcasts from shows were not uncommon at a time when televisions were not yet a prevalent fixture in American homes. Other stars that drew crowds at the Dream Bowl were Guy Lombardo, Sammy Kaye, Frank Sinatra, June Christy, Jo Stafford, Rosemary Clooney, Kay Starr, and Shep Fields.

As was said, the building is still standing and is still in use, a fact that speaks to the stability of its original construction. Gene Traverso, the son, told me that so solid was the foundation and flooring, that years later tradesmen observed that it was of sufficient strength to support a second story, if one was wanted. We get the picture of a floor that supported easily the step and movement of dancers, while its smooth wood finish allowed for, if you had it in you, the graceful sliding of feet and the sway of bodies in tandem which, propelled by the music, lasted—one dance form to another—from 1941 to 1969.

The article by Pam Hunter refers to a nine year "lull" between the close of the Swing Era (1954), and the beginning of the Country/Western period in 1963. As we'll see later, it was actually a four- to five-year lull. All my trips to Vallejo, then, would have taken place somewhere between approximately 1954 to 1959, which spanned my ages 7 through 12—an eternity for any kid. It was a time during which scheduled events were few in number, so my memory that there didn't seem to be much happening turned out to be right. Still, all those sightings from the car happened during the day. Not available to me, at that point in my life, was any concept of a night-life during which the club would come alive.

Years later, I had the good fortune to meet with co/owner John Zanardi's daughter Louise, who told me that she remembered helping her father hang posters, when she was young, to advertise upcoming shows, and I do recall two rare sightings of such posters: one for Fats Domino and another for Johnny Cash, hung on telephone poles near the venue, circa 1957. Still, long stretches went by during which no posters were hung, no flyers were sent out, and no name appeared on the marquee, whose vacancy dramatized in a sad way the inactivity of this one-building ghost town. That was my impression at the time. As to its current circumstance in that triangular sector of land exactly one mile in length on its longest side, you can pick your sentiment: 1) the building these days is no longer alone in the field, or 2) it has lost its singular status, surrounded as it is at the time of this writing by sixteen neighboring structures that now fill up the area and block it from view. It needs to be emphasized that that corridor between Napa and Vallejo during the fifties had very little development on either side of the highway, with just a few structures here and there, making the big white building east of Hwy. 29 that was the Dream Bowl highly noticeable.

That "lull," mentioned by Hunter was, however, a long way off from those days when big bands and Swing were at the high point of their popularity. The extent of that popularity is brought home in *The Musicians: A Chronicle of Vallejo Bands 1920-1949* where we are told that the same performers that came to the Dream Bowl also played in Vallejo at the Casa de Vallejo and other music venues in town: "The residents of Vallejo were fortunate to hear and dance to these well-known orchestras. Not to be outdone, the local musicians formed big bands of their own. Carrying over from the thirties were the existing bands of Ted Muller, Hal Hay, George Lambro, Lou Boss Jr., Joe Pallotta and Keith Kimball." The book goes on to list fourteen new Swing bands, in addition to those just mentioned, that were formed in Vallejo in the 40s, with an average of eleven band-members each. Twenty Swing bands in Vallejo! I was astounded by this discovery. These incredible statistics show that at the time, the music was very much alive and well.

In an addendum to *The Musicians: A Chronicle of Vallejo Bands 1920-1949*, longtime Vallejo musician and President Emeritus of the Vallejo Musicians Union Gene Gelling offers his "reflections" on the book from a musician's point of view. Gelling talked with Midge Lund, who co-authored the book, and they both saw "…musicians as a specialized group…with their own expressions…" when talking about those moments when everything came together smoothly. "Cookin' or ridin'," says Gelling, when:

> A solo artist retreats into that little world all his own… chords flow along easily, embellishments weave in and out around the melody and you hear a composition being born on the spot. On an 'up' tune the drive can be tremendous. On a slow number the figurations can astonish you to the point you almost forget to breathe. Those things are never planned. They just happen.

Benny Goodman

In looking at the impressive list chronicled in *The Musicians: A Chronicle of Vallejo Bands 1920-1949* of performers who played at the Dream Bowl, we find quality bands that demonstrated night in and night out, that they were capable of getting into the "flow" that Gelling talked about so eloquently. The band among them that became the most famous nationally was the Benny Goodman Orchestra.

For my parent's generation, the Swing bands were a major part of the musical background of their time, attested to by their widespread popularity. In ballrooms, in movies, or on radio, exposure to this music was part of one's everyday experience. My parents were born into the roaring twenties, and grew up in the decade that was referred to as the "Jazz Age." That exciting age and its excesses ended with the stock-market crash on Wall St. in 1929 followed by the Depression lasting another decade and more, but somehow Jazz survived. It survived because people scrimped and saved so that they might buy a record or go to a show, because now the music served as a release from hardship brought on by tough economic times. The Jazz of the Swing bands accounted for much of the profits in the music industry, which grew from ten million in 1932 to fifty million in 1939 and became as popular as it would ever be. It provided a valuable backdrop to World War II, a touchstone as it were, a strong link between the events and the music that came out of them, which remained firm in the minds of those who experienced that ordeal.

It was not however, part of the musical background of my youth during the mid-fifties, so for me this music was brand new and for that reason it was one of the more captivating listening experiences to which I gave attention. With repeated listening sessions, it struck me that this music was energetic, well-composed, capable of producing many moods, and performed with great skill.

Popular bands earned the recruiting power to attract the best musicians, and because there were so many talented musicians in Goodman's band, a significant number of them went on to successful careers of their own. Among these are drummer Gene Krupa, trumpeter Harry James, and vibraphonist Lionel Hampton. Other notable band-members were the innovative guitarist Charlie Christian; pianists Teddy Wilson and Jess Stacy; and Fletcher Henderson who was acknowledged as a skilled arranger and had been a band leader of an all-star cast in his own right during the previous decade. It was he who was responsible for the techniques that were foundational for arranging that many of the big bands would make use of in the years that followed. Because his importance was often overlooked, Henderson was the subject of the book: *The Uncrowned King of Swing*, by Jeffrey Magee. Meanwhile Goodman—with the help of Henderson and the band members—reached the point with great effort where he actually did come to be known as the "King of Swing."

There are no reports of Goodman being an easy man to work for, but that proved beneficial to the listening audience as they would always experience a well-prepared unit up there on the bandstand. In a PBS documentary, various band members talked about being on the road. Singer Helen Ward recalled a logistics nightmare of lengthy backtracking, playing engagements in Meadowbrook, New Jersey; Rocky Mount, North Carolina; and Manahoy, Pennsylvania on successive nights. Jess Stacy claimed they "…played fifty one-nighters in a row…" which, when I first heard it, sounded like exaggeration; but I was convinced when vocalist Martha Tilton said of a two-year stretch, that the band: "Never had a night off; not one."

Goodman was always looking for ways to improve the band, and worked tirelessly to expand his own musical development as well. He wanted the great drummer Gene Krupa for the band and successfully recruited him. Pianist Jess Stacy reports that he had a gig playing in a "...gangster joint..." in Chicago in which, unbeknownst to him, Goodman had seen him play. Goodman contacted him shortly thereafter because he had been impressed with his skills, and over the phone asked Stacy to come to work for him. Stacy didn't believe it was for real. He said, "Are you kidding me. Somebody's putting me on. If you're Benny Goodman, send me a wire or write me a letter, [he pauses] which he did." I found it amusing that this scenario of skepticism leading to a missed connection repeated itself when, at a later date, Benny called Lionel Hampton who was in California at the time, to ask him to join the band. In his autobiography (with James Haskins) Hampton recalls that his trombonist, Tyree Glenn (by Hampton's account, a practical joker), "...tells me that Benny Goodman's on the phone...so I just ignored Tyree. Over the next week or so, Tyree kept shouting 'Benny's on the phone from New York,' but I thought he was joking." Things were finally worked out when Lionel's fiancée Gladys, answered one of Benny's calls.

The band got some early exposure on the NBC radio show *Let's Dance* in 1934. Still a regular on the show in early 1935, they would perform after bands led by Xavier Cugat, and Kel Murray, on the last spot on the broadcast at 12:30 AM. In an interesting turn of events, this less-than-ideal broadcast time that was too late for most people on the east coast, would help them—as we'll see—in the months that followed, because in May of that year, the band would hit the road. There was a strike at this time at Nabisco, which sponsored the show, and because of this the show was cancelled. Soon after, the band got work at Manhattan's Grill, but it did not go well there. The Goodman Orchestra was filling in for Guy Lombardo, and the crowd expected the "sweet" music for which the Lombardo band was known; Goodman's band was a disappointment for those in attendance.

As the tour moved across the country, poor receptions continued. By August 1935, Goodman found himself with a band that was nearly broke, disillusioned, and ready to quit. This assessment is backed up by comments from band members, and Goodman himself in the documentary. According to pianist Jess Stacy, at their first gig on the tour in Lansing, Michigan, there were eighteen people in attendance. Making matters worse was the fact that the interested parties that night were all local musicians; it made the failure all the more stinging. A similar failure awaited in Denver. Goodman admitted at this point that he was "…about ready to give up the ghost." It's something of a miracle that the troupe stayed together because they weren't locked as a group on a bus, as many bands had done, but instead caravanned in several cars which made the scrapping of plans much easier. It's not clear from the documentary if Goodman was all in on calling it quits, and then, after talking it over, reconsidered, but Jess Stacy does say he pleaded with Benny to continue traveling "…over the mountains and see what happens…" all the way to California. They did indeed press on to California, a decision from which many would benefit, for it proved to be a pivotal moment in the band's history.

It turns out that the seemingly unfortunate time slot on those NBC radio shows was just right for folks out on the west coast. They were therefore primed for the music when the band arrived to perform it in person, and were apparently more accepting of its comparatively harder edge. However, the Benny Goodman Orchestra didn't exactly run the table on their trip west either. After Jess Stacy's comments on his plea to continue on to California, he said there were 10,000 waiting for them when they got to the Palomar Ballroom in Los Angeles, California. Stacy might have also commented on the previous night's engagement in Pismo Beach, but if so, it was not part of the documentary. The disappointing response to the show at Pismo Beach had temporarily shaken their collective confidence, which had been uplifted the previous night by very enthusiastic crowds in Oakland, California, at McFadden's Ballroom. The people in attendance at Oakland bested the crowds at Palomar that happened two nights later, and they represented the first groundswell of fandom that would rapidly grow in the months that followed.

What was it like to have been there? In a 2009 article in the *San Francisco Chronicle*, Jesse Hamlin talks about those early performances and revives comments about the exciting performance at McFadden's by Herb Caen, well-known and long-time columnist with the paper. He was in attendance that night, and had this to say:

> From the first note, the place was in an uproar. Krupa riding his high hat like a dervish, James puffing his cheeks till surely they must burst, those saxes playing like one, the rhythm always burning and churning and driving you out of your mind, and then, just when you thought nothing could get hotter, Benny's clarinet rising like a burnished bird out of the tightly controlled maelstrom and soaring to the heavens, outscreaming even the crowd."

In that description, Caen explained the impact and power of the band as it begins to ride the crest of its creative strength. He conveys an insider's take on the lofty levels achieved by the musicians that evening, beyond his acknowledged skills as a writer because, as pointed out in another *Chronicle* article by Paul Wilner: "...Caen used to sit in with local combos displaying his talents as a drummer, as well as a master of the three-dot item." Caen captured vividly the excitement of that night and gave us a sense of the band's sizeable potential in an early stage of its fulfillment.

In every account however, it is evident that initially, at that defining moment two nights later on August 21, 1935 at the Palomar, the band, a bit unsure of itself, was reluctant about "...soaring to the heavens..." right at first. They opened with subdued "stock arrangements purchased on the trip," which drew tepid response. We have to remember that Goodman and the band members were still smarting from the previous night's poor response in Pismo Beach. According to Willard Alexander, the booking agent for the band at that time, drummer Gene Krupa said, "If we're gonna die, Benny, let's die playing our own thing," and this is corroborated by Goodman's background voice in the documentary, where he can be heard to say in regard to that moment: "Let's play what we know, let's go for broke." So they went instead with arrangements by the aforementioned Fletcher Henderson and Spud Murphy, livelier ones no doubt than those "…stock arrangements…" with which they began, and it was to this more authentic rendering that the 10,000 who came, joyously and excitedly demonstrated their approval.

Months earlier, the west coast had benefitted from the NBC broadcasts. Now the favor was being returned west to east and all points in between, as the Palomar shows were sent out live on the radio across the nation. A popular movement was under way; critical mass heaped on the momentum begun in dramatic fashion by the 10,000 at Palomar. As the documentary follows the snowballing enthusiasm the band was receiving from avid fans, Tony Bennett comments that: "People dancing in the aisles was something new." And "dancing in the aisles," would become a long standing go-to phrase used by commentators in describing an exciting performance by a band.

The Goodman Orchestra's popularity grew quickly to such an extent that Benny and his band members no longer had to worry about being accepted, a very liberating experience for any musical group in any era, regardless of type or size. An exclamation point to their widespread appeal takes place three years later, on Jan. 16, 1938, in what can be seen as a coronation of their level of achievement when they performed at Carnegie Hall.

On that occasion, however, there would be new considerations beyond the summit of their popularity; they found themselves having to prove their worth as if at a first audition because of the historical weight and reputation that was Carnegie Hall. Was it not America's most famous proving ground for serious music? In the minds of the musicians that night then, something more than popular entertainment was called for, and it was admitted by various band members that everyone was nervous. As they stood collectively in this tense state about to take the stage, the ice was broken by Benny's brother, bassist Harry Goodman, with his mock commandeering call to: "Follow me."

The occasion asked that they demonstrate to a nation why this music called Jazz deserved serious consideration, and for that task they were thrust into the role of representatives. There was a lot at stake, because if they did put in a winning performance, it would help to ensure a successful future and at the same time bring honor to the Jazz heritage in its entirety; the way the concert was set up shows they were thinking along these lines. I think it's fair to assume that no one was more sensitive to the enormity of the moment than Goodman himself, with his deep conviction that Jazz, like classical music, deserved serious consideration—an opinion supported by the fact that he had involved himself in crossover projects playing and commissioning classical pieces at various times during his career.

Irving Kolodin, the band's booking agent who worked on the Carnegie project, provided a captivating account of the events before, during, and after the concert, which served as the liner notes for the original recording. Involved in the planning of the event, he explains, apologetically, that the first part of the show: "Twenty Years of Jazz," was his idea. He feared that the idea "…probably caused more trouble in listening to old records and copying off arrangements than it was worth," but the effort was made to give listeners a sampling of developments from its earliest days up to the present moment. "For a little freshness…" said Kolodin, new arrangements by both Fletcher Henderson and Edgar Sampson would be included in the lineup of songs for that evening. A jam session was included in the first half of the concert that involved members from the equally important Count Basie and Duke Ellington bands together with Goodman personnel.

As to the viability of a pure concert, without dancing, Kolodin knew that it had already been done successfully a few times. In his liner notes, he observed that: "Nightly at the Pennsylvania Hotel (now the Statler), the number of those who stood around the bandstand, or sat at tables listening, far outnumbered those on the

15

dance floor." Still in the planning stages, he was gathering up testimony to assure potential backers that it would be a success. He was thoroughly convinced the program would succeed, but it's interesting to note that Goodman didn't share his confidence, evidenced by the fact that he didn't think getting tickets would be a problem. Kolodin tells us (in a dignified spin on scalpers), that Goodman "...had to patronize a speculator..." in order to get tickets for family members who had decided in the last week that they wanted to attend. Benny never dreamed it would sell out.

Owing to the uniqueness and importance of the event, a sense of decorum held sway as the evening unfolded. There had to have been present regular patrons of Carnegie who might otherwise not attend a Jazz concert but had sufficient interest to have a look since it was taking place in their own back yard so to speak; they were perhaps willing to let their hair down slightly for the occasion. The other portion of the ledger might be numbered by those more accustomed to letting their hair down at dancehalls, but who, on this night, committed themselves to keeping their locks neatly in place and in the process helped bring about warm feeling at the half-way place of their meeting, adding in some measure to the success of the evening. Kolodin quotes, but does not name, a "...critic of the Times... (who next day wrote, 'When Mr. Goodman entered, he received a real Toscanini send-off from the audience.')" Further indications of this cooperative attitude are found in Kolodin's own comments on the show-stopping performance of "Sing Sing Sing:" "I don't suppose that Louis Prima, who wrote the tune, was around Carnegie Hall that night. It is not often that Bach or Beethoven is rewarded in Carnegie Hall with the hush that settled on the crowded auditorium as Jess Stacy plowed a furrow—wide, deep and distinctive—through five choruses of it."

A word about Kolodin: Once upon a time, I responded to a very attractive subscription offer, and one of several bargain choices I selected was the magazine *Saturday Review*. This was pure dumb luck as I knew very little about the magazine. I would come to the opinion quickly, after an issue or two, that I had made a worthwhile investment. Norman Cousins was its editor, who added to his notoriety by writing *The Anatomy of an Illness*, a book which recounts his recovery from a debilitating condition (after a series of failures with traditional treatments) in which laughter, he discovered, played a key role in his improvement. Working for him on the magazine was a very talented group of contributors who covered a variety of topics on art and culture. It was not uncommon to have a respected writer doing a review of another fine writer so that the review in itself was an elegant expression inspired by the quality of the work under review.

Beginning in 1947 and lasting beyond three decades, Kolodin wrote regularly for the magazine, and distinguished himself by being one of the first critics to focus on, and write a book about, recorded music. *A Guide to Recorded Music* appeared in 1941. Born in New York City, Kolodin was a tough task-master with a sharp wit. He wrote informed reviews on both classical and jazz recordings and performances, working for the *New York Sun* for eighteen years and for *Saturday Review* for thirty-five years, earning the respect of his colleagues and having a very successful career as a critic who was particularly influential during the decade between 1950 and 1960.

In the photographs I've seen, Kolodin is impeccably attired in well-tailored suits; with pipe in hand, he conveys a dignified presence. It is altogether fitting then, that a man of his stature was on hand so as to give an account of what took place on this very significant evening for Jazz.

"Daddy, what's this?"

Had it not been for Benny's daughter Rachel asking that fateful question after rummaging around in a closet in their home, where she found a pile of recordings, a fuller accounting of the events of that evening would never have become available to a larger audience as the original recording offered only a portion of what was performed. And as for those performances, surely all the elements for a magical night were in place, but there are never guarantees in this regard. Luckily, the fates obliged both in its unfolding, and in its preservation. After Goodman counted off "Don't Be That Way," Kolodin says: "From then on, one climax piled on another."

For me, hearing this music as I did, some twenty years after the time of its performance, was memorable on several levels. It was a joyous family occasion, mixed, I think, with the gravity of the moment at Carnegie that finds its way to us through the music—most dramatically by the piano whisper of Stacy during his wonderful solo, which forces you to come closer where you are then held captive for the dramatic finish to their "show-stopping" "Sing Sing Sing."

By the time Goodman and his orchestra came to the Dream Bowl after its 1941 opening, it was still a very popular band that had undergone many changes in its lineup, and had seen the inevitable departure of many of its more famous members. While it was no longer possible to see the Goodman Orchestra all-star line-up play together, patrons of the Dream Bowl could still take advantage of all that talent spread out in new clusters. These new groupings afforded them additional perspectives of the individual musical ideas these talented men now showcased as bandleaders themselves. I'm talking about Harry James, who formed his own band in 1939, and Gene Krupa, who formed his in 1938, just two months after the triumphant performance at Carnegie Hall. Both of them came to the Dream Bowl prior to Benny's own appearance. Then there was Lionel Hampton with his own group who always brought excitement whenever and wherever he performed, and added, after Goodman, his name as a band leader to the historic lineup that performed at the venue.

Thanks to the wonderful world of YouTube, some of these performances can be seen. There also exists a two-CD set of the Carnegie Hall Concert which offers nearly everything (thanks to daughter Rachel) performed that evening, and the music captured on the recordings of this significant moment in history would be a great addition to any collection. It is very thoroughly compiled, and since much of the material in this box-set was previously unreleased, there are insightful notes from Turk Van Lake, who played with Benny in the 50s and 60s. Van Lake, at age nineteen, was one of those who attended the concert. There are also comments by Phil Schaap, who had much to do with the restoration and re-mastering of these important recordings.

Goodman did achieve much acclaim, but I think his skills and love for the music still may not have been fully acknowledged in the manner he deserved. He was not flamboyant and his appearance might have suggested banker more than swinging musician, but this is an ideal moment in which to avoid judging a book by its cover. He wanted black musicians in his band because they were talented men, and he didn't care if prejudiced people didn't like it because he was a decent (albeit occasionally cold) man and the music came first. He, along with Teddy Wilson, Gene Krupa, and Lionel Hampton made up a quartet that was a separate feature to the full band, and which was one of the earliest integrated combos to ever perform live.

At the Carnegie concert, the quartet came out to perform three songs at about the half-way point of the evening. One of them was the Gershwin brothers' "I Got Rhythm," which they performed at breakneck speed. I have to believe that the triumph here was enriched beyond the very-demanding musical one because of what it stood for socially, and man! did they raise the roof in the process.

From Ken Burns' *Jazz*, in episode five, "Swing: Pure Pleasure," a quote is narrated from a *New Republic* magazine article by Otis Ferguson, who writes:

> They played every night and they made music you would not believe. Not a false note; one finishing his solo and dropping into background support, then the other. All adding inspiration, until they get going too strong to quit. This is really composition on the spot, and it is a collective thing, the most beautiful example of men working together to be seen in public today.

Other performances of the same song exist on YouTube, some with Jess Stacy in place of Teddy Wilson, and they're certainly worth a look see. One in particular (running time 3:53) is from some sort of TV network gathering of invited guests including singer Peggy Lee, who earlier had been a vocalist in the Goodman band, comedian Alan King, and other celebrities. The energy developed by the quartet is so jacked-up that the rather inhibited and stiff gathering is eventually overcome and can no longer sit still in their seats; it is truly wonderful stuff.

The Goodman Orchestra on that night really left an important mark, most dramatically with "Sing, Sing, Sing," which showcased everything the band was capable of doing. It's long running time, over twelve minutes, allowed for all the differing moods the arrangement offered. Several solos were taken, all of them great, and the ensemble passages were delivered powerfully and were kept energized by drummer Krupa's relentless drive. It was the first time I experienced a musical piece of such eye-opening length. Kolodin tells us it was during the performance of "Sing, Sing, Sing" at Palomar that fans went wild over the instrumental tour-de-force for the first time. That response demonstrated why the piece quickly became the rousing finale, frequently used, to bring shows to an end.

Vocalist Helen Ward recalled in the documentary that on a performance of it one night, Krupa "refused" to stop playing, forcing the band to crank out more choruses which (I'd like to think), was a factor in it becoming the extended piece it was. And lastly, with respect to its performance on January 16, 1938, Kolodin had this to say: "At this concert, with the end of a hectic evening in sight and no lingering concern about the success of the program, the band seems to be playing at last for its own pleasure only, with rather remarkable results." Indeed so, Mr. Kolodin, indeed so.

I've had enough opportunities to verify what I remembered as a great evening by checking it against the vast history that exists in recorded archives, to know that sometimes my memory is unreliable. I also believe there is reward for being in attendance at a live performance, because even an incredibly good home sound system cannot match the powerful PA and elaborate stage setups typical in large arenas, nor can it provide the added elation of a group experience. For the Carnegie Hall performance by the Goodman Orchestra that January night in 1938, however, there is ample evidence that those in attendance were dazzled and uplifted, and recorded evidence demonstrates they had every reason to be. This is the state in which I make concerted and continuous efforts to locate myself. These remarkable moments are gratifying, inspiring, and life-affirming, and that is why my wife and I attend as many concerts as we can.

Beginnings

Human beings are very good at listening to music. Personally, I love the experience of seeing and hearing a musical performance. Wall Street traders would greatly envy the return on investment I experience when I listen to an inspired piece of music, if it could only be made available to them. Very little is required to reap the benefits music generously provides. The only thing anyone needs to do is pay attention.

That we have the capability of being deeply moved by music is fascinating. The raw tools of our senses are great gifts we have been given: the wonderful receiving and delivery systems that are our ears; the incredible processing center between them; and outside them a host of musicians, men and women, providing the captivating sounds that pour in. Our amazing sensory equipment—geared precisely for music appreciation—can be enhanced further by an active and interested mind. Before birth, the capacity to hear is with us at twenty weeks, and after birth our ability to familiarize notes and organize sounds begins early. There is no shortage of evidence demonstrating our skill in this area.

Daniel Levitin, author of the 2006 book: *This is Your Brain on Music*, is a neuroscientist who beforehand worked as a session musician, a sound engineer, and record producer. These skills struck me, when I first heard him interviewed on radio, as ideal qualifications to be a valuable teacher for the things I hoped to address in this book, and, as an added bonus, I discovered when reading his book that we had listened to and liked a lot of the same music.

For starters, with regard to our capabilities to hear and understand music, Levitin says: "Music listening, performance, and composition engage nearly every area of the brain that we have so far identified, and involve nearly every neural subsystem." He then specifies that "The brain extracts basic, low-level features from the music, using specialized neural networks that decompose the signal into information about pitch, timbre, spatial location, loudness, reverberant environment, tone durations, and the onset times for different notes (and for different components of tones)." And while we do not all have the ability to sing on key, Levitin tells us "A majority of people in our study— nonmusicians—were able to sing songs within 4 percent of their nominal tempo."

A single note has many tones and the one with the lowest frequency is the called the fundamental and all others are called overtones; descriptions that reflect in a straight-forward way the spatial relations of lower and upper frequency ranges, and the beauty we know that's possible within such structure. Levitin points out that "The brain is so attuned to the overtone series that if we encounter a sound that has all of the components, except the fundamental, the brain fills it in for us in a phenomenon called *restoration of the missing fundamental.*" A note is not "trumpeted," into our brains in merely mechanical (hydraulic or pneumatic) manner, but is given shape and interpretation by our unique physiologies and minds. Factors of infinite variety make up the neural patterns and pathways carved by our experiences early on and are continuously modified thereafter, which explains why a song might affect us differently after the passing of time.

With respect to the development of a musician's skill and the mood-enhancing effects brought to a musician, Levitin adds this personal observation: "…if I'm playing an instrument I like, and whose sound pleases me in and of itself, I'm more likely to pay attention to subtle differences in tone, and the ways in which I can moderate and affect the tonal output of my instrument. It is impossible to overestimate the importance of these factors; caring leads to attention, and together they lead to measurable neurochemical changes."

The evidence is that most of us (90% it is said) take advantage of this natural ability to enjoy music. Thank goodness for that, because to be so supremely equipped, and not make use of such a gift seems almost sinful, so my passion regarding the value of music appreciation and celebration makes what follows an undeniable case of preaching to the world's largest choir.

As for my own placement in the world of music, I came into it in 1947. Looking at all the music that was available from that time to the present is to witness a rich mixture of various styles, some that continued to develop, and others that emerged brand new. I was fortunate enough to hear good samples of the music from my parent's generation: the Swing bands and the popular singers of their day from records, radio, movies, and television variety shows. The Swing era was followed by the Be-Bop era in Jazz, which I began to pay attention to in the early 60s along with other styles that came after: Hard-Bop or Post-Bop with Sonny Rollins, Art Blakey, Horace Silver and others. Then there emerged the "birth of the cool" with Miles Davis, Gerry Mulligan, and Stan Getz, and that was followed by the Avant Garde with Ornette Coleman, Cecil Taylor, John Coltrane, Albert Ayler, Charles Mingus, and Eric Dolphy. Those names constitute only a small sampling of the many musicians associated with those genres which I reference with reluctance, since there is so much in Jazz one should not attempt to categorize.

With respect to the music of my generation, I like to think I had a head start thanks to my two slightly older sisters, Paula and Shirley, who watched Dick Clark's American Bandstand religiously, had top-forty radio going much of the time, brought home 45s that they (and I) played to death, and who were on top of the music scene in that unmatched way only teenage girls can be. I'm sure some of that enthusiasm rubbed off on their pest of a brother who always wanted to hang around with the big kids.

As for recording technology, we were just beginning to come out of the dark ages. 78 rpm records were still available, but were on their way out. Record players had speed ranges of 16-1/2, 33-1/3, 45, and 78. One was supposed to be able to play a stack of records, but this could be risky business. The clunky mechanisms would sometimes fail, and if, for instance, it failed on the first occasion, the tone arm and needle would come down on the turntable itself. Sometimes a second or third record would drop along with the one that was supposed to, and chaos would ensue. Better systems were available, but in our house it was through modest home equipment that my sisters and I heard and saw the birth of Rock and Roll, along with the more adult music to which we were exposed.

Of crucial significance, in all of this, was the fact that my mother played piano (and cello when she was in high school), and without exception, instilled in her children an appreciation of music. She also instructed us when we were quite young as to how it worked, sitting patiently with us at the piano, explaining and demonstrating just what was going on. This experience was of the utmost importance. Daniel Levitin tells us that neuroscience has shown that "The brain undergoes a period of rapid neural development after birth, continuing for the first years of life…basic structural elements are incorporated into the very wiring of our brains when we listen to music early in our lives." Completing this family of music lovers in our home was our younger sister Lynda, a gifted singer/musician who still performs, lending her pure voice and guitar skills—along with those same talents from Kathleen Potthoff, Dawn Rose, and Mark Lawson—to the beautifully blended harmonies of the local Napa band Sweet Burgundy.

In the late 50s, Paula and Shirley teamed up with another pair of sisters from Napa, Janet and Diane Pierson, to form the Trim Tones. They entered local talent contests as a quartet, singing Andrew Sisters style harmonies on songs like "Moonglow," "Picnic," and "Sentimental Journey," while my mother accompanied them on piano. They sang beautifully, and had the double advantage of the close harmonies of siblings. I remember being thrilled to see them up on stage at the Napa Fairgrounds and proud because they were my sisters. I count it as a great gift that I was party to these experiences, and I welcomed music, which was an enjoyable and ever-present accompaniment to my life during these formative years. It would remain so with ever increasing enjoyment and appreciation as my life went forward.

As an introduction to these chronicles, I don't want to mislead anyone into thinking that ours was the ever-happy household. It wasn't, and my parents ultimately divorced, my mother sacrificing (as married people were more apt to do in the 1950s), her chances for happiness so as to keep the family together. But these facts do not detract from those moments of enjoyment, and if anything they enhance what I now fondly re-capture. On rare occasions at our home, my mother would play piano along with one of my father's co-workers who could play saxophone and clarinet, and there'd be enthusiastic singing.

The joy inherent in these musical moments was apparent early on, but the fact that there could be something beyond that experience, something magical, was demonstrated to me by our next-door neighbor. He happened by one day, not long after he and his family had moved in. This probably occurred on a weekend as I remember everyone was home and he came to the open front door, to say hello in neighborly fashion. My mother was playing the piano, so I'm sure (as you'll see) he was drawn by the music. He was invited in, and in short order was singing along with the rest of us. Now, this man had a very inhibiting speech impediment, and struggled mightily in conversation, but he sang fluently with apparent ease. I would come to understand later that, appropriately enough, this man was a musical-therapist, and was living testimony to—and a dramatic embodiment of—the therapeutic value and enriching possibilities that music, in unique fashion, could provide.

Rounding out these entertaining moments involving music were times when another of my father's friends (from his days growing up in Lincoln, Nebraska), Ronnie, a long-haul truck driver, would bring a delivery to northern California, and stay with us a day or two until his next job. With him he brought great records from his collection of Swing bands, and his considerable dancing skills. These skills were accommodated for by the old-fashioned technique of clearing the living-room furniture as far to the side as possible, and putting on the music. He needed some room because he was a big man—big and tough-looking—but he loved to dance and he was good. I'm reminded of the fact, one I noticed in the 50s and 60s, that tough guys had no qualms about singing and were often in school choirs, which says something about music's disarming effects. In *The Rest is Noise*, Alex Ross's thorough investigation of music in the twentieth century, I found support of this idea: Ross says, "The New York Police Athletic League reported (in the 1930s) that singing classes had proved surprisingly popular among juvenile delinquents; the boys were suspicious at first of this 'sissy stuff,' but soon were singing out at full strength."

So there in our living-room, and these circumstances accompany my hearing Benny Goodman for the first time, we had what I think was the most ambitious hoedown our street had to offer, with feet flying everywhere in sync with the music pouring out of our little console. Swing music, it should be remembered, was tailored specifically for dancing. I was able to get an idea of what it must have been like then, to have the larger experience of being able to actually dance with one of those great Swing bands right in front of you at the Dream Bowl. My older sisters, teenage girls then, took turns as jitterbug partner to Ronnie, and loved it. I remember nothing but smiles, and why not? There was music and dance in the house and it was good. I like to think that had an advanced alien research team been hovering above Fairview Terrace just east of the Napa Fairgrounds with their sensitive scanning equipment, they would have detected from 10 Hoffman Avenue a force-field that registered on their sensor screens a healthy spike indicative of the enthusiasm within, displayed as a fiery glow radiating out from walls and windows. With hindsight I can see the great value of those experiences.

There may be no accounting for taste, but I think you can account for someone having an interest in the creative process involved in artistic endeavor. I've already talked about the importance of the nurturing environment that, as I grew up, was firmly in place for a life of music appreciation, but I think this was helped by other factors as well.

I was born in Napa at Parks Victory Memorial Hospital. One memory of that hospital is of the ether mask approaching my face before I went down for the count (and we did count backwards; remember?) for what was the near-automatic tonsillectomy that children of 1950s vintage experienced. And having recently read in Tom Robbins' *Tibetan Peach Pie,* that he lost a younger sister in 1939 because she had been overdosed with ether, I'm much more appreciative of the fact I made it through. Another memory, reinforced as I grew older, was of the dreary architecture of the building, but Parks Victory was, more importantly, a building of function whose existence was the result of generous efforts by doctors and concerned citizens. Its less-than-cheerful facade was more than offset by the good works happening inside: the stilling of pain for patients in general, and in particular, assistance administered to a young mother, my mother, giving birth that fourth day of February, 1947.

With respect to the mystery of why something affects us deeply, and to the "…other factors…" mentioned a moment ago, I offer the following: I consider myself a fortunate individual who was twice favored by circumstance.

First, I would not be here at all if my father, who earned a Purple Heart, had not fought to stay alive, digging his fingers into the ground (he would tell me years after the fact), because he felt death upon him after being hit by shrapnel during WWII in the battle of Hurtgen Forrest in Germany. It came to be, therefore, that I was the outcome of what must have been, at least for a time, the happiest of occasions: couples re-uniting after the war.

Secondly, in my embryonic state, I represented the yet-to-arrive other gender that families often hope for. And to these factors I would add the collective mind-set, not to be discounted for anyone born in the late '40s, that in general was more positive and optimistic, as a result of the comparatively prosperous economic period following WWII, when Americans felt better about their standing in the world.

I'm a firm believer in personal responsibility for the development of one's own good fortune, but salute with reverence and humility these facts of formation that lend themselves, I'm convinced, to cheerful outlook and disposition. I think these bits of fate add good measure to the psychological endowments and physical apparatus conducive to music appreciation with which nearly all of us are by birthright granted, and which we make use of much of our lives.

In her article recounting the history of the Dream Bowl, Pam Hunter did not talk about any of the Rock bands that came there during its final period; the article made it sound as if the Country and Western bands were the last ones to perform there. Granted, there was not much of a sample size, nor much in the way of documentation, but I was there for two concerts, so I have at least two eyewitness accounts with which I'm quite familiar. My own experience at the Dream Bowl came in February of 1969, during a moment very near those "final breaths" to which Hunter referred. What I witnessed, however, were new breaths; musical voices from San Francisco, that were fire-breathing and powerful in their emergence, and, as it would turn out, long and lasting in their influence: The Grateful Dead and Santana. Opening for the Grateful Dead was a local band from Napa called Amber Whine. We'll talk with one of Amber Whine's founding members, percussionist John Hannaford, in a while, who'll tell us about his Dream Bowl experiences.

The Grateful Dead made a powerful and lasting impression that 22nd day of February, 1969. It was the second time I was in the presence of amplified music, and this time at much closer range, as the first occasion had been an outdoor concert. Their sound system was amazing, their concept was strikingly new, and they were serious about delivering their music with as much intensity as was possible for young men with electric guitars and amplifiers to do. That is to say, the mission was accomplished with colossal force. I recall these things reliably because my mind, on this occasion, was not altered by so much as a sip of beer. I already had an abiding interest in music, and because of that memorable night, the search for that element of magic for which I'd already been given a small taste, would from that point on, be one of increasing demand.

I'll say more about the Grateful Dead later, but before we get too far from Benny Goodman, I need to talk about having heard a radio program, the title of which was "Grateful Dead in the Gone World." It was an offshoot of either "The Deadhead Hour," or "Dead to the World," (shows I listened to regularly) both hosted by David Gans, and was part of a fund raiser for radio station KPFA. So I'm listening to the program, and those shows typically featured plenty of live performances, and I start hearing the Carnegie Hall version of "Sing, Sing, Sing," which fades out, then in comes a jam from one of the Dead's live performances, then back to the Goodman Orchestra, and so on with an emphasis on those sections featuring the percussion of the Dead's double drums, and the driving beat continuously provided by Gene Krupa which crop up intermittently from both bands. This was a highly entertaining and surprising moment for me since I was a fan of both bands. I don't recall—or may have missed—any introduction concerning what was about to be played, and I thought the mash-up worked beautifully. I began to wonder about the program's genesis.

Sometime thereafter, I did some landscaping work for the retired Head of the Solano Community College English Department, Kathy Rosengren. Earlier, I had taken a literature course at SCC that had been under her direction, and she was gracious enough to take a look at what I was working on for the book at that time and gave me some valuable guidance. I had mentioned the Goodman/Dead combination segment I'd heard on the radio and she suggested that I make an effort to get in touch with the people who had put the show together. I took her advice and remain grateful that I did. First I emailed David Gans, explaining to him what I was working on, and asked him about that particular show. Gary Lambert was a person who had been involved with a number of Grateful Dead-related activities for radio including several interviews, and who also became the editor of the *Grateful Dead Almanac*. Gans, in an email reply, thought Lambert had been the instigator in this sordid affair, so he passed along my query to Lambert.

I had concluded my letter by saying (and asking): "I am seriously involved in trying to honor these and other related musical efforts in this book. I would greatly appreciate any recollections you might have regarding what made you think that these two bands would be interesting to place side by side. I loved it." In short order, I received a very generous response from Lambert in which he went out of his way to provide me with an account that was loaded with interesting and entertaining facts. It was everything I could have hoped for, and more. First, he told me that it had been done before "…in the early 70s, on a…radio station in Pittsfield, MA, the late, lamented WGRG." His brother Glenn worked at the station, and later worked for KSAN in San Francisco, and took part (I remembered seeing him) in "…several broadcasts of Grateful Dead shows, including the Closing of Winterland." Lambert explained that "The GD/BG connection took root in our minds…after a particularly amazing Dead show…at the Capitol Theater in Port Chester in November of '70." His brother, with him that night, asked after the show: 'Y'know what the music reminded me of tonight?' "And without a moment's hesitation, I said, 'The Benny Goodman band, from around 1938?' 'Exactly!' my brother replied." He then explains how it came to be that he and his brother were synched-up in this sentiment:

> When we were growing up in Queens…around 1961 or '62, I'd guess, our parents took us to see the King of Swing…at a short-lived Bronx amusement park called Freedomland. And so I found myself right up against the stage ('on the rail' in Deadhead parlance), at the feet of King Benny the Good, for my first real live Jazz experience. From that night on, I was hooked on live music—a healthy addiction that fully flourished in my teen years…and peaked with the introduction of the Grateful Dead into my life.

I got quite a kick out of and could relate to his appreciation of live music and the fact that it had taken root. So also, with his confession that seeing Jerry up close "evoked a familiar feeling of joy and wonder very similar to the one I felt gazing up at Benny Goodman when I was 10 years old. …sometimes, seeing Garcia peering over the top of those wire-rim glasses with twinkling eyes, I imagined that he *looked* a little like Benny!" He concludes by saying

> …later, when we came across a great live 'Good Lovin'' on a bootleg LP, it seemed only natural that we'd both detect echoes of Gene Krupa's epic solo from 'Sing Sing Sing.' I don't think those echoes were mere coincidence, by the way: Mickey Hart has always cited Krupa as one of his earliest drum heroes; and when I had the pleasure of working on the first Planet Drum tour in 1991, one of the highlights was bringing the show to Carnegie Hall, where Mickey was thrilled to realize that his drum kit was going to occupy the same spot on that hallowed stage that Krupa's had on that fabled night more than five decades earlier. I wondered out loud how it would sound to crossfade Krupa with Mickey and Bill, and

Glenn decided to give it a shot on the air. Worked like a charm. So when David and I were coming up with ideas for the KPFA marathon years later, I thought it was an idea worth reviving.

So, thanks to the Lambert brothers for producing that invigorating revival, and thank you Gary for providing essential information. In a related Goodman/Grateful Dead experience, my wife and I, in May of 2011, attended a fund-raiser in behalf of the Marin Symphony that was held at the Marin Veterans Memorial Auditorium in San Rafael, California. In a companion book for sale the night of the event, the development of the program we were about to enjoy is talked about in detail. The book's cover, fit for the occasion, was adorned with a tuxedoed skeleton conductor, and proclaimed, from top to bottom: *"First Fusion—A New Renaissance"* "Marin Symphony presents First Fusion—A Symphonic Collaboration with Bob Weir & Very Special Guests—Featuring the Music of the Grateful Dead."

The evening brought together lovers of the symphony and lovers of the Dead, and I'm happy to report, the place was packed. The guest conductor with whom Bob Weir collaborated was Giancarlo Aquilanti. According to Nicholas Meriwether, who edited *First Fusion*, Aquilanti earned a "...Master's degree in composition from California State University Hayward...a doctorate in composition at Stanford (and)... is now the director of the school's music theory program." As for the handling of the compositions chosen, Weir said, "I introduced Giancarlo to the Dead's M.O., which is state a theme then take a little walk in the woods. He got that pretty quick, so that's the approach we used."

Aquilanti commented that, "I didn't know him personally, so I didn't know what to expect. But I was really impressed at how knowledgeable he is not only of that particular kind of music, but music in general. His suggestions, and the comments he had about my orchestrations and about the form, were always very thoughtful." Aquilanti used the computer program "Finale," which provides a sonic model; a close approximation of how an orchestration will sound, so that together they could go over the material and make improvements. "So I'd play these for Bob," Aquilanti said, "we'd spend hours and hours together up at his house. He'd listen and he'd give me some feedback and we'd go back and forth."

The collaboration then, in terms of the make-up of the audience, and the presentation of a different style of music in a place where classical music was the norm, was reminiscent of the scenario at Carnegie Hall that took place in January, 1938. The performances were wonderful, and the spirit of cooperation and extra effort for the occasion was palpable with all participants (sixty-eight musicians and fifteen vocalists), enthusiastically doing their part for the good cause that it was.

About the time of my graduation from High School (1965), my mother married George Simmons, a very decent and generous man. He had lived in a house right where Kelly Road intersects Highway 29. A small cozy home was also on the property which, when we were young, was temporarily home to all but one of the four children our mother had during her first marriage. As their wedding approached, George had a new house built on that same property which was very close to the Dream Bowl. That intersection—so near the dance hall that I had passed those many times in my youth—was now a place of permanent proximity for our family where many parties, holidays, family re-unions, weddings and farewells would take place. Adding to the growing regard and fascination I'd had for the old place, was the fact that now the Dream Bowl had become a neighbor as well.

I want to mention here a brief encounter that will become more meaningful when I start talking about the great Duke Ellington. Please just file away the following account for later: Because of its closeness to both a major road and highway, it was not uncommon for motorists needing direction or experiencing car problems, to pull off near our highly noticeable bright green house and ask for help which George would frequently provide. My mother told me a bittersweet story about an elderly couple who sought help one night, but not of the typical sort. They came to the door, and inquired about the Dream Bowl. They were dressed very nicely and they had come to recapture a lovely evening shared there many years ago, and they were quite disappointed to find it closed.

The Dream Bowl was not grand in appearance from the outside, but pleasing enough within, and like Parks Victory Hospital it was an un-fancy building of purpose. Its name however, in the architecture of elucidation, was a stroke of design genius, perfectly capturing the essence of 1940s affection with big bands, dance and romance. And wasn't *that* what that couple had come back hoping to find? What that couple wanted, I'm convinced, was to rekindle the captivation and enchantment suggested in that name, a name ideal for summoning love's refrain. Who knows, if you just go to this dance, maybe some magic would actually take place, and you would in fact meet that girl or boy of your dreams. Too syrupy you say? Not so. Louise (Zanardi) told me it was true that many servicemen from all over the country met girls at the Dream Bowl and for that reason wound up settling down here to begin lives with their sweethearts.

In an effort to flesh out those people normally found in the "Acknowledgements," which I fear often gets passed over, I want to talk about the events that went into the development of this book as we go along. In the quest for this story and the finding of facts, I was first led to Guido and Rosey Colla by my mother. They were friends, and they ran into one another at a restaurant; by chance, the Dream Bowl came up in conversation. My mother knew I was interested in its history, and arranged a meeting in her home. That meeting with the Collas, whose long life together had its beginnings at the Dream Bowl, marked the beginning of this book. They told me that they went to the Dream Bowl during their courtship. Guido served in the military during WWII, and after that met Rosey in 1946 and they were married two years later.

What they told me that night brings home just how vibrant music and dance were throughout the U.S. at that time, and especially in Northern California, as they recalled venues in Boyes Hot Springs, in Rio Nido along the Russian River, where they saw Lionel Hampton and Count Basie. There was also the Memorial Auditorium in Sacramento, Sweets Ballroom, the Ali Baba, and McFadden's in Oakland, and the Casa de Vallejo where they were entertained by Bob Crosby (Bing's brother) and the Bobcats.

As for their experiences at the Dream Bowl, they recalled hearing about events on local radio. The shows took place on the weekends, and lasted until one in the morning. There was a full bar, they said, but minors were welcomed, and they surprised me by reporting that underage people were stamped on the hand, something I thought to be a more recent invention. The various groups performed from a raised stand at its southern end and they recalled that there was not an in-house master-of-ceremonies, as each band took care of that on their own. When I asked about memorable performances, they recalled Alvino Rey with the King Sisters, and the Jimmie Lunceford Orchestra, who impressed many that had heard and seen them perform, as time will show.

Alvino Rey was a stage name the Oakland-born Alvin McBurney took on to take advantage of the Latin music craze in New York where his career as a musician began to take off. Hired by Gibson Guitar Corporation in 1935 to help develop pickups, Rey had also done pioneering work in amplification and is a figure guitar geeks would find fascinating as he was that very rare animal: a guitarist who was also a big band leader. He developed the "talking guitar" effect, which helped keep him in demand as a studio musician. While there have been a number of different ways to bring about the effect, many of us have heard a version of it, if, for example, you remember from *Frampton Comes Alive*, Peter Framton asking the very enthusiastic audience at Winterland in San Francisco with his guitar: "Do you feel-----like we do?" You may also have in your collection that great recording *Blow by Blow* on which Jeff Beck does the same thing on his instrumental version of the Beatles' "She's a Woman," or Joe Walsh's "Rocky Mountain Way," and there are other examples. Once again I found out that a technique that I thought my generation could lay claim to, had been in existence for a long time, in this case, since 1939.

The talking guitar had a gimmicky appeal that helped Rey become popular, but his success wasn't just because of the gimmicks. He was a very skilled musician as well. Adding to the good fortune of his career was the fact he met the singing King Sisters on a radio show and they joined forces in more ways than one. The King Sisters: Alyce, Donna, Luise, Marilyn, Maxine, and Yvonne sang very well, and each had Hollywood glamour to go with their sublime voices. Alvino and Luise fell in love, got married and remained together until Luise's death in 1997, the year of their 60th anniversary. The sisters had ties to the Bay Area, as they performed on radio in Oakland, and auditioned for the position vacated by another popular female group, the Boswell Sisters, at radio station KGO in San Francisco. With Alvino Rey's distinctive guitar sounds and the dazzling King Sisters fronting the band, it's easy to see how a lasting impression was made on the Collas and others.

It was a great start, with the aid of a bit of luck, to be able to meet and talk with the Collas. Helping to ensure that the effort be kept alive, Guido suggested at the end of our time together that evening, that I get in touch with Vallejo musician Babe Pallotta whose number he found for me in the phone book right on the spot. Happenstance, as I've tried to gather information for this book, has been my friend often enough to make me recall something mythologist Joseph Campbell talked about on more than one occasion in his lectures. He frequently quoted Arthur Schopenhauer, and from an interview with Michael Toms recounted in the book *An Open Life*, Campbell says:

There's a wonderful paper by Schopenhauer, called "An Apparent Intention of the Fate of the Individual," in which he points out that when you are at a certain age—the age I am now [Campbell was in his 80s]—and look back over your life, it seems to be almost as orderly as a composed novel. And just as in Dickens' novels, little accidental meetings and so forth turn out to be main features in the plot, so in your life...And then he asks: "Who wrote this novel?"

It had always been the case at the Dream Bowl that it was a venue where you could see local bands along with those of national prominence. Love of music, and its appreciation, brought together a wide variety of individual band members and fans all circling around one another in a weave of living stories.

Babe Pallotta was a member of one of those local bands, and I had the privilege of meeting and talking with him about his musical career shortly before his passing in May of 2006. When I met him, he had respiratory problems and had to use an oxygen tank but otherwise seemed perfectly fit, with lively, intelligent eyes, good cheer, and gentlemanly manner. Later I would see pictures of Babe when he was in his twenties. He was a handsome man, and had preserved those handsome features and pride in appearance. He was a sharp dresser and still had some dark strands of what must have been, when younger, a head full of jet-black hair. He told me he began playing accordion when he was eight years old. Several relatives helped him learn music, including his father who also played accordion. He eventually joined his older brother Joe, a drummer, who formed his own band.

According to *The Musicians: A Chronicle of Vallejo Bands, 1920-1949*, Joe tried to earn a spot in the Al Chester Band from his home town of Crockett, and in one of my favorite lines from the book, they report: "Trying out for this group, Joe was told he played too loud, and being miffed, decided to organize his own band, using his relatives to form a combo." Over time, this grew to a twelve-piece orchestra for whom "Work was sporadic at first, but by 1941 the orchestra started a 25-year run of steady work, an incredible record for a local band."

An interesting tie-in to Napa and Vallejo histories is the fact that Babe, as reported by the *Vallejo Times Herald*, played baseball for the Napa Merchants in 1942 before being drafted into the army; he also played at the Turf Club during timeouts at 49ers games at Candlestick Park during the eighties, where in person I saw them and heard their crisp orchestrations swirled around by the ever-present winds of Candlestick. Babe told me that also playing in the Joe Pallotta Band for a time was blues guitarist Roy Rogers—who grew up in Vallejo and played with blues legend John Lee Hooker who also made his home in Vallejo for a few years—and trumpeter Marvin McFadden, another local musician who has also played with Huey Lewis and the News. And speaking of the News, Johnny Colla, a founding member of that same band, is the son of Guido and Rosey. On Feb. 7, 2008, my wife and I attended a Vintage High production of Miss Saigon, in which our granddaughter Caylie sang and danced. In the pit orchestra was none other than Marvin McFadden on trumpet and flugelhorn. Caylie's father, Mike Soon, is a chemist working for Caltest, which houses its offices in a building where, once upon a time, music and dance took place. They called that place the Dream Bowl.

Babe told me that they won a battle-of-the-bands competition and became the "house band" for the Dream Bowl, and he recalled times when they would work as many as five engagements in a single day. I asked him about his own recollections as a listener. Were there bands that performed at the Dream Bowl that stood out? The band that impressed him the most was Jimmie Lunceford and his Orchestra. His face became more animated as he thought back. He mentioned that their musicianship was of very high quality, as was their presentation.

In an essay by the late Ralph J. Gleason, critic and author, he talked about being impressed deeply by the Lunceford Orchestra, first as a young man, and later as a life-long fan. Gleason said, "The songs were all played, regardless of their simplicity or complexity, for dancers, basically. After all, these *were* dance bands and, except for its one brief tour of Europe just before World War II broke out, I doubt if the Lunceford band ever played a concert. They played dances and they played stage shows; the concert era for big bands came a good deal later." This is an important observation.

While Gleason was attending Columbia University, a fellow student had played him a Lunceford recording, and he flipped, becoming an instant fan. It was a great pleasure to discover that he, a man whose work and person I greatly admired, had written about Lunceford in *Celebrating the Duke*, a portion of which I read in the compilation *Reading Jazz*. His passion for the music, so strong at that age, comes right off the page:

> They used to appear on blue-label 35 cent discs every couple of weeks at the bookstore on the Columbia campus—two sides, 78 rpm, and you had to be there right on time or the small allotment would be gone and you would have missed the new Jimmie Lunceford record. If you were lucky you got one, ran back to your room in John Jay or Hartley Hall, sharpened your cactus needle on a Red Top needle sharpener, the little sandpaper disc buzzing as you spun it, and then sat back in ecstasy to listen to the sound coming out over your raunchy, beat-up Magnavox.

As regards the Lunceford band, and the performing style of the time, Ralph Gleason added this:

> True big band freaks, of whom I was one, were absolutely dedicated to the Lunceford band. It had—and still has—a very special place in the memories of those who date back to the Era of Good Feeling of the 30s, when the big bands symbolized a kind of romance and glamour and exotic beauty long gone from the world of entertainment... and when I got to the Big Apple and found that you could actually get to see a band like this in person at the Apollo or the Savoy Ballroom or the Renaissance or the Strand or Paramount theaters, I simply couldn't believe it. It was just too good to be true.

For people from Napa and Solano counties, the Bay Area, and beyond, the Dream Bowl was that place where those same bands and performances could be experienced, and where one could be part of what was "just too good to be true."

A bit more needs to be said about Gleason, who was born in 1917 and lived until 1975. I became interested in him because his name just kept popping up in the printed material to which I'd been drawn. I couldn't help but notice from those excerpts cited above, the urgency with which Gleason, the exuberant student, retells his dorm-room activities, and although his demeanor was quite laid-back, his level of interest in music, demonstrated in his long career as a journalist, never relaxed over time. It was one of several reasons why I held him in such high regard. His work would be of considerable importance as he always seemed to be part of the vanguard able to tap into and accurately report valuable changes as they unfolded in Jazz, in Rock, and elsewhere.

I found him to be a reliable guide for those things that proved to be worthwhile, and I was equally impressed with both his appreciation and celebration of music. In April of 1966, I started subscribing to the Jazz magazine *down beat* (to which Gleason was a contributor), and before that had been buying it off the rack since February of 1964. In the early 60s, Gleason hosted a quality TV show called *Jazz Casual*, filmed at KQED studios in San Francisco. In addition to his work as a critic and journalist, he had helped organize both the Monterey and Berkeley Jazz Festivals. Especially endearing for me was the fact that in his commentaries on music, he was one of the first, if not *the* first, Jazz critic to take seriously the things that Rock bands were doing, and there were many aspiring musicians, particularly in the Bay Area, who deeply appreciated Ralph's influence in bringing respectful consideration to what they were trying to accomplish.

In their 2017 50th Anniversary Year issue, *Rolling Stone's* Andy Greene talked about the magazine's "…nine major…" interviews with Bob Dylan over the years, saying: "*San Francisco Chronicle* columnist Ralph Gleason was one of the first critics to recognize the singer's immense talent. 'Genius makes its own rules,' Gleason wrote in 1964. 'And Dylan is a genius, a singing conscience and moral referee as well as a preacher.' Three years later, when Gleason and Wenner started a new magazine, they named it largely in honor of Dylan's "Like a Rolling Stone." In similar manner, Gleason had given Johnny Cash his first review by an important critic, praising a performance of his in 1956.

Rolling Stone editor Paul Scanlon, in his Introduction to *Music in the Air—The Selected Writings of Ralph J. Gleason*, quotes Gleason from an article in *American Scholar* from the year 1967:

> 'Forms and rhythms in music are never changed without producing changes in the most important political forms and ways.' Plato said that. 'For the reality of politics, we must go to the poets, not the politicians.' Norman O. Brown said that. 'For the reality of what's happening today in America, we must go to Rock 'n roll, to popular music.' I [Gleason] said that.

When I read that, it made me think of a Bay Area radio personality who went by the play-on-word name Travus T. Hipp. The host of a talk-show, he was a savvy observer of the political scene, and would always say, when callers asked what they should be reading, that "I don't recommend books, I recommend Rock 'n roll." It was apparent however, that both these men were quite well-read, but as with caricature, you exaggerate to draw attention to important aspects of the subject at hand. I had first heard Hipp on AM radio, but he went over to FM (KMPX then KSAN) in the early days of underground radio which was happening in 1967, so it occurred to me that Gleason was probably listening to Hipp, and Hipp was probably reading Gleason in the *SF Chronicle*, and elsewhere.

Both men, I would add, did pioneering work in the early days of Rock. Chandler Laughlin III, Hipp's real name, in addition to his work in radio, was a key figure in the swirl of activity that took place, famously, in Virginia City at the Red Dog Saloon with the band The Charlatans. The shows at the Red Dog, which began in June of 1965 and ran for six weeks, were a model for the ballroom/concert scene that came about in San Francisco. They involved, for the first time, both the poster art advertising the event and light-shows accompanying the music. Gleason was one of the first respected critics to take an interest in, observe, and report on what was happening.

In a special addition to the *SF Chronicle* about the 2013 opening of the SF Jazz Center, Paul Wilner (who commented earlier on Herb Caen), was talking about "…the Bay Area's vibrant, and eclectic, Jazz tradition. And the late *Chronicle* Jazz critic Ralph J. Gleason served as a tireless guide and cheerleader for West Coast sounds. When the '60s came around, Gleason led the charge for the San Francisco sounds of the Jefferson Airplane, the Grateful Dead and their wild and crazy contemporaries, adhering to Duke Ellington's admonition that all great music is 'beyond category'." I was still very much interested in Jazz but was becoming equally interested in Rock, and I can assure you, there was considerable snobbery in evidence in the Jazz press. When *down beat* did start covering Rock, its announcement expressed reluctance that had the tone of a disclaimer.

You could gather from Gleason's reviews that he was a careful listener, and this was further evident in the respect he had earned among the fraternity of musicians. An anecdote talked about by Steve Allen during his on-camera musings as he was bidding farewell to his pioneering place on late night TV is another demonstration that Gleason was always paying attention. More than any other host of his time, Allen, a musician himself, was interested in and supportive of musicians. He had produced the show *The Jazz Scene* (1962) hosted by singer Oscar Brown Jr. (one of the few programs on TV specifically about Jazz), and his own *The Tonight Show* was always a haven for unique musical presentations. I recall, for example, a show on which Henry Mancini was a guest for the entire night; on that same show, the very talented Jazz combo, the Cannonball Adderley Quintet, performed, after which Mancini gave great praise. I thought to myself at the time, we sure could use more shows like this, because during the 60s, that sort of public validation for Jazz musicians from a respected member of the music mainstream, seldom occurred.

Despite Allen's own skills as musician—he could play any instrument—he was still primarily known as a comedian, and because of that his records had always been snubbed, routinely and unfairly, by the critics. To prove a point, Allen contrived a hoax, and made a recording of Jazz improvisations on piano and overdubbed a third part; another hand. For the liner notes, he invented a person with an intriguing biography: a reclusive black pianist just recently discovered and here, now, for the first time, were the recordings. The record received splendid reviews, and the wool had been successfully pulled until Ralph J. Gleason listened to it and noticed a few too many notes happening for two hands. All along, Allen had intended to reveal what he had done, but Gleason's attention to detail put an end to the prank. Steve Allen was eventually accorded a measure of respect as he earned a Grammy Award for Best Original Jazz Composition for "Gravy Waltz," in 1964.

My own sense of urgency, like that which Gleason had for Jimmie Lunceford's music, began to develop when my interests shifted from my baseball card collection to *down beat* magazine. In my youth, I'd often walk to Towey's market across from Tulocay Cemetery on Coombsville Road, not far from our home, and eagerly buy a pack of baseball cards. Who's inside this time? Now, as a young man, it was with that same anticipation and hope that I went to the corner of First St. and Coombs in downtown Napa, where a magazine rack located in front of Miller's drugstore was one of the few places the magazine was available, and where they, too, had a "small allotment." I clearly remember my steps quickening with greed as I neared the corner. *Let me not be late; just one more issue for yours truly, if you please. Good lord how I enjoyed getting that latest issue. Who's on the cover this week?*

As can be seen, Gleason's listening-to-music routine involved the use of inexpensive playback equipment too, and his years as a student at Columbia were a decade and a half further back in the dark ages of sound reproduction. Still, the ideas were sufficiently conveyed so that the "ecstasy" was experienced. Eagerness for the essence of the musical message is useful in hearing past the scratchiness of a poor recording. I'm reminded of comments by mandolin virtuoso David Grisman, who along with Jerry Garcia (future lead guitarist for the Grateful Dead) immersed themselves in Bluegrass one season, going to music festivals, and always seeking that rare recording that captured something great. When Grisman and Garcia did a radio interview with the aforementioned Gary Lambert and talked about their Bluegrass pilgrimage, Grisman described some of those rare recordings they acquired in their travels as "...sounding like frying eggs,"—a great description—and if you grew up in the fifties, you know exactly what he's talking about. The more important point was that even though they didn't sound all that great, they were still worth having if they conveyed something of the magic that had occurred.

Recording technology was not an issue, however, where live performance was concerned. With respect to the Jimmie Lunceford Orchestra, the theatrics were impressive, choreographed in precise manner and delivered with great flair, but the music never suffered because of the effort to incorporate "showmanship." No matter what acrobatic feat the musicians were up to, the music still cooked madly. Evidence of this is contained in Gleason's report from Columbia, because just hearing the music was enough to captivate him. He had not yet seen the band.

Another respected critic from Gleason's time, Leonard Feather (1914—1994), the noted Jazz historian whose prolific output in books, magazines, newspapers, and liner-notes was well-known, and a musician/composer in his own right, said of the Lunceford Orchestra in his *The Book of Jazz*: "The musicians not only worked well together, but even waved the brass derbies over their horns in perfect unison. To some this meant that the band was too correct, to the point of stiffness; yet the Lunceford band in person was as exciting a sound and sight as can be observed on any bandstand today." It should be mentioned that subsequent generations of black artists would understandably find such an approach disturbingly clownish, but whatever the impetus might have been, that stylized delivery was part of a well-organized package. Still close enough in time to be influenced by vaudeville, it was, as Ralph Gleason said, a "...stage show..." typical of Lunceford and most bands from that era that caught the attention of a young musician in the making, as we'll see in a moment. Even in the period following the end of the Swing era, performances were still being described as "revues": a succession of events which could include dancers, singers, skits and parody. One might remember that before Tina Turner became a hugely successful solo artist, she was part of what was called the Ike and Tina Turner Revue.

In addition to her work with Sweet Burgundy, my sister Lynda has joined the Second Street Band, playing guitar, keyboards, and singing with fellow musicians Nigel Bates on drums and vocals, and John Ray on bass guitar. On lead guitar and vocals is longtime Napa guitarist Larry Otis, whose unique stylings and slide-guitar skills earned him a position (in the mid-sixties) with the Ike and Tina Turner Revue. Otis explained to me exactly how their "Revue" worked. "First it would be just the band before the Ikettes, Tina, and Ike came out," warming up the crowd with the instrumental "Memphis Soul Stew," then the band shifted into Jessie Hill's "Ooh Poo Pah Doo" as the Ikettes came out singing and dancing. Then Tina herself came out amid powerful flashing lights, as Ike too, took the stage with his guitar. With Tina dancing as only she could, along with the Ikettes, the band backed it up with a riff which served to introduce the stars and the beginning of the show full-force with one of their well-known songs, which was always done with great energy, flair, and solid musicianship.

With regard to the Jimmie Lunceford Orchestra, in addition to great musicianship, one was given the various components that were part of a revue, sometimes all at once; that had, I'm sure, a great deal to do with why they were so well-remembered. A YouTube video shows a featured male vocalist (the entire band did backup vocals), a featured female vocalist, and a segment with three male tap dancers. Adding to the fun, two horn players bounced down off the bandstand and did a dance routine of their own, hot-footing it while continuing one-handed, to hold onto their respective tenor and baritone saxes; no small feat.

Presiding over this multi-faceted and precise performing entourage, Lunceford himself was a man who seemed perfectly suited to be a band leader. A large man of fairly serious comportment, he was the calm center against the sometimes frenzied activity that surrounded him as he yet maintained control. The baton he used to lead the band was oversized and caught one's eye as did much of what went on with this band. It was clear that a great deal of planning and rehearsal had gone into the preparation of these shows. The drummer was up front, in the center, and on a raised stand, the height and width of which was designed so that it functioned also as a niche under which the back portion of the piano fit snuggly. That raised stand was equipped with what was, for its day, an extravagant drum kit with tympani, gong, glockenspiel, tubular bells, and an array of smaller tuned drums aligned in the front of the kit. Every bit of it got used with crossover moves and stick tosses that added punctuation to the musical statements being made by the band, and yet the drummer's contribution was a show all by itself.

There was so much going on that it wasn't until a third or fourth look at a YouTube video clip that I saw the amazing things the drummer was doing. Gleason goes on to say, "...maybe they would do 'For Dancers Only' for half an hour...making the whole audience meld together into one homogenous mass extension of the music." And I can easily imagine such a state as I discovered, in listening to a three and a half minute version of "For Dancers

Only," the sensation of a gradual yet sustained increase in energy generated over the course of the song. Imagine what could be done over a 30 minute span. Sounds like the stuff of a memorable evening.

Helping Lunceford make musical arrangements that stuck in one's mind was secret-weapon Sy Oliver, who composed "For Dancers Only," having joined Lunceford in 1933. Skilled arrangers are rare and Oliver strikes me as one of the most talented and unsung heroes in this overlooked but highly important profession. Arrangers are not often asked to come out and take a bow. Coming up with ideas for an entire band concerning what each section should play—the tempo, duration, and so on for every instrument—is very challenging. Just as great athletes do not automatically make good coaches, even the most virtuosic and gifted soloist may not be able to transfer that talent into written parts for everyone else in a band to maximize what is possible, for the best sound, collectively in an arrangement. It's definitely a special talent.

In 1939, Sy Oliver was hired by Tommy Dorsey, the same year Fletcher Henderson was hired by Benny Goodman, making him one of the first black arrangers to work for a white orchestra. We had, in our family collection, a recording that had the album-title song "Yes Indeed." The album was a compilation of recorded works by the band from 1939-45. Dorsey had a great band which included Frank Sinatra as its featured male vocalist from January 1940 to January 1942, and the Pied Pipers vocal quartet led by the silky-smooth stylings of female vocalist Jo Stafford, who remains a favorite of mine. Another famous bandmember for several years was the great drummer Buddy Rich. One of the surviving accounts regarding his arrival was that Rich became more eager to join the Dorsey band (in 1939) when he heard about Sy Oliver coming aboard.

When, as a teenager, I first listened to their version of "Yes Indeed," which was done in February of 1941, I thought—and I don't know how else to say it—this is one of hippest things I'd ever heard from white musicians particularly from such an early period. Don't get me wrong; those who performed it—and believe me, they nailed it—deserve credit, but many years later I learned that the song had been composed and arranged by Oliver, and that he traded lead vocals with Stafford, which certainly had a lot to do with the way it sounded. It is readily available on YouTube, and if you give it a listen, you'll hear just what a fine arrangement it is. It starts out quietly, the melody stated without accompaniment by trombones with, perhaps, understated help from the reed section, then trumpets join the brass section, a line of counterpoint is added by the reed section, and then they build the conversation further, exchanging harmony-rich riffs of call and response. Then there's an unexpected and subdued interlude in the middle (which Ray Charles used as the beginning in his album-title-tune version on his 1958 recording of the same name) to settle things down so as to allow proper recognition of the incoming singers. Their strong singing is helped by spare but perfect piano lines and always-effective hand-clapping, which also sets up the more ambitious sections at the end when the band kicks back in and ends with a big flourish. Please check it out. (running-time 3:32, look for the starlit cityscape)

That "young musician in the making" I mentioned earlier whose attention was grabbed by Lunceford, was pianist Horace Silver. Silver successfully blended blues and Latin rhythms in his unique and varied compositions, pleasing both musicians and audiences alike. Silver credits The Jimmie Lunceford Orchestra with helping to cement his decision to be a musician. He writes about this in his autobiography, *Let's Get To The Nitty Gritty*, but I first heard an account of it from Silver himself, on KCSM's *Jazz Profiles* with Nancy Wilson. His mother had passed away when he was nine, and his father took him to Rowayton, Connecticut "...almost every Sunday to Rowton Point," an amusement park and they'd eat hot dogs and ride the rides. On one of these occasions in 1939—he was still nine years old—"Jimmie Lunceford and His Orchestra came up on a Greyhound bus. I said, Dad could we please stay to hear one number. We waited half an hour or forty minutes just waiting for them to get set up at the dance pavilion." Silver goes on to say that "...blacks were not allowed inside at this time." The pavilion was not totally enclosed, so you could stand nearby, hear them and see a little. "They started playing, and the music sounded so good. The Jimmy Lunceford band was so together, they were hitting it so precisely, and the music was swingin' and it sounded so good. I begged and pleaded with my Dad to stay for one more tune, and we stayed for three or four tunes. It was when I heard that Lunceford band, *that's* when I said to myself that's what I want to be: a musician. They were dressed nice, the singing was good—the playing was good. It was just one hell of an outfit, and that's when I made my commitment to be a musician." And I must add that I'm so glad I was able to actually hear him say what he did, because reading those same words in print does not do justice to what really transpired.

As he was recounting this memory in rapid pace, I could hear the excitement in his voice reinforcing the impression they had made. It reminded me of the enlivened expression I witnessed in Babe Pallota's face when he talked about Lunceford's orchestra standing out among the bands he'd seen at the Dream Bowl. In the PBS television documentary, *Ken Burns Jazz*, Artie Shaw, a man who did not hand out praise easily, said of the Lunceford Orchestra: "Tremendous band, always at its peak."

And finally, in the opinion of Lunceford himself: "A band that looks good, goes in for better showmanship and seems to be enjoying its work, would always be assured of a return visit."

For Horace Silver, the depth of the impression the Lunceford band had made on him was reflected in the serious tone of his voice at that moment, and borne out by his compelling compositions, energetic soloing, and the successful and influential career that followed.

There are many stories about individual musicians and bands of all types, big and small, who play all manner of music, that for one reason or another, never got the recognition they deserved. The Jimmie Lunceford Orchestra, although well-known, probably should have been more celebrated than it was.

At the end of my talk with Babe Pallotta, he suggested I talk with Mrs. Zanardi, the widow of John Zanardi, and he supplied me with her phone number. Shortly thereafter I made the attempt. Mrs. Zanardi was not in good enough health to do this, but when I explained what I was doing to the considerate care person in the home, she helped me get in touch with Zanardi's daughter, Louise.

It would be difficult to assign a comparative degree of importance to any of the various moments that thread this story together. I can, however, pick a favorite and that would be the exchange I had with this caretaker. For one thing, she, probably more than all others, deserves recognition, and also because it seemed to be the thinnest of threads. I say that because I remember now a moment of silence after she told me that Mrs. Zanardi was not able to talk on the phone which was nearly the end of things, a heartbeat or two away from utter separation, Grand Canyon-like in its effect; but then her voice began again, doing one more thing, per her inclination, for this stranger on the other end of the line yet to realize, in its fullness, the value of this moment. Without her help, several crucial connections would never have happened. So to Debbie, the "at night" caregiver, I appreciate greatly what you did for me.

Soon after getting the information from Debbie, I met Louise who welcomed me into her home. She seemed genuinely pleased that someone was taking an interest in this part of her family history, and during the course of that enjoyable evening, she provided important information that added to this complex chronicle, such as: the partners were already planning and promoting dances in rented halls before they built the Dream

Bowl; that money saved for a house was used instead to buy the plot of land on which to build; that the "airplane-hanger" design was, by her recollection, the first of its kind for a ballroom as duplications would follow. Louise went on to say that they planned the dances so as to coincide with swing-shifters getting off work from nearby Mare Island Naval Shipyard in Vallejo. They also tried hard to get an access road off Highway 29 for a more convenient front entrance, but could not get it approved, most likely because of traffic safety considerations. She added that her mother would often stay late, until 2 AM after shows on Saturday nights, readying the snack-bar and preparing for the next show, but never missed the 9 AM church service later that same Sunday morning.

Once again I was fortunate to have one person I met lead me to another. Ironically, Louise did not have any photos of the Dream Bowl herself, but she knew someone who did. She had, only a few days before, gone to a shoe-repair shop seeking the skills of an endangered occupation: a cobbler. The owner was Richard Bean, but his shop, then located on Tennessee Street in Vallejo near Scotty's Restaurant, was home to more than shoe repair; it was also a shrine to music. The unique and (for me) memory-evoking equipment of his trade was on one side of the store, while the other was gloriously decked out with posters, photos, glam shots, arcane memorabilia, best-wished autographs, and more. What Louise had noticed during her recent visit, among the grand array of collectables, were two 8x10 glossies of the Dream Bowl. She told me I ought to check it out. I was familiar with its location so the following day I went to the shop. Richard and I hit it off, and like everyone else I've met on this road, he was cordial and eager to help.

Adding to the significance of this moment was the fact that my father's best friend Harry Henderson had for many years owned and operated a shoe-repair shop, on Main St. near the Napa Courthouse. They met after both were injured during WWII, a bonding experience if ever there was one, were on the same ship coming back home, and were in the same military hospital in southern California where they recuperated and—I strongly suspect—as soon as they were able, raised hell. Harry was outgoing and friendly, had a devilishly infectious laugh, and was always kind to me and my sisters. Whenever I went into his shop, the operation, sights, sounds, and smells never failed to fascinate, and this eye-catching display of equipment was enriched greatly by Harry himself who, naturally hyper to begin with, was never long without a cup of coffee and/or cigarettes. He worked like a madman behind the long counter where he could, at all times, be seen moving briskly from machine to hand tool and back, never wasting a moment. Harry seemed representative of the men my generation grew up seeing, guys in khaki or grey work clothes working hard, I mean really, really hard. So whenever it is shown that America has declined in a variety of social indicators, I am reminded of the rock-solid infrastructure we had of men in the '50s who worked extremely hard (that thing for which there is no substitute), and much is explained.

These memories were re-kindled when I walk into Richard's shop, not having been in one for over forty years. The added impact of this trove of treasures from the world of music made it a stimulating experience on several levels, and it turned out a useful and important one too. He lent me the photos of the Dream Bowl that Louise had seen along with some printed materials, and you can probably guess what happens next: he went to his Xerox machine, and made a copy of a phone number, on the spot. That phone number belonged to Raymond Sweeney, who worked for Black Jack Wayne during the Dream Bowl's Country and Western years. Raymond, I found out, was eager and excited to talk about the Dream Bowl when I called him shortly after meeting Richard. Things were starting to shape up.

If the notion of meeting someone at a dance was not already a standard feature in the psyche of most Americans, there was no shortage of effort in moviemaking and/or songwriting to place it there permanently during the 30s and 40s, and it didn't end there. Each of the following popular songs involves dancing. In the 1942 movie *Orchestra Wives*, the highlight to an otherwise terrible movie was when Paula Kelly and the Modernaires back up Tex Beneke as he sings "I Got a Gal in Kalamazoo," and he meets that girl at a school dance. Julie Andrews says it all when she sings, in the movie *My Fair Lady*, "I Could Have Danced All Night." In the recording by the Drifters (who did "Up on the Roof"), "Save The Last Dance For Me," was an impassioned plea contained in the title, and straight from the heart of its lyricist, songwriter Doc Pomus. And finally, the Beatles pledge undying love to a girl on the first cut of side 1 from their debut American album *Please Please Me* in the song "I Saw Her Standing There."

"Kalamazoo" was a #1 hit, *My Fair Lady* was successful on Broadway, and later as a film, and "I Could Have Danced All Night" was recorded by many artists. "Save the Last Dance," was recognized as being in the top 25 of all time popular songs, and one of many written by the great Doc Pomus. Pomus was one of those Brill Building lyricists working in New York like Carole King and Neil Sedaka, who cranked out scads of simple (deadline) ditties needed quickly for, say, a "B" side for the heartthrob of the moment and other vocalists. But Pomus had also written more serious and finely-crafted songs, and had earned respect as a genuine blues aficionado/singer that often was the only white person in the New York clubs where he performed early in his career.

The significance of the activity of dancing and its effect on couples is sensed strongly by Pomus who, I would learn in Alex Halberstadt's biography of Pomus *Lonely Avenue* (the title of a song of his made famous by Ray Charles), was a larger-than-life figure, despite the restrictions brought on by polio. He did not like keeping his very loyal and very beautiful wife, actress Willi Burke, from dancing—which she loved—because he could not join her on the floor. And while the lyrics may appear initially to reflect male possessiveness typical of the era, what we really get are the insecure feelings he, nevertheless, could not keep himself from having because of his condition and when you learn this, the song's lyrics are altogether transformed:

> But don't forget who's takin' you home
> And in whose arms you're gonna be
> So darlin' save the last dance for me

In *Ken Burns Jazz*, from "Episode Four—The True Welcome," dancers Norma Miller and Frankie Manning talk about the wonderful times they had during the late 30s leading up to the Swing Era going to the grand events. Miller recounts a uniquely exciting and life-changing moment, one of many uplifting stories in that series, when as a teenage girl, she was swept off her feet, literally, as she stood eagerly outside the Savoy Ballroom, by a famous dancer of the day whom she recognized, a dandy named Twistmouth George.

Miller talked about spending evenings as a teenager on the fire-escape outside her family's hot apartment, as many in that situation had done, seeking relief from the stifling heat the day had imposed, and from that cooler vantage point she became mesmerized by the shifting silhouettes of dancers through the shadowed back-window shades of the Savoy, just across the way, longing for the day when she would be allowed in. Typically, people too young or otherwise unable to get in would gather across the street outside the Savoy and dance to the music that could be heard leaking out from within the Ballroom. The famous Twistmouth, said to be one of the innovators of the Lindy Hop, called out to Miller in the crowd one afternoon, and to her astonished surprise, invited her inside to partner with him in a dance contest. She deliriously agreed. She was then provided a breathtaking look at the experience in full swing, taking part in the contest and being transported around the room in dance—aloft much of the time—and then escorted in her now elated state back out to the front of the ballroom, and to the world outside. Very little of the initial moment was lost in its re-telling, because it was reflected in her beatific smile and breathless expression, as palpable now, as it must have been then. "It was the greatest moment in my life," said Miller.

The pair went on to talk about the first time they were finally old enough to attend an evening performance when the great drummer Chick Webb and his Orchestra were holding court regularly at the Savoy, a band Benny Goodman had said outplayed them in a Battle-of-the-Bands face-off. Dancer Frankie Manning described the excitement that had been building for years, of his first night entering the club through its front doors with a half-dozen friends, going together up the steps and into the Ballroom as one could hear the ever-loudening music, but not yet see the band nor others in attendance. As you reached the top of stairs and came through the door "…your back was to the bandstand, and as you turned around the stairwell…" all would dramatically be right there in front of you intensifying that first surge of excitement of seeing the musicians and the dancers as they filled the room with sound, movement, and energy, and from the perspective of those dancers already on the floor, the look of newly-arrived couples, fresh and eager to join them on the dance floor as they made their way into the crowded gathering, adding to the excitement and fun.

The Savoy had two stages, and narrator Keith David tells us in the documentary that: "In the Savoy Ballroom, as one band wound up a set, the second band took up the same tune; the music never stopped." Frankie Manning, like Norma Miller, talked in still-excited manner about witnessing that scene for the first time: "It looked like the floor was getting into the mood of the dance club—the floor was just bouncing up and down—the people were bouncing up and down. It was just such a wonderful time in our life to come up there and be exposed to this kind of music—Oh wow!"

I recall pianist Eddie Palmieri (in remarks made between songs at a performance at Yoshi's, Oakland) talking about his involvement in similar oft-recurring and energized scenarios in Latin Jazz clubs in New York in the early 60s, in which bands would raise the intensity of the music to inspire and challenge dancers, who would then respond in kind, forcing the band to crank it up yet further, and on the ever-ascending contest would go, long into the night.

While Miller and Manning reminisced, both of their faces brightened with each recollection, the years peeling away with every moment they recalled, adding to the vigor that's always evident in people who have spent their lives dancing. Here they were, some fifty years later, still smiling, and yes, still dancing, which is what our couple are going to be doing tonight because they are here, at the entrance, ready for an evening with the remarkable Duke Ellington and his Orchestra, at the Dream Bowl.

Duke Ellington

Duke Ellington's presence commanded respect; he deserved that and more. He was a tremendous talent whose musical legacy is vast, rich in quality and innovation, and whose influence is widespread. A strong case can be made for him being the most important figure in all of Jazz.

I so wish I had seen him live, and the fact is I came close. I took several day classes in 1974 at Solano Community College: English Composition, Sociology, and Survey of Jazz. Those classes were a bit of a challenge as it was my first time returning to school in a serious way, following my graduation in '65, and those classes during the regular school day lacked the comparatively casual dynamic that night classes had. Adding to the difficulty was the fact that I was working swing-shift at Ace Hardware's Distribution Center in Benicia, lugging freight from 4:00 PM until midnight, and getting to bed about 1:00 AM. Those morning classes (8:00 AM) came pretty early.

The instructor of the Survey of Jazz class was John Kolarik. Mr. Kolaric was a wonderful, easy-going teacher and mentor to a lot of local musicians. He was a talented trombone player who also played upright bass and who continued performing into his 93rd year, in Vallejo and elsewhere, right up to the time of his passing in May of 2016. Thanks to the help of John Mikolajcik, a fellow grad from Napa High's class of '65—a fine trumpet player and percussionist (steel drums) in his own right who would eventually become part of the Music Deptartment at SCC—I was able to contact Mr. Kolarik. Thirty-six years after those classes I would call Mr. Kolarik to ask if he had any Dream Bowl recollections. He told me that he went to see Harry James, and it was so hot, literally, that it was the only time he could recall seeing a band take off their suit jackets during a performance. For our class, Mr. Kolarik was planning a trip to Sacramento for anyone interested, to see Ellington, but the show was cancelled because the Duke himself became ill. I didn't know it then, but this was very near the end of his time. He died on May 24, 1974.

I grew up hearing his music. Both my parents liked Duke Ellington, especially my mother, who because she played piano, appreciated all those beautiful things Duke was doing as an accompanist, a soloist, and a composer. The album *Ellington Indigos* was in our family collection, and that recording was a mix of Duke's own compositions and standards. I listened to it often. There were beautiful versions of "Solitude," "Willow Weep for Me," "Prelude to a Kiss," and "Tenderly;" dreamy slow-dance tempos one and all. I remember Ellington quoted in the liner notes, describing altoist Johnny Hodges' solo on "Prelude" as "excruciating ecstasy," a phrase I was too young to appreciate fully, but one I was moved in the direction of by my imagination, cultivated by the lush tones spilling into one another in one cascading phrase after another, delivered uniquely by Hodges with his signature sound.

The Ellington band was loaded with great musicians, many of whom spent nearly their entire careers with Duke. A famous moment in Jazz involves the Ellington Orchestra at the Newport Jazz Festival in 1956, which caused enough of a stir as to be a boost in his career that had dropped off a bit in the mid-fifties, and led to Ellington appearing on the cover of *Time Magazine*. During their performance of "Diminuendo and Crescendo in Blue," Paul Gonsalves takes an extended tenor-sax solo, and this leads to an exhilarating demonstration of group-mind as the audience finds itself in a collective state of aesthetic arrest wrapped up in spontaneous creation and release. As is known, the phenomenon had several factors that coalesced, led by Gonsalves and the band, then joined and augmented by an attractive woman in stylish dress who, caught up in the spirit, rose from her reserve box seat to dance with abandon, and causing nearly everyone else there to likewise get out of their seats and move to the music, until all were absorbed completely in that magical moment when briefly and miraculously all that mattered was movement—of sounds and bodies. Living as we do in the twenty-first century, we are now more used to such occurrences, but I can't emphasize enough the startling significance of such a thing happening in 1956!

Psychotherapist Francis Weller, author of the book *The Wild Edge of Sorrow: Rituals of Renewal and the Sacred Work of Grief,* who effectively helps people in dealing with grief, talks about the importance of ritual: "The ritual is the most ancient art practice that we have." "When we enter into the ritual process, it triggers some deep memories in our experience...we have always done this communally and we have always done this in some type of ritual context." "So what we're trying to do is bring back the primal or primary function in process for really setting our grief down." And so it was that memorable afternoon.

Significant in this event at Newport is the fact that Paul Gonsalves played for a long time, twenty-seven choruses they say. There is a rise and fall of energy through the course of the solo and the first time I listened to it, I thought I heard a period during which he had run out of steam, but he persists, important in any endeavor, and is rewarded with another level of exceptional force, and this becomes the supreme moment that everyone, from deep within, was after.

Physicist/Philosopher David Bohm, who was on several occasions interviewed by Michael Toms, the host of Radio Station KPFA's Sunday series "New Dimensions," studied dialogue (notably with Jiddu Krishnamurti) and experimented with it, thinking it was highly important because group discussion allows the development of unique ideas not possible otherwise. He did enough work to know that things did not always go smoothly, but he never lost faith in the idea, and had seen, that given enough time, "...troublesome points..." could be worked out, and a deeper level of ideas and consideration could be realized.

The very entertaining Bay Area performer Josh Kornbluth, whose introspective monologues and interactions have delighted audiences, eventually added music with a four-piece band to his shows, and says of this development: "When you get right down to it, the show is about a monologist learning that real meaning only exists for him through dialogue, and playing music together is the most heart-direct kind of dialogue I know."

So on that day, out of doors, under the sun in beautiful Newport, Rhode Island, at America's longest running Jazz festival, Duke Ellington and his orchestra sent out sound waves from their instruments which dramatically affected those right in front of them and then diminished as it headed toward the bodies of water that surround Newport and flow to the great Atlantic Ocean nearby, and a dialogue between dancers and musical diviners was given adequate time to transcend "troublesome points," and some core requirement, from which we are estranged by a cover of time, was achieved and everyone came away richer for it.

Now let's return to that elderly couple asking about the Dream Bowl, standing expectantly on my mother's front porch with their evening yet before them. I'm permitting myself a tweak of reality here because I can't bear to send them back to where they came from, and this re-writing of history allows their evening to go off without a hitch. I'm imagining their discussion after seeing an ad for the show went something like this:

> Husband: "Hey, hon'. The paper is advertising the schedule of bands playing at the Dream Bowl this month. We haven't been there for so long. What do you think about going?"
>
> Wife: "Oh, I don't know."
>
> Husband: "Aw c'mon, what do you say? Let's go dancing. It'd be fun."
>
> Wife: (Now reconsidering) "Well, what band could we see?"

Husband: "Well, let me see—it says here, in two weeks it will be Duke Ellington—how about that?!"

Wife: "Hmmm, that would be lovely."

Husband: "All right then, in two weeks, Duke Ellington and his Orchestra."

Tonight at the Dream Bowl, let us, like our elderly couple, relive a moment in the late-30s. It is not a concert performance which, as Ralph Gleason pointed out to us would happen "a good deal later;" it is a dance. And for our couple tonight just the relaxed strains of a familiar song bring about not as primal a display of human connection as had happened at Newport, but one certainly as timeless and basic in its more private and intimate choreography, and equally important for its participants. Maybe they hear something like "Where or When," to start off their evening, and it produces smiles to go with the steps that are returning to memory. The instruments play the melody only, but in each of their heads, they can hear the lyrics they both know well:

> And so it seems that we have met before
> And laughed before
> And loved before
> But who knows where or when

Tonight though, defying the odds and the song's lament, our couple does remember where and when; right here at the Dream Bowl, and they are reminded of a time when love was new, and the promise of life ahead, making possible down the road a moment of tenderness uniquely achieved and realized by them this special night.

Count Basie

This music we're talking about: they didn't call it Swing for nothing—and no band was more deserving of the title than the Count Basie Orchestra. I'm sure anyone lucky enough to have seen them at the Dream Bowl got their money's worth. I can't imagine an occasion in which the robust sound they achieved did not Swing. Receiving high praise from distinguished editor Robert Gottlieb, who deemed their partnership as having produced one of the best Jazz autobiographies, was: *Good Morning Blues*, as told to Albert Murray. Murray, by the way, was one of several writers who provided commentary for *Ken Burns Jazz*, and he always offered thoughtful information that came from a sympathetic ear and an understanding heart. In the book Basie talked about a performance at the Reno club in Kansas City, and his remarks match up nicely with the comments made by Gene Gelling, quoted in the first part of this book, when he talked about bands "cookin."

John Hammond, a writer and an energetic crusader for Jazz, had come to see the band and meet Basie, whom he had praised in *down beat* magazine. Recalling that evening, Basie had this to say: "The band played exceptionally well that night too. I don't know, but all of a sudden it just sounded like the guys turned on another button or something. I don't think it was because John was there either, because nobody knew who John was. It was just one of those good nights when the band was solidly in the groove and could go on and on swinging like that forever."

With Basie's famous relaxed demeanor leading the band, one might wrongly assume a casual approach in his direction and the way the band operated, but Basie thought it important to dispel any such notions. In a 1939 interview with *down beat* magazine, he said "I'd like it known that the band works hard—rehearsals three hours long are held three times a week, on average…" Still, Basie saw to it that flexibility was equal partner to discipline and said of the "standards" they played in addition to original material, "…one of the boys or I will get an idea for a tune…and at rehearsal we just sorta start it off and the others fall in. First thing you know, we've got it. We don't use paper on a lot of our standards. In that way, we all have more freedom for improvisations."

One of my more recent and enjoyable discoveries in Jazz, although he has had a lengthy career, is the music of Eddie Palmieri. He is a pianist, but, as I heard him tell it from the stage of Yoshi's in Oakland, his wish, as was the wish for many budding musicians interested in Latin Jazz, was to be a percussionist, and follow in the footsteps of band leader Tito Puente. This initial desire comes through in his approach to piano, and as an accompanist he really propels the band with compelling, and continuous drive.

In like manner, William Basie wanted to be a drummer, but switched exclusively to piano at age fifteen. He always wanted people tapping their feet when his music was played, something a drummer is always doing, so an emphasis on rhythm as a component of the Basie style was more pronounced in his arrangements and delivery—a distinctive quality of the band that would remain over the years—and Basie would compile over fifty of those years as a leader of big bands, maintaining that leadership while many other bands faded from existence. That's plenty of time to be a positive influence for younger up-and-coming musicians. Grateful Dead guitarist and vocalist Bob Weir said in an interview, one of the great things about music was that you could continue to do it as you got older. The example he gave was that of having gone to see Basie and his band sometime in the 1970s. His assessment: "They swung like angels." A few years earlier, drummer Bill Kreutzmann saw Basie at the Fillmore Auditorium in San Francisco, saying in his book *Deal*, "His drummer was Sonny Payne and watching him play was fascinating and inspiring. I was staring at Sonny in total awe when I felt someone tap me on the shoulder. It was Mickey Hart. I had never seen him before, but he introduced himself as a fellow drummer and friend of Sonny's."

Helping in a big way was the stellar cast of musicians that Basie always had on hand. Tenor saxophonist Lester Young was one of the most influential players on that instrument, and together with Herschel Evans formed one of the greatest 1-2 punches in big band history. This double tenor sax alignment in which two lines of counterpoint conversation emerge from the soloists was designated as one of the Basie band's "innovations;" if it was not exclusive to them, it certainly was a feature in the Basie band more than any other.

Driving and supporting those remarkable soloists was a great rhythm-section. In his *The Book of Jazz*, Leonard Feather contrasts what he feels to be an over-organized Lunceford band to the Count Basie Orchestra, saying they: "...offered more informality and longer solo opportunities in a looser setting than any other band of the '30s. The free-flowing rhythm section, with Freddie Greene's guitar, Walter Page's bass, Jo Jones' drums and the leader's piano, was the key to the rhythm miracle achieved by Basie."

Another of the "innovations," said to be attributable to the Basie Orchestra was "riffing" within a big band. I think of this as the band having the collective mind-set of a soloist. They seemed to me to be more of a band's band. The band's approach and focus was more directed to what kind of groove they could find or what excitement they could generate rather than the expected accommodation for dancers that the period required, which, by the way, was still easily accomplished, as they shot for something more. In today's parlance, although it's sometimes used in dismissive fashion, we might think of them as more of a "jam band" than other bands from the period.

That a "riff," a term still in use today, was used in an innovative manner by the Basie band, is supported by an entry that I found when poking around for various definitions of the term. One said, "Riffs can be as simple as a tenor saxophone honking a simple, catchy rhythmic figure, or as complex as the riff-based variations in the head arrangements played by the Count Basie Orchestra." Those "head" arrangements are the ones Basie referred to when he or one of the band members comes up with idea on the fly which sounds right while rehearsing one of their numbers.

At the rhythmic center of all this (minus two years in the military) from 1934 to 1948 was Jo Jones. There were many years of playing and practice to hone his craft, and no one made it look as easy as Jo Jones. He was a great drummer, and his solos involved body-language that ideally emphasized accents as he struck a snare or cymbal. He was the essence of smooth.

Wynton Marsalis, in *Ken Burn's Jazz*, talked amusingly about how Basie's sparse piano style, making subtle statements in very economical fashion, came to be. In the early years of his career, he and the band would play supper clubs where arrangements were tight-knit and intimate, with tables so close, that socializing and having a little taste now and then was as important as the music. So there were two conversations going on: one with patrons, and one with the band; a little here, a little there. The entire band projected a relaxed command over their musical assignments, as demonstrated by their leader, and no one ever said that dour expression need be partner to expert musical execution. For the Basie band, it never was. They looked like they were enjoying themselves, which is the best encouragement for others to do the same. What more could you ask for?

These days, Gary Giddins is my favorite writer on Jazz. A blurb about his book *Weather Bird* says it best. "Giddins is opinionated but generous, with the laudable ability to capture the essence of a performer's style in vibrant language that makes the music described seem almost audible."—Publisher's Weekly.

In an essay on Big Bands from the same book, Giddins, as usual, makes sensible observations. He begins by saying despite the attention given big bands, the critics "...are frequently ignorant of its workings." He adds, "Orchestration, the least examined of the Jazz arts, (recall comments on arranger Sy Oliver) is widely regarded as a species of behind-the-scenes arcana, like film editing; only writers with distinctive styles and onstage roles - Ellington, Gil Evans –excite acclaim."

Giddins then talks about a 5-CD compilation of 75 recordings made between 1941 (the year in which our story begins) and 1991, put together by Bill Kirchner. Of the collection, Giddins says, "His intention is to show how the death of the Swing Era liberated big bands, and to induce wonder at the postwar accomplishment."

Giddins concludes by mentioning a number of other big bands that, in his opinion, should have been included, but goes on to add: "Of course the inclination to quibble underscores Kirchner's point: When the Swing Era died, big band music blossomed." Giddins, mid-way in the essay, reminds us of the difficult task, financially, of maintaining a traveling big band following WWII, yet despite this, the creative pursuit of what was possible through orchestration with a large ensemble did continue, and while "blossom" may not convey, in the sense Kirchner uses it, the Hollywood-linked popularity achieved by some of the Swing Bands (Goodman, Harry James, and Artie Shaw), it is the continuation of the search for new musical possibilities that ultimately matters. So that exciting period called the Swing Era did come to an end, leaving a remarkable legacy of great music, and with its connection to the war years, it remains a time rich in meaning and in memory, especially for those who were there to experience it.

Country and Western

Recall now that I walked out of Richard's shoe shop armed with information for my next contact. I met Raymond Sweeney at Epie's Restaurant in Sacramento. We sat down, had some breakfast (my favorite meal by far), and as always in that situation I was reminded of the scene in the movie *Lillies of the Field* when Homer Smith, the character played by Sidney Poitier, finally with pocket money for the first time in a while from a recent construction job, orders a huge breakfast, and finishes by asking the waiter to "...keep the coffee coming." On this morning, I didn't put in a special request, as Homer Smith had, but I kept sliding that cup over making it an easy pour for the waitress, and said "yes please," each time she asked "more coffee?"

As regards the interview I got that day, Raymond Sweeney was ideal. He was off and running long before the coffee took effect, and I rarely needed to ask questions; he was sharp on details and chronology to boot. His father played saxophone, but he himself never learned an instrument. Still, as he became a young man, he "...wanted to participate..." in some fashion in the music world. He described himself in the mid '50s as "...anti-country music...," but in 1956 while listening to KOBY radio, he heard that mainstay guitar riff that started off many of Johnny Cash's songs, and he begin to change his mind about Country music after all. Like me, he had gone by the Dream Bowl while riding in his parent's car, was likewise curious, asked his father what went on there, and after hearing what it was all about, expressed a desire to go. This was 1954. By his recollection, two years later his father took him to see Cash and this corresponds with information provided online at Infocenter.com, which lists 4,281 concert entries spanning the years 1955-1999. It shows Cash coming to the Dream Bowl on December 10, 1956, January 7, 1960, and February 7, 1960. Raymond then told me "...after that first show, I got hooked." Considering Cash's popularity, this was an amazing first time experience for him, and he told me that he was "...totally absorbed with it." He remembers that inside the Dream Bowl, there were "...benches around the walls...," and that they served "...just beer and hamburgers in the back."

This, at the mention of beer, is as good a time as any to acknowledge that despite the entertaining activity going on inside, you still had the competitive urges of the men plus the availability of alcohol, so you knew that eventually there was going to be trouble, and occasionally a fight would happen in the parking lot. I spoke with long time Napan Don Townsend, who, like my father, worked at the Sheriff's Department. He told me he worked security at the Dream Bowl because it was out of the city limits. Since the Sheriff's Dept. had jurisdiction for Napa County, they would be hired to police these events. One night, Don told me, he and a partner had to break up a fight, and one of the combatants had a hook for a hand. His partner that night volunteered to take the other guy, and Don had to deal with the one who remained. A bit of history is in order here.

Don grew up in Napa, was a Hall of Fame athlete at Napa High, was a quarterback on the football team, and also played baseball and basketball. He went to USF, was on the football team as a freshman quarterback in 1949, and after a knee injury, decided against football when head-coach Joe Kuharich told him that he "would make a good guard." Kuharich coached until 1951 when USF famously went undefeated, and the team was loaded with great players who went on to stellar careers in the NFL, among them: Ollie Matson, Bob St. Clair, Gino Marchetti, and others. Don reminded me (I had known the story), that an invitation to the Sugar, Orange, or Gator Bowls would be extended to them only if they left their two black teammates Ollie Matson and Burl Toler home, but the team stuck together and would do no such thing.

Don focused on baseball for his three remaining years. I first became aware of his athletic skills when the Peace Officers formed a softball team, and I got to be the batboy. Townsend, who played first base, was big all over, but had great agility. After college, he played AAA baseball as a left-handed pitcher on the Fresno farm team of the St. Louis Cardinals, and had the team jacket to prove it before the days when anyone could go into Big-5 and buy one. I remember him pitching batting practice at Kiwanis Park, but very little batting was taking place. Man, I'll tell ya, he was bringing the heat. No one was catching, and balls were slamming up against the backstop. I volunteered my services, got my glove and scooted my skinny little posterior back behind the plate. Next thing I heard was a chorus of concerned adult males, my dad among them, saying, "Mike: No!" I was too foolish to think of a foul tip, straight back into my unprotected body.

One night at a game at the Napa Fairgrounds where the city-league had its games, Don was upset with himself for striking out, and tossed the bat toward the rack. It had a little too much force and carry, and it speared right between the diagonals of the cyclone fence that separated field from stands. I went over to retrieve the bat, but could not pull it out from the fence and needed help to remove it. I also remember a fracas at home plate after a collision, when Don interceded and pinned the other party against the backstop. The fracas ended right then and there. So he was definitely the right guy for the job that night in the Dream Bowl parking lot.

After a victory, the team would reconvene at Catania's on Silverado Trail, not far from the Fairgrounds, for pizza and beverages. There was plenty to listen to at these gatherings, and I kept my ears wide open. In a *Sports Illustrated* article by Rich Cohen on *The Sports Writers on TV*, he talks about John Roach who created the talk show which had three veteran sportswriters: Bill Jauss, Bill Gleason, Ben Bentley, plus a young Rick Telander. Cohen tells us that: "In their meandering talk Roach heard echoes of his childhood, the just out of earshot babble of his father sitting around the poker table in the basement with his friends. If you're a kid, up past bedtime, hearing just the scraps, the high-frequency blue talk and profanity...well, you'll chase that the rest of your life." What would have been the "blue" nature of the conversation was toned down a bit, I'm sure, because of my presence there, but I have to say I got more than "just the scraps," as I still heard some pretty juicy stories. I had enough sense to keep quiet so as not to jeopardize my being able to come another time. I got to do everything but drink the beer.

Don would also tell me that long before he was on assignment there, when he was still in high school, if it was somebody he and his friends wanted to see, (he mentioned Tommy Dorsey and Stan Kenton) they would drive out to the Dream Bowl parking lot early so as to be able to position their cars right by the windows, which would be open, and they'd sit on the car fenders to watch the show.

By the time Don was doing security there, it was during the Country and Western phase. Only when I started putting information together for this part of the story, I hit a research bugaboo, as some of the things Raymond Sweeney was telling me about his first-hand experience with Black Jack Wayne were not matching up with what Pam Hunter reported in her article for the *Napa Register*. For one thing, she named Gene Traverso's friend and business partner as Lou Zanardi instead of John Zanardi, and as mentioned earlier, she didn't say anything at all about the various Rock bands that performed there in its final two months in 1969, even though the article was printed in 1973. Granted, there wasn't much of a sample-size nor documentation, so even though it was the most current period of the dancehall's history, when I started looking around for information about those last two months the task proved to be quite difficult. Had I not gotten lucky, I might still be scratching my head. So in her defense, I'm guessing Hunter had similar trouble, but unlike me, she did not have the luxury of working without a deadline. The detail that hung me up the most, however, was that Hunter wrote that "...in

'63…Country Western moved into the Dream Bowl under the management of Black Jack Wayne," but I've found evidence that he was doing shows there several years earlier.

Raymond Sweeney told me that he would listen to Black Jack Wayne's radio show on KNBA in Vallejo, and he remembered Wayne talking during his broadcasts about up-coming events at the Dream Bowl. This was 1960, when Raymond, age twenty, was a first-year law student attending classes in San Francisco while living in Richmond. Because of his growing interest in Country music, he wrote Wayne a letter, sending it to the station, suggesting that he ought to send out a newsletter every month to people attending shows to let them know about artists that were scheduled in the near future. Wayne read the letter out loud in its entirety on his show, and Raymond's mother happened to be listening at the time. Wayne asked on the air that Raymond get in touch with him.

I think it's fair to say that Wayne, the shrewd and experienced promoter, saw an advantage to be gained, and from Raymond's point of view, there was his opportunity to "participate" in the music industry. He did in fact meet with Wayne, who suggested he do a "newspaper" rather than a "newsletter." Raymond told me that Wayne said "…I'll back you financially," and more specifically that he would pay for the first month's issue, which Raymond said cost $150.00 for 500 copies. As for getting reimbursed, Raymond's words to me on the matter were, "That didn't fly," but he didn't seem too embittered by the experience. In fact, he talked about what a great promoter Black Jack Wayne was, and said that after he stopped managing the Dream Bowl, it went downhill.

Additional information as to the timeline came from a Rockabillyhall.com entry by Jerry Key of the Key Brothers. Giving a brief history of their career, Jerry talked about an audition for Wayne. It's a good story:

> One day a neighbor heard us practicing because we were so loud and our window was open…It so happened that he was an executive at KROW Radio Station in Oakland; the largest

> Country radio station in the Bay Area. He asked if we would
> be interested in auditioning for a man named Black Jack
> Wayne, a disc jockey at KROW Radio, band leader and
> promoter of music all around the Bay Area...Wayne, he hired
> us to join his Country band as Rock 'n' roll performers. That
> began our career. [He continues] We would perform every
> Friday night at a large dance hall in Haywood [*sic*], California.
> Saturday at 5pm we would sing on the One-Hour Black Jack
> Wayne Television Show on Channel 2, San Francisco. Then at
> 8:30pm every Saturday night we would sing at another large
> dance hall called The Dream Bowl in Napa, CA. We would
> open for all the top Country acts of that time, such as: George
> Jones, Johnny Cash, Ray Price, Lefty Frizzell, Gordon Terry,
> Freddy Hart and many others.

No date is provided for these activities, but Jerry goes on to say
that Wayne, thinking it might boost their notoriety, gave them the
name The Cobra Brothers. Here's Jerry Key again: "As the Cobra
Brothers we had a large following of Rock 'n' roll fans in the Bay
Area. Mr. Wayne produced our first record "Everybody's
Looking" and "Night Time" on the Black Jack label. The record
did very well locally." With a little more research, I found that the
date of issue for that recording was May, 1959, so the brothers
were performing at the Dream Bowl *before* this date.

The other bit of sorting out I had to do was that it looked as
though Wayne might be working at two radio stations circa 1959.
KROW, which as stated by Jerry Key played Country music, was
nevertheless considered Top 40 in the industry. From the
California Historical Radio Society website, I learned that in May
of 1959 the station was purchased by Gordon McLendon who
owned several other radio stations and was based in Dallas. With
his "right hand man," Don Keyes, they flew to San Francisco to
seal the deal. According to McLendon, they initially intended to
maintain the same Top 40 format as the other stations in his
"stable" had. In a taxi ride through the city they were utterly
charmed by San Francisco, and both wanted it to be home to their
newly acquired radio station. The two holed up in their hotel and
began research by listening to local stations. Don Keyes recalls

"...KFRC, KOBY, KEWB, and of course...KYA , the Voice of the Bay." I remember these AM stations and KSFO was also popular during this period. They decided to change the format to "Easy Listening" with a content formula that was repeated every quarter hour. This meant that they didn't repeat the same records, but they did repeat the same style or type of records. Don Keyes tells us "I also began hiring staff consisting of old-school, heavy-voiced announcers." This fact, I assume, spelled the end of Black Jack Wayne's tenure at the station. While they were making major changes, they also changed the call letters to KABL which would thereafter, whenever voiced, always call to mind the icon of the "City" by which they had been so impressed.

I was so entertained by the way they pulled off the change, I just had to include it herewith: For three days leading up to the May 11, 1959 change of format, they deliberately kept playing the same one awful song. The song was described in the CHRS account: "As noted by Mr. Keyes in his narrative, the changeover from KROW to KABL was done with a helping hand from the goofy Rockabilly-style theme from 'The Giant Gila Monster,' a prototypical 1950s straight-to-drive-in movie produced by B.R. and Gordon McLendon. The song was incorporated into the so-called 'stunting' with supposedly straight intros, such as 'Here's Frank Sinatra to sing his latest hit,' or 'Now Teresa Brewer steps to the mike with this old favorite.' Each time, the listener was rewarded with yet another mind-numbing spin of 'The Giant Gila Monster." It must have been dramatically soothing when they finally did unveil the "easy" listening for which that station became so well-known. Then they had to deal with the fact that the station was located and licensed in Oakland; there were legal issues affecting their desire to make it a San Francisco station. McLendon came up with yet another bright idea: "...the station began the long-term practice of announcing itself as: 'This is Cable, K-A-B-L, Oakland, on your San Francisco dial—960...in the air, everywhere—in San Francisco.' So, as of May 11, 1959, "Easy Listening" was in at what was formerly KROW. Black Jack

Wayne was out and shifted the focus of his radio promotional efforts to KNBA in Vallejo.

For his part, Raymond Sweeney continued to put out the *Western News* out of his own pocket because he thought it was important, and he enjoyed doing it. When I walked out of Richard Bean's shoe shop, I had an armful of several of the issues Raymond produced, once a month, for eight years until December of 1968. Financial problems arose around that time with Dream Bowl management, and some of the events advertised in *Western News,* scheduled for the first month of 1969, never came to pass.

As was mentioned, Black Jack Wayne was a good promoter, having both a radio (KNBA) and a television show on KTVU, Channel 2. KTVU was a fledgling independent small-market network in those days featuring local programming, with the ubiquitous Walt Harris seemingly doing everything. The professional wrestling they televised was announced by Harris, and had such celebrities as the tag-team of Pepper Gomez and Luis Martinez, "Champion" Ray Stevens, the big heel with platinum-blonde hair who called everybody "pencil necks," and the ever-entertaining Shiek who, I remember, once assaulted both Jim Wessman from Gateway Chevrolet *and* the '54 Chevy he was pedaling during one of their (always live) commercial breaks, sending the comically suave Wessman, casually perched on a ladder, flying from his roost.

Walt Harris, with his avuncular look, glasses, and conservative suits would look quite at home in an accounting firm, but there he was taking insults from Ray Stevens, and later that evening, you'd see him doing the Channel 2 News. Roller Derby with the Bay Area Bombers was also featured on KTVU, and Harris was the announcer there too. The celebrities on the Bombers were Charlie O'Connell (who we spotted one night in Ruffino's restaurant in Napa) and Ann Calvello. I was age nine when our entire family went to one of the matches at the Oakland Auditorium and I got to see Ann, Charlie, and the rest of the Bombers in person. It was totally fun—maybe the most fun thing I ever experienced in my youth. I think the script for that day involved speedy Ralph Valladares passing the entire team on the last jam of the final period, to squeak out a victory. It was the first time I ever lost my voice from yelling. I say these things about Channel 2 to show that a live broadcast from the Dream Bowl was exactly the sort of thing that could be seen on the station during these early years. Raymond told me he knew of no other promoter who was doing live TV broadcasts at that time in the Bay Area.

Raymond recalls events for which the 5-acre parking lot would be full, and cars would have to park off the side of Kelly Road and Hwy. 29. Gene Traverso, he said, arranged to have a van drive out to pick up the guests to save them the long walk from their cars. Raymond also remembered seeing a limo for Johnny Cash, attached to which was a small trailer that held Marshall Grant's upright bass, and sure enough, on page sixty-seven in Grant's book *I Was There When It Happened*, he tells us that a "...buddy built us a little solid-steel trailer that we could tow behind the car..." and "...when we got that little trailer, we were able to put everything in there, and life on the road got a lot more comfortable."

As for what musicians were paid, Sweeney remembers Judy Lynn receiving $750.00 for a performance, $1250.00 for Faron Young, who was known as "The Hillbilly Heartthrob," and the highest amount he remembers an artist being paid was $1500.00 for Johnny Cash. Young and Cash, incidentally, were born a day apart. Singer Brenda Lee was one of the well-known performers to come to the Dream Bowl, and fellow Napa High classmate Dan Oliveres told me he had a memorable evening attending her show. Dan had come with an older friend or relative as he was too young to drive but, as was said earlier, minors were welcome. Brenda Lee was born in 1944, so that made her two or three years older than those of us graduating in 1965, but she began performing at a very young age. I remembered Dan from our senior year as he took part in the Winter Show reading his own poetry; later in his life, he wrote and performed his own songs. At the Dream Bowl that night there was another act on the bill, and when Brenda Lee was finished with her set, and while the other band was playing, she was itching to dance, and looked around for a partner near her own age. Dan looked like a good choice, so he got to dance with the lively Miss Brenda Lee.

The shows, periodic live broadcasts, and telecasts under the guidance of Black Jack Wayne, continued until 1967. Raymond told me that Lee Stefenoni, nicknamed the "Petaluma Cowboy," stepped in to manage what was at the time being called Club Dreambowl. They moved the stage closer to the front entrance, brought in tables and chairs, and added an eighty-foot bar with five stations. In the April, 1968 issue of *Western News*, Raymond concludes an article on the club by saying: "Travel out to Club Dreambowl on the Napa-Vallejo Highway, seven miles out of Vallejo and enjoy yourself. There is a very large neon sign on the road which all can see. Have a good time and have a good meal at the H & H Café on the premises."

Bob Wills

Close to the end of the Country and Western period at the Dream Bowl were two shows with that great entertainer Bob Wills, on December 7 and 8, 1968. Raymond told me that the Bob Wills shows were scheduled, he recalled, "...against the advice of Black Jack Wayne..," who didn't think people would "...walk through the mud in December..," to come to a show. He turned out to be wrong, and the shows were well-attended. It is fitting that the conclusion of this era, and Raymond's part in it with it the *Western News,* involved Bob Wills, because Raymond, who has passed away since we met, was a huge fan of Wills. He told me during the interview that he wanted to write about him, and actually did spend some time gathering material to use in a book, so this portion of the book is done with Raymond in mind.

Bob Wills was definitely an intriguing subject for biography, someone whose life as a musician was something in which I was already quite interested, even before I met Raymond. He struck me as one of those people who was destined to be a band leader. His appeal was such that he built up over the years a loyal following of the sort that people would attend his shows no matter what sort of weather there was. He obviously loved what he was doing and being on stage in front of a band was purely natural. His joy in this activity was permitted full expression, and his personality maximized the contagious enjoyment possible at a music performance. In addition to his ebullient presence and popularity as a band leader is the interesting place I think Western Swing holds during the Big Band era, and Wills is generally regarded as the main architect in the development of Western Swing. While his music may not be seen as the pure Jazz of the Big Bands, I think that for that reason it was a more unique hybrid of various styles. It was not marked as much, I think, by direct lifts from earlier black traditions of folk, blues, and Jazz, yet the influence is still there to be heard.

The fiddle, his instrument, was most often used where there was dancing; Wills, throughout his long career that lasted fifty-eight years, did everything he could to keep the two activities together. On the bandstand, if he wasn't fiddlin', he'd be dancin', always with a big smile. Professor of History, Charles R. Townsend author of *San Antonio Rose: The Life and Music of Bob Wills*, wrote the liner notes to *Bob Wills: For the last Time*, a recording made in 1973 which was indeed his last. Townsend tells us: "From the time he was three years old, he played with Black children and later worked with Blacks in the cotton fields." Wills himself is then quoted, saying: "I don't know whether they made them up as they moved down the cotton rows or not, but they sang blues you never heard before." Townsend adds, "One of his favorite artists was the 'Empress of the Blues,' Bessie Smith, and he rode nearly fifty miles on horseback to see her in person."

Wills began assembling bands in 1930, and made his first recording in Feb. of 1932. He was listening to all forms of popular music, soaking up what he liked with particular attention given to the music that dance-bands were playing, and was one of the first to want to use horns in a string band. This was enough of an anomaly at the time that life was made difficult for Wills and his band because, as Townsend pointed out, "Musical 'experts' said the mixing of horns and strings would not work and announced that Wills absolutely did not know what he was doing. The musicians' union would not allow him and 'his boys' to join the Local for several months after they arrived in Tulsa because, as the union decided, they did not play music and were not musicians." Ray DeGeer was a saxophonist with Wills who Townsend tells us also played with "Gene Krupa, Red Nichols, Charlie Barnet, and other Swing bands." DeGeer says, "There were many bands that played cleaner and musically better. But they didn't have the spark. I think the uninhibited aspect had to do with [Bob's success]. It gave it life. Everybody had himself turned on." This description is worth remembering as are the remarks of Irving Kolodin talking about the "...remarkable results..." achieved when the Goodman band played "...for its own pleasure only..." when later, we take a look at the Grateful Dead.

In terms of his ability to assemble musicians, Wills was the Western Swing equivalent to Benny Goodman. After Wills' passing, Merle Haggard reassembled the Texas Playboys, as the band was called, revived Wills' music, took it on the road, and in the process earned a cover story in the May 1990 issue of *down beat* magazine, the first time a Country singer had been on its cover.

Bob Wills loved horns, and as with other Jazz orchestras of the day, there was ample opportunity for solos. Wills, along with his fiddle-playing, sang lead on occasion, added backup harmony, kept up a running stream of hollers and ahhaaas to keep everything loose and fun, and led the band with his bow.

I inherited from my late father-in-law Alton (who was raised in Temple, Texas, was a fan, and as a young man had seen Wills perform) a taped interview with band member Johnny Gimble, who would become an award-winning fiddler in his own right, and who talked at length about joining the band in 1949. Gimble said that an invitation to join that band was, for a musician of that period and from that area, the equivalent of a ballplayer being asked to play for the New York Yankees. Tiny Moore had been in the band since 1946, played fiddle and had also done pioneering work on electric mandolin. In 1972 Moore recorded with the aforementioned David Grisman, and worked with him again on the recording *Back to Back* with Jethro Burns, which Grisman produced.

Being new to the band, Gimble wanted to know what was expected of him and asked Moore for advice. Gimble said there was an expression used in those days in recording studios which was "how do you want us to act," that is to say, what attitude were they to take musically; what would Bob want from them? To illustrate, and answer his question, Moore said, "I'll tell you a little story." He described the first practice he went to, and during a solo break in a song, he got the Bob Wills bow pointed at him. As you might suspect, his attempt at a solo was a bit tenuous in this first effort, and Moore said he played a "straight lead." Moore said that Wills called on someone else to solo, and he "eased over to him," (and the verb form is important, as Wills did not wish to embarrass him in front of the others) and said, "Son, when I point to you, I want you to play all you know." He held back no more. Alton Stricklin, his piano player for many years was quoted in Townsend's liner notes: "When he told the piano player to 'tear it up,' you went into orbit." Added Wills himself: "When I gave Al the chorus, it's just like winding up a toy and turning it loose. You didn't know which direction it would go."

It needs to be stressed that improvisation was as important to these Western Swing musicians as it was to musicians playing simultaneous to them in smoked-filled clubs on the hip streets of New York City. Gimble talked about having to "originate things," when he was first learning his instrument. He admitted not knowing much about chord structure in the beginning, that he "started from scratch" and learned "the hard way," and this manner of development is a prevalent scenario that turns up frequently whenever innovative musicians are described.

It is safe to say that anyone riding over forty miles on horseback in order to see Bessie Smith is someone sincerely interested in the Blues, and it was an important component of the Bob Wills style. When I first heard the Blues song, "Sitting on Top of the World," (not to be confused with the bouncy popular song with the same title) it was by the British power trio Cream off their 1968 double album *Wheels of Fire*. I knew nothing about its origin. It had been on an earlier release by the Grateful Dead (March of 1967) from their self-named first album, and although they would turn in some exceptional Blues interpretations throughout their career, their version on this recording was so nervously up-tempo that any Blues feeling had been scared off. The Cream version was a more straight-ahead Blues that so many of those British bands had worked hard to understand and respectfully render. It originated in 1930, according to Wikipedia, and was recorded that same year by the Mississippi Shieks, and was described as a "...popular crossover hit for the band." There is, in fact, a very impressive list of musicians who have recorded it down through the years, including the Bob Wills band, who honor the original version as much as anyone.

There was a time when a record was identified according to the style of dance it best suited, and it would be right there on the label: Fox Trot, Waltz, etc. Whether by design or just an outgrowth of the influence of the music of the day, I felt the original version had the feel of a waltz to it, and the Wills version preserves both that feeling and the fiddle as lead instrument.

In the *down beat* cover-article on Haggard, nicely crafted by Tim Schneckloth and augmented with clear contemplations throughout by Merle, the importance of improvisation and the best situations from which it might flow are analyzed. Having just seen a performance by the 13-piece Merle Haggard and the Strangers—which was loaded with several veterans from Wills' Texas Playboys—Schneckloth noted their approach to be "...loose and exciting, yet it stays coherent and, well, *tight.*" During the interview after the performance, Schneckloth mentions that description, and asks Haggard: "...what do you call a band like that?" His answer: "I call it Country Jazz. It's freewheeling, and it's certainly Jazz, since everything we do is ad-lib."

Some of my favorite moments in music come from things played that contribute appropriately to the overall makeup of a performance: a rhythm guitar line that aids a solo, or a soloist adding supportive backing lines to the vocals. By rights then, I had to be interested in the legacy of Eldon Shamblin, who established himself as one of the great rhythm guitarists of all time. Haggard talked about Shamblin, saying "He's the greatest man in the world for coming in low key…he's such a great complimenter. Whether he's playing Jazz, Country, whatever, people want to know, 'Who is that guy that's setting everyone up?'"

As further evidence of the importance of improvisation to Haggard's approach and execution, he states that when he's tried (for TV shows for example), to lay everything out and rehearse it, "…I'll tell you, it's the hardest thing I've ever had to do. I can't work that way." I remember Jerry Garcia claiming more than once in interviews that it was "…constitutionally impossible for me to play a song the same way twice."

With respect to my contention that the Western Swing bands offered a unique delivery of Swing music, Schneckloth observed that such bands had fewer horns than the brass and reed sections typically found in bands like Goodman and Ellington, and "As a result, the western Swing bands have traditionally used unorthodox voicings in ensembles." In those situations, the string instruments would fill in or help out, providing, in their way, what a horn might have done, and in that process brought about fresh inventions, the occurrences of which would have been less likely had the regular instruments been used.

Concerning Haggard's own eclectic style, he claimed Jimmie Rodgers as an influence and learned that Rodgers himself had been influenced by singer Emmett Miller, about whom Haggard comments, "He had a little group together that included Jimmy and Tommy Dorsey, Jack Teagarden, Gene Krupa, and Eddie Lang. They were all in Miller's group, but nobody knows what happened to him." Miller's obscured history was brought out in Nick Tosches' book *Where Dead Voices Gather.*

At the end of the article, Haggard makes this suggestion: "I'd just like to say to the readers of *down beat*: If they like good plain Jazz with no b------- electronics involved, come around and see what we have to offer. They may be surprised." Indeed they might.

Bob Wills and the Texas Playboys, like the Benny Goodman Orchestra, had moments, early on, when it looked like they might not be able to continue, but they both turned the tide in dramatic fashion. A reference to the high point of their success as a band is found in an entry from Wikipedia which says, "For a very brief period in 1944, the Wills band included 23 members, and around mid-year, he toured northern California, and the Pacific Northwest with 21 pieces in the orchestra. Billboard reported that Wills out-grossed Harry James, Benny Goodman, 'both Dorsies, et al' at Civic Auditorium in Oakland, CA (Oakland again!) in January of 1944."

By the time Wills was making appearances on December 7th and 8th of 1968 at "Club Dreambowl," it was after he had disbanded the Playboys in 1965. That December 7th date marked the twenty-seven year anniversary of the Dream Bowl's scheduled opening. Wills was making the rounds performing solo with local house bands backing him up. He was on his last legs, and a few months after those shows, and on May 31, 1969, Wills had a stroke from which he would not recover. For Wills and many other musicians, an unhealthy lifestyle—so often a partner to life on the road—enforced its toll. In Wills' case, too many stogies and too much drink hurt him, but however we might view such tendencies, they were part of the human package that was the Bob Wills that many came to know. It was *that* man who initiated, time after time, the following situation, and for a first-hand description, let's listen to Bob's pianist Al Stricklin recalling in his book *My Life with Bob Wills* his initial trip with the band after having just joined. Concerned about attendance (and getting paid) for a gig in Glen Oak, a remote spot fifteen miles east of Bartlesville, Oklahoma, he begin to relax as people started showing up about 8 PM:

> Cars were piling up outside. Some people were coming on foot. Some were riding horses. By nine, they were having to

turn them away. We started playing. Bob hadn't arrived yet. And nobody paid us much mind. About thirty minutes later, while we were playing, I heard the damndest racket I had ever heard. There was applause, yelling and whistling. People were just going wild. Bob Wills had finally arrived…When Bob started, the applause drowned out the music. Bob was grinning and playing, and every so often he'd point that fiddle bow of his at one of the boys and tell him to get with it. We would. And again would come that wave of applause. Maddening. Deafening. I had never heard or seen anything like it. It wasn't a dance. It was a show. What people call today 'a happening' (Stricklin wrote the book between 1973 and 1976).

It is important to mention that the two dates talked about here happen just two weeks after the excitement that occurred at the Palomar with the Goodman Orchestra. Dare we say that something was in the air?

Stricklin talked about his experiences the day before on September 6, 1935, his first playing date as a member of the band. Traveling to Tulsa to meet the band for a noon broadcast at the Barrel Food Palace, he and his wife Betty had to fight through the huge crowd that had gathered to get to the bandstand where the band was already playing. Mind you, this is his first gig:

I don't know why, but suddenly in the middle of a number, Bob looked out and spotted me in the crowd. He said, "Hold it boys, look who I see in that crowd. It's old Al Stricklin. Let him through, friends." Two things impressed me about that. I had never been called Al before. The other thing was the way that Bob had that crowd eating out of his hand. I have never seen any other person who could hold a crowd of people spellbound the way he could.

Not long after that great, confidence-building welcome, Stricklin's heart sank as soon as he began playing because the piano was in terrible condition, and it really limited his ability to play well. After the performance, he'd been told that later that afternoon there would be a rehearsal and a meeting. Feeling bad about the way things had gone, he strongly feared that at that meeting he'd be told that his services were no longer required, and he and wife would have to head back to Texas, with $14.75 between them of the $20.00 they'd started out with when they began their trip—a decision that required great courage, considering the risk. Nevertheless, he showed up to the meeting on time. Sitting in a chair where he, as he recalled "...had a good worry on," Bob approached and said:

> Al, I want to apologize for that old piano at the broadcast. I know it was impossible to play and I want you to know that I think you are great and we are really glad to have you." He squeezed my shoulders and continued, "Al, I'm promising you. That piano will be repaired or replaced by tomorrow." I'll never forget the feeling that came over me after that. More than thirty-seven years later I can still feel it. That man had magic. He could turn you on and make you want to perform the impossible.

He had touched many lives that way. Bob Wills: Quite a guy.

Johnny Cash

"The biographies of great artists make it abundantly clear that the creative urge is often so imperious that it battens on their humanity and yokes everything to the service of the work, even at the cost of health and ordinary human happiness. The unborn work in the psyche of the artist is a force of nature that achieves its end either with tyrannical might or with the subtle cunning of nature herself, quite regardless of the personal fate of the man who is its vehicle."

-Carl Jung (*The Spirit in Man, Art, and Literature*)-

"…I work hard on my music. I put in a lot of thought. I lose a lot of sleep"

-Johnny Cash-

It comes as no surprise now, that out of all the performers that came to the Dream Bowl, Johnny Cash would attract the most people. I say that because his star-power rose to the point where he had his own TV show, and even if you didn't watch the show, you were aware that he had one. I was not watching much TV in those days, from the summer of 1969 to the spring of 1971 when the show had its run, but looking back on the guest lists of those shows, I wish that I had. Great guests included Louis Armstrong, Bob Dylan, Joni Mitchell, Merle Haggard, Ray Charles, and Eric Clapton. The excitement Cash generated at the Dream Bowl in the late fifties happened long before his popularity grew to the point that he was a household name.

Except for an occasional crossover hit record—and Cash had his share of them—I was not hearing Country music around the house, growing up, and I did not go looking for it. On those rare occasions when I did hear it, it didn't do much for me. As time passed, I gradually became aware that Country and Rock musicians were listening to and borrowing from each other. That sort of cross-pollination was going on all over the place. Tony Williams, famous for becoming the drummer in the Miles Davis Group when he was still a teenager, was a person I wrongly assumed had to have been exclusively steeped in Jazz, but he talked about listening to and being interested in Led Zeppelin and other Rock bands of the 60s and 70s. No surprise then, when he formed one of the first Jazz/Rock fusion groups—Tony Williams Lifetime—comprised of Williams, John McLaughlin, and Larry Young. Bassist Jack Bruce (from Cream), would join the trio on its second album.

Ray Charles, the first musician about whom I was fanatic, recorded a very important breakthrough album, *Modern Sounds in Country and Western Music*, in 1962. It was hugely successful, and for that reason, Ray did not focus as much on writing original material from that point on. The biggest selling single, "I Can't Stop Loving You," had been buried on the album, the next to the last cut on side two, because producers didn't think it had any potential to be a hit on the radio. Boy, were they wrong. Despite the comparatively long running time of the song (4:13), it was heard constantly on the radio, and the songs "You Don't Know Me," and "Born to Lose," also got considerable air-play. Ray was new to the ABC Paramount label having come over from Atlantic Records, as had John Coltrane, and executives, knowing how successful he had been as a rhythm and blues artist were not thrilled with Ray's plan to do an album of Country songs on his first effort with the label. Wisely, they deferred to Ray's wishes, helped by the fact that he had already earned a measure of artistic autonomy (and royalty percentage per recording) uncommon in the industry. As A&R person Sid Feller said, even though Ray stuck to the original melodies "… when Ray Charles sings it, it sounds like a brand new song." The impact of the record was far reaching, causing Country music to be heard in quarters where that had never been the case, and by people who had confined their interests to Country artists alone and were now hearing great interpretations by a black musician. This was a huge development. More than one person in the music industry has talked about how beneficial that record was for Country music in general. Among them, Buck Owens recognized the recording as a major influence; later (1966), Ray had a big hit with "Crying Time," a song by Owens; and Willie Nelson said the album "did more for Country music than any one artist has ever done." Doug Freeman, an editor of the Austin Chronicle which focuses on activities in "The Live Music Capital of the World," commented on the "...melding of Country and R&B..." by writing: "With his 1962 *Modern Sounds in Country and Western Music*, Ray Charles created the benchmark for crossing the line, highlighting the similarities in sentiment often overshadowed by sound." In quite skillful fashion, Freeman really nailed it with that important observation.

As a result of my having become so interested in his music, I learned more about the man himself, and because of that, I would say that Charles took the whole development in stride. He never sensed any great separation in gospel tinged blues, "crying sanctified," as Blues singer Big Bill Broonzy once described his singing—an approach for which the descriptive word "soul" was first used—and a sad Country song, because he liked a good song that told a story, and moreover, he listened to and enjoyed all types of music. This was also true for Charlie Parker, who seldom listened to Jazz, as it was for Frank Zappa who seldom listened to Rock. I think it is possible for any sighted individual, that that ability to see might (unfortunately) aid in bringing about certain prohibitions to enjoyment between different styles of music that Ray Charles was able to see past because he heard (only) the music and the soul(s) behind it.

I still prefer Ray's original and earlier recordings on Atlantic, but *Modern Sounds* was full of great songs all of which he skillfully rendered. For a long time, I thought the coolest thing I had heard by any musician was Ray's piano intro on "What'd I Say," one of his songs recorded on Atlantic. I loved the sound of that electric piano, still do, and being the innovative musician he was, he had to have been one of the few musicians using that instrument in 1959. He showed you several styles, and did them all very well. He had great soloists who could hang with any major Jazz acts, and his singing just really got to me. In terms of infusing and delivering a song with emotional power, he was one of the best ever; by itself, that would have been enough of an accomplishment, but he was awesome as a live performer to boot. One of my most prized possessions is *Ray Charles in Person,* a recording from Herndon Stadium, Atlanta, Georgia, 1959. It's killer from the first note through five songs and two instrumentals.

In addition to his playing, singing, composing, and performing skills was the fact that he was also a great arranger capable of transforming an innocuous ditty into a much more potent version of its former self. An example is "You are my Sunshine," featuring Marjorie Hendricks and the Raelets. Showcasing how good Ray's band was, the arrangement features the band providing a great groove, a smooth-sounding riff to back up Ray's initial vocals. There follows a middle section of the entire band soloing as one, that leads into Marjorie Hendricks bracing solo and the piece then concludes with Ray's trademark passionate pleas. Check it out (running time 3:01). Sunshine indeed—with an exclamation point. Marjorie Hendricks, by the way, could belt out a song with as much force as Ray and I was disappointed when she was not talked about at all in the important documentary *Twenty Feet from Stardom,* which focused on female backup singers and the painful obscurity that usually comes with the job.

Because of the structure and standard delivery of "You are my Sunshine" with which we'd all become familiar, the song seemed absolutely beyond a more soulful interpretation, but Ray totally re-designed it. Often, we're not comfortable with a song's re-arrangement and say it has been "butchered," but Charles' version, nearly unrecognizable in its new form, was a mutation that gave it more life and stature, something he had accomplished on numerous occasions with a variety of songs. So with his unique arrangements and winning style, Ray Charles had made a very important contribution that paved the way for more mixing of musical styles, and I'm so glad I was along for the ride.

I still regard the work of Ray Charles as having been a very good place to begin a life of interest in music, considering the directions to which I was drawn from that point forward. Out of the various musical exchanges in which different musical traditions became friends and borrowed from one another, it became undeniably evident that there was some wonderful stuff going on in Country music, and this made possible the larger impact that a Johnny Cash could bring.

In Nicholas Dawidoff's book, *In the Country of Country,* he recounts an interview with Sam Phillips from Sun Records, where Cash started out saying that Phillips "...excitedly..." told him more than forty years after the fact: "Nobody I'd heard sounded like him." "Even if you didn't like that voice, it got your attention." Dawidoff adds his own opinion, "It still does. Cash's untrained voice has a natural ability to express suffering. The deep, affectless bass-baritone that struggles to keep up with even a medium tempo...lodged somewhere between talk and music, his singing is flat and artless and grim, the way the white poverty-stricken South was flat, artless, and grim."

That describes his voice to a tee alright and his voice certainly invokes and evokes the hardship of his surroundings. Grim though it was, he did something very creative with it and rose above those things thought to be obstacles. We've heard about bleak circumstances which served as incubator for artistic accomplishment so often that we're forced to regard such a scenario as offering equal possibilities when compared to an environment where artistic endeavors are encouraged and taught in stimulating locales. What, then, constitutes the ideal environment from which artistic creation can emerge? What comes to my mind in this regard is Frank Zappa talking about being bored to death when he was living in Lancaster, CA in the

Antelope Valley of the Mojave Desert. If you were to be entertained, you had to come up with something on your own, and if ever there was a champion in the world of music for DIY it was Frank Zappa, and it began there in the desert.

According to Dawidoff, Johnny began writing songs in Dyess, Arkansas at age 12. He joined the Air Force at age 19, in 1951 and kept writing. By 1954, he found himself in Sun Studios literally alongside Carl Perkins, Elvis Presley, and Jerry Lee Lewis. Roy Orbinson was at Sun at this time too. Sam Phillips, that clever old cuss, was haulin' in the gold. He made the mistake however, of not protecting his claim very carefully. Cash and Perkins left for Columbia, and Elvis went to RCA. At about the same time Cash left, Orbison went to Monument Records and according to Cash in his autobiography, Phillips, having found out through the grapevine that the two of them had signed other options, phoned Johnny at home, and Orbison was there at the time. Neither had admitted what they'd done when Phillips had asked them on an earlier occasion if it was true. Now Sam, plenty irritated, wanted an explanation, and, says Cash, "…wanted to know why I lied." Johnny told him "…he hadn't been truthful with me about a few things (which itself wasn't true)…, so I thought I'd just pay him back a little." Then Phillips, who Cash says is now "…even madder…" wants Orbison on the phone and proceeds to read Roy the riot act, and Orbison, unable to contain himself, busts out laughing, as did Johnny. You can just see the smoke coming out of Phillip's ears as he slams the phone down. I say that because having seen Phillips several times in interviews, I noticed he always had a glint in his eye like that of an explosive preacher on the verge of delivering fire and brimstone.

Cash continued to work on the craft of songwriting. The combination of his serious approach to songwriting, his unique voice, commanding presence, honesty of delivery and love of occupation accounted for his popularity. From Dawidoff's *In the Country of Country*, he goes on to say, "From 1955 to '57, Cash was prolific. He wrote in cars, at rest stops, in waiting rooms, and in time those songs have come to be one of the most influential bodies of work in both Country and Rock history…"

In a 1973 interview with Robert Hilburn from *Rolling Stone*, Cash said, "Good talent will always be heard. There's nothing going to take the place of the human being. They can get all the Moog synthesizers that they want, but nothing will take the place of the human heart."

Cash's well-known personal history is filled with troubled moments, and Johnny himself would be the first to admit that he was a sinner, prompting Dawidoff to comment, "For years Cash has vacillated between Saturday night and Sunday morning…" but he always professed his faith and was equally courageous and willing to praise Jesus as he was to condemn war. There is a photo, a famous one by Jim Marshall, of Johnny and June Carter Cash nestled up to one another. I don't know the circumstances, but it looks like a moment on the road, where one can get weary, and they were providing one another sanctuary—what Cash's friend Bob Dylan would call "shelter from the storm." They are tenderly close in embrace, not a false display of affection for the cameras, but a moment of their own creation that functions as a shield to the outside world, their love rising above that world and allowing a mutual and honest display of vulnerability; but, adding to the story that the picture tells is the tension that is being projected as well, as the storm clouds were never far off where Johnny Cash was concerned.

Regarding the development of his musical style, Johnny sensed that it would be helpful to check out other life circumstances to enrich the experiences he had pretty much tapped out around his home, and says in his autobiography with Patrick Carr that he "loved driving into Orange Mound, the black part of town, to sit on Gus Cannon's porch and listen to him sing and play guitar." Well, just who is Gus Cannon? Along with (evidence will show) a great many others, I had been touched by him, but did not realize it until I began working on this book. It took a long time to find out.

It's 1963, I'm sixteen and it's my turn in the chair at the barbershop on Silverado Trail right across from Food Fair Supermarket where my mother was a clerk for nine years, a significant situation which ensured that I never got away with any shenanigans when I was at Alta Heights Elementary School which was but a few blocks away. Many of the moms residing in the area shopped at Food Fair, where all pertinent information regarding behavior at school by off-springs was pipelined to my mother posthaste. Information sharing on-line is sluggish compared to a network of mothers at the local market. My mother was always, therefore, armed psychic-like, with the events of the day, and would meet me at home after school with stern looks of accusation the moment I walked in the door. *Damn, how does she know?*

So, I'm getting my haircut, and this song comes on the radio. I'm hearing it for the first time and I really like it. I liked it so much that I clearly remember thinking, in that moment, that *this song is going to be a hit.* It was a simple song; repetitive but catchy. It sounded as if there were several guitars being played. It's worth recalling that in 1963 folk music was quite popular, as popular as it was ever going to get, and "Tom Dooley," for example, had been a hit for the very successful Kingston Trio. The TV show Hootenanny which debuted Oct. 12, 1963 was ABC's second-most popular show, running for three seasons, and featuring, almost exclusively, folk groups. Students on college campuses were mostly listening to folk bands. Later, this period of popularity, would be referred to, amusingly, as the "folk scare," where all manner of liberal and progressive ideas were lurking in the lyrics that likely contributed to its short shelf-life. Also relevant, I would contend with regard to Folk music's lack of staying power, was the feeling expressed by David Byrne, in his book *How Music Works*, that "The Folk scene was low energy too, as if the confessional mode and Folk's inherent sincerity was somehow enervating, in and of itself."

The telecasts of the shows done on various college campuses were loosely described as live performances. The "live" audiences could have been described perhaps more accurately as 500 or so movie extras, but I watched the show often enough to see some genuinely achieved exciting moments. I remember the "house" bassist, a black musician I discovered later was named Norman Keenan. He always seemed to please the vast variety of musicians he had to support, ones I'm assuming with whom he was not acquainted—an ability helped, I'm sure, by his background as a Jazz musician. Often I'd see the featured performer walk over to shake hands with this man whose playing was always perfectly appropriate and tasteful. Those were wonderful moments because most of the guest artists were white, and a handshake uniting different races was still a pretty big deal on TV in 1963.

The song that I heard that day during folk music's moment in the sun was "Walk Right In," by the Rooftop Singers; two guys, one gal, a common arrangement for folk groups. The ringing guitars that were so noticeable throughout the verses and during the instrumental break that sounded to me like several guitars, turned out, I would learn later, to be only two, but both were 12-string guitars; it was probably the first time I had ever heard that particular instrument.

I once heard an interview with British singer/songwriter Nick Lowe, who, incidentally, would in 1979 marry June's daughter and Johnny's step-daughter Carlene Carter. Lowe had the popular single "Cruel to Be Kind." He was discussing a record on which he was working at the time, and he talked about using an acoustic guitar in the recording, and "...like the Everly Brothers, give it a good thrashing." Think of the beginning to "Wake Up, Little Susie;" that's a good thrashing, and so it was too, with "Walk Right In." There exists a YouTube video of the group singing their hit on TV, and they do a very solid performance of it which surprisingly did not involve lip-syncing, making their live performance a rare exception in those days.

After hearing it in the barbershop, it became obvious soon thereafter, that I wasn't the only one who liked the song. It was an early "crossover" hit that spent two weeks at #1 on the Billboard Hot 100, went to #1 on the "Easy Listening" chart for five weeks, peaked at #4 on the R&B chart, went to #23 on the Country music chart, was #1 in Australia, in the top ten in the UK, and was record label Vanguard's most successful record of all time. The writer of that song, who'd also put out the original version, was the man Johnny Cash was listening to on that porch: Gus Cannon. Cannon had made a recording of it with his Jug Stompers in 1929.

I once heard the very talented guitarist/singer/songwriter Bonnie Raitt, who my wife and I had the pleasure of seeing at the Paramount Theater in Oakland, say to Terry Gross on her radio show "Fresh Air" that guitarist Roy Rogers, a frequent collaborator and guest musician in her touring band (mentioned earlier as having been a onetime member of Vallejo's Joe Pallotta Band and later with John Lee Hooker), had a unique modern style as a blues guitarist. He was also, she went on to say, "…deep in the trenches…" which accounted for the fullness of his style. Johnny Cash has spent considerable time in those trenches of his songwriting background, and therefore brings with him great believability in the delivery of a song. In performance, he gives the impression of singular importance to that particular song as he sings it to you, because he's had the living to back it up. When Sinatra serves up an invitation for a romantic excursion in the song "Come Fly With Me," he sings it with conviction because we know he had the means, and had done that sort of thing more than once. It's not every singer that can live up to the words he or she is singing to us, but by being the writer of a song, an edge is earned regarding the impression that can be made. Even after the demise of Tin Pan Alley-like song factories and the rise of the singer/songwriter, the likely case remains that most songs sung are done so with lyrics by someone other than the singer's. It well could be that that singer might capture admirably (or even in superior fashion) the emotional content of the lyricist's message, but for me there is added appreciation if I know the singer has written the song. One of the famous song pairings delivered in live performance by the Grateful Dead is "Scarlet Begonias" to "Fire on the Mountain." I am particularly fond of how the band performs it live because there typically is a long instrumental development between the two songs which is often very adventurous.

"Scarlet Begonias" is a song in which the narrator tells us about his encounter with a woman, but an extension of this relationship is not in the cards. There's an attraction to the woman and we're told, in complimentary fashion by the narrator that, "I knew without asking, she was into the blues." There were a number of plus factors, but he confesses in the end that, "I had to learn the hard way, to let her pass by, let her pass by." Then in what feels like a state-of-grace amid mild elation that comes out of a personal decision made in a sea of contradiction, he steps back out into the world at large as "The wind in the willows played tea for two— Sky was yellow and the sun was blue—Strangers stopping strangers just to shake their hand—Everybody's playing in the heart-of-gold band, heart-of-gold-band." As much as I love the many interpretations I've heard of that song over the years by the Dead, it was still quite moving to hear it done by Robert Hunter himself, who penned those words. The version I heard was sparse with perhaps just guitar accompaniment, giving the lyrics precedence, and his voice is similar to Cash's, low, and also like Cash's (and this was pointed out by Dawidoff) as near to recitation as it is to singing, but very unique and penetrating.

I first heard Johnny Cash's "Big River" performed by the Dead. It's up tempo, one that the Dead have done in conjunction with their own "Cumberland Blues" whose tempo is the same, going from one into the other as if they were conceived together.

That up tempo, according to Cash, was at the suggestion of Sam Phillips. Cash had wanted to do it as a slow blues, but went with Sam's instincts which Cash admitted were very good. I can't imagine it being done in a slow manner. I feel that there is a playful quality to the story that probably would not be permitted by the song structure if it had been done as the slow blues he originally envisioned.

The song caught Bob Dylan's teenage ears, perhaps helped by the fact that his home state, Minnesota, is mentioned in the lyrics, which made a lasting impression on this soon-to-be songwriter. Dylan told Nicholas Dawidoff when he heard the lyrics to the chorus in Big River "…that they seemed to him '…just words that turned into bone.'"

> Now I taught the weeping willow how to cry
> And I showed the clouds how to cover up a clear blue sky
> And the tears that I cried for that woman
> are gonna flood you Big River
> Then I'm gonna sit right here until I die

Those lyrics caught my attention too, and something else when I checked online to see the song in its entirety. I was looking at the verses written out and I saw that Minnesota, where their paths crossed, is shown in parentheses. Then I checked out a Grand Ole Opry TV performance by Johnny on YouTube, and I swear, the way he emphasizes the word, as an aside, he makes you see those parentheses. Check it out and see if you don't agree (running time 2:14).

Cash, Marshall Grant, and Luther Perkins were all strumming acoustic guitars when they first formed as a band, and Marshall had the idea of changing the instrumentation around. They had heard Elvis on the radio and thought they ought to make a recording so that they, too, might be heard on the radio. Luther Perkins borrowed a used Fender Telecaster electric guitar from a friend and store manager Sid Layworth, who at the same time sold a similarly worn upright bass for twenty-five dollars to Marshall Grant. Grant didn't know a thing about the bass, and I loved learning that someone helped them tune it, after which Grant used adhesive tape to mark the strings so he knew where the notes were. Luther Perkins was going to have to play lead-guitar, something he had never done before. They then embarked on what we would come to know as a very successful collaboration; even though they knew they were not stellar musicians at the time, they had the all-important element of commitment. As Marshall said, "(But) almost every weekend without fail, John, Luther, and I would get together and have fun working with our instruments and trying to get better. We just kept at it, and after several months, the three of us decided it was time to go looking for the company that was recording Elvis."

The key phrase there is "just kept at it." They built their group sound from the ground up, and maybe they didn't know what they were doing, but it didn't keep them from carving out something unique. According to Grant, it helped: "You know, most times an inability to do something can stop you from achieving whatever goal you may have set. But in our case, our *inability* to play our instruments was suddenly becoming a positive."

In addition to that stripped-down instrumental backing, the "boom-chicka-boom sound" that became so famous, the three musicians also developed a winning formula for their live performances. Johnny had more than enough charisma to handle the "front man" requirements of the group, delivering the songs with emotion and adding flourishes with his guitar, holding it high up to the mic while he played and occasionally strumming up the neck of the guitar. Marshall Grant was likewise a very energetic presence on stage, bouncing up and down, slapping bass strings, and chewin' gum. For his part, Luther Perkins' demeanor and function was like that of bassist John Entwistle from The Who. If you have every band member jumping around, maybe it has the effect of canceling each other out, but have one member stand like a statue, and you've achieved some effective contrast. For both Perkins and Entwistle, their physical activity was limited to their fingers, and Entwistle would in precise and subtle manner raise the neck of his bass guitar just enough so that the energized and stage-roving vocalist Roger Daltrey would not collide with it. Luther Perkins, for his part, would just move those stoic eyes ever so slightly to give fans something to talk about later. The band had personality.

All this helped to establish a successful career, but it sure didn't hurt to have the savvy Sam Phillips come up with a winning manipulation or two. We already talked about his suggestion that "Big River" be played faster, and Phillips had also done that on another very important song for Johnny Cash and the Tennessee Two. In February of 1956, they had four songs that were doing well: "Folsom Prison Blues,"[*] "So Doggone Lonesome," "Hey Porter," and "Cry, Cry, Cry," and Johnny was ready with his next song to record, "I Walk the Line."

They recorded it for Phillips at a very slow tempo. He told them he loved it, "But do me a favor. Just do one more take for me, and let's move the tempo up quite a bit." Johnny was insistent about wanting "to keep it as a slow ballad." According to Grant, Sam came back with: "I don't have no problem with that, John, I just want to hear it one time for my own personal view." Two months later, after a performance on the *Louisiana Hayride* (Bob Wills had been the guest on its very first show: April 3, 1948), they were driving back after the show listening to KWKH, when on the air came the new recording—and it was the fast version. Grant said, "We were furious..." They confronted Sam the next morning. Grant tells us that Phillips, seeing the three of them charging into his studio, said (while holding both of his hands up), "Wait, guys, wait! I know what you're thinking! But give me two weeks. If it don't do what I think it's going to do, I promise you right here, I'll pull the record..." Two weeks later, back on the *Hayride* again, they dutifully play the up-tempo version. "People

---

[*] For an important perspective on Folsom Prison Blues, as well as an engaging look at his love for Motown Music, I highly recommend Bruce Jenkins' book *Shop Around.*

just loved it!" "Driving home," Grant added, "we kept twisting the radio dial back and forth, hoping to hear our new song, and in a two-hour stretch we heard 'I Walk the Line' thirteen times on thirteen different radio stations." How great it must have felt to be riding in that car! They were no longer upset by that duplicitous little trick that ol' Sam had played so smartly.

What makes "I Walk the Line" or any other song popular still remains a mystery. There is no formula for a guaranteed hit. It is agreed, for instance, that the Kingsmen's "Louie Louie" is not a particularly distinguished piece of music. A very basic song, the recorded version that became so well-known was the result of the first and only "take" in the studio, and band members (stunned that they were not allowed to try again) tell of problems with microphone setups and mistakes in its execution, but it had to have had something right. In Dave Marsh's interesting 207-page look at that one song, *Louie Louie*, he quotes from a phone conversation he had with lead vocalist Jack Ely, who commented on the song's success saying: "A very wise person once told me, 'The spirit of love is in that record.' 'At that precise moment the six people involved were in love with that song and you can hear that on the tape.'" Marsh then reports: "Told that this seems a very precise definition of what's going on within the grooves of the fabled Wand 143, Ely sighed and even on a transcontinental telephone line, you could feel his face squinch up somewhere between a smile and a grimace. 'That was my mother,' he said."

Sam Phillips was right, I think, in saying that the voice of Johnny Cash got one's attention. In the book I'd read by Al Stricklin, who'd been Bob Wills' piano player, I discovered a scrap of paper while working on this portion of the book. On it I had jotted down some ideas having to do with the notion of someone, centuries ago, attempting alchemy in a dimly-lit and crudely constructed laboratory. By today's standards such long-ago undertakings lacked order and precision, but of equal value, regardless of the state of science of any era, was the attitude and approach of the alchemist himself. That attitude was an essential part of the potentially correct mixing of elements that might produce something extraordinary, owing to honesty of purpose. That attitude was an equally important component of the experiment at hand, along with the tools and materials of his profession, the combination of which gave transformation a chance. With respect to the alchemy of song then, even with that impressive delivery from Cash, you're getting more than just his voice; it's the whole package of a life and roads traveled brought together into a compelling whole. With respect to songwriting or composition, one cannot apply the hurtful things people do to one another to the act of songwriting itself. Yes, you can tailor the lyrics to reflect a tale of woe, but that reflection isn't what's going on between the writer and that which is written in the creative moment. You can't be mean to a song. You can't hurt its feelings with an ill-considered response.

The one sin I know of is neglect. According to a Wikipedia profile, the great drummer Edward Blackwell, most famous for being a member of Ornette Coleman's groundbreaking quartet along with Don Cherry and Charlie Haden, liked to make use of an ancient adage from the Orient: "Neglect your art for one day, and it will neglect you for two." Let us recognize then, with respect, the sanctity of songwriting and creativity, and hold sacred the purity of behavior, artist to craft, that seems to hover above the shortcomings found elsewhere in life.

Juxtaposition is a clumsy word that's difficult to pronounce, and as for its appearance it's as if someone reached into the Scrabble pile, tossed up a handful of letters and out came this word, its arrangement befitting its meaning. I mention the word because we've all seen that music used in TV and film often makes a dramatic impression, provided it's a movie we find engaging and one that brings about some measure of surrender on our part opening us up to greater emotional impact. Arthur Schopenhauer, in *The World as Will and Idea*, had this to say on the matter: "This close relation which music has to the true nature of all things can also explain the fact that when music suitable to any scene, action, event, or environment is played, it seems to disclose to us its most secret meaning, and appears to be the most accurate and distinct commentary upon it."

In the *Sons of Anarchy* television series, such a moment occurs in the episode in which Jax goes to Ireland where his recently-kidnapped infant son has already been adopted. He intends to reclaim him, but when, from a distance, he sees the love the new guardians are giving his son, he has second thoughts because he has always struggled internally with the fate he imposes on his son because he, the father, is the leader of a motorcycle gang. As anyone knows who saw the series conclude, this is a prophetic moment. While he follows the parents, carefully staying out of sight, the song "Alesund" is playing in the background by Sun Kil Moon, with its composer Mark Kozelek, formerly from Bay Area band Red House Painters, on vocals.

Thanks to my son Michael (who later would be in a band with drummer Anthony Koutsos from R.H.P), I've been introduced, over the years, to many interesting bands, among them the Red House Painters, and therefore I had heard Kozelek when he was still with that band, but I'd never heard "Alesund," until that moment in the show. It's an achingly beautiful song, but Kozelek has a murmuring manner of singing his lyrics and the recording has a vocal track in both left and right channels a slight bit out of phase. It sounds great but all those elements combined make the words difficult to make out. When I later used closed-captioning and learned what the lyrics were, it became clear that they didn't relate to the scene at all. "Alesund" is similar, in sentiment, to the Dead's "Scarlet Begonias." He meets a girl (they are both musicians) and they hang out together pleasantly. It probably could have turned into something, but for some reason, like the narrator in "Scarlet Begonias," who decides it's better to "...let her pass by," Kozelek's narrator tells us he does not pursue the relationship and its possibilities. He leaves the partying group of friends and ducks back into the darkness and Norwegian winter in the port town of Alesund. What the song does have, however, and this did relate to the scene, is an emotional pull. There's something about a compelling scene, and this certainly was one, that enables a piece of music or a song to hit you with greater impact because of the context, like the angelic voice of the opera singer when Andy Dufresne takes over the record player in *Shawshank Redemption*.

In the movie *Silver Linings Playbook*, the main character, played by Bradley Cooper, is struggling with bi-polar issues as he desperately seeks reconciliation with the wife from whom (by restraining order) he is separated, instead of moving on and recognizing the growing love for the new woman in his life. This new person, played by Jennifer Lawrence and for which she received the Academy Award for Best Actress, gets him to be her partner in a dance competition which he agrees to do if she'll deliver a letter to his ex. While they're practicing for the competition and slowly getting to know one another, she plays Bob Dylan's "Girl from the North Country." I had heard Dylan perform it before, but I either had not known about the version used at this moment in the movie, when Cash joined Dylan in a duet, or did not remember it—and I was surprised. It did "work" after all, in the scene as a paean to intimacy and as possible encouragement to place a former lover in the past. In that meaningful moment, it occurred to me that these were, quite possibly, the two most recognizable voices around during the course of my adult life. Was the intonation always right there? Did they achieve proper harmony? The more important question for me was: would the impact for this scene have been greater had some other singers delivered it in place of Dylan and Cash? I answer—not on your life.

More recently, on the TV drama *The Blacklist,* as an episode nears conclusion, the main character (Reddington, played by James Spader), is going around settling scores with people who have it coming. All the while, Cash's "When the Man Comes Around" is playing during the dialogue-free succession of scenes. It was not a song with which I was familiar, but there was no mistaking that voice or its somber mood. The impression of Cash's song in that moment was so strong that it got me thinking; yes, it was seemingly the ideal song for that moment, and in this case the lyrics did fit with the action, but I wondered if there was some other mojo at work that increased what I thought was its undeniable power to reach out and grab the listener. There was. This song was one of Johnny's final recordings, and part of a very fruitful collaboration with producer Rick Rubin. In Robert Hilburn's biography, *Johnny Cash,* he quotes Tom Petty who said "Rick was just over the moon about working with Johnny. I don't know if any record meant more to him than Johnny's." That's one aspect of the achievement.

I knew a bit about Rick Rubin, enough to know that he had been a part of a number of successful recording projects involving different styles of music with a variety of artists, Tom Petty among them. He was respected in the industry, and coaxed good effort from the people with whom he'd worked. Hearing Rubin in interviews, it doesn't take long to realize that he is intelligent, his perspectives are insightful, he knows what he's doing, and perhaps as important as those just-mentioned qualities in his role as a producer, he is a bear of a man. He's soft-spoken because he needn't yell. Rubin's formidable presence made me recall Adam Smith's entertaining 1975 book *Powers of Mind* about self-help trends in America which had a chapter dedicated to a man Smith identifies as Swami Hal.

Unlike Rubin, Swami Hal was gruff and loud. But size does matter. According to Smith, Swami Hal was American, abrasive, gigantic, bearded, and offensive, but was nevertheless the genuine article. "I went to India, I took my vows, I'm a renunciate, that's what a swami is, and that's what I am." He ran a little ashram in a remote spot deep in the woods somewhere off the grid in the Northwest. He had, said Smith "...a few followers and some juvenile delinquents who had been farmed out to him by despairing civil authorities."

Smith asked "...what the young incipient hoods did?"

"They meditate," Hal said. "And they work on the farm."

Smith asked, "Because it's a religious principle?"

"BECAUSE I'LL KICK THEIR ASSES IF THEY DON'T AND THEY KNOW I CAN DO IT," Hal boomed.

I reprint it just as Smith had in the book, all caps and bold like Hal himself and I laughed so hard when I came across it. The point is I don't think there is going to be much barking-back from any musician if and when Rubin, towering over them, feels the need to lean on them a little to get done what needs to be done.

With Johnny Cash however, there was no such requirement. What the two of them were working on was the final chapter of a remarkable story from the world of music. So we have, as mentioned earlier, the enthusiasm of Rubin for the project, combined with Johnny's awareness that his time was running out—another factor of compelling significance. There's no missing the sense of urgency that is present in that moment. Rubin kept after Cash to do what he (Johnny) wanted to do. Johnny marshalled his strength giving every last ounce of energy he had to the project, all the time in terrible pain, particularly his jaw, which after an earlier operation had never healed properly. About his work on *American Recordings,* Anthony DeCurtis, from *Rolling Stone,* said in a beautiful description befitting Johnny's history and strength of effort on the recording: "Not a feeling is flaunted, not a jot of sentimentality is permitted, but every quaver, every shift in volume, every catch in a line resonates like a private apocalypse." Wow!

A collaboration (initially suggested by Rubin) with Tom Petty and all the members of the Heartbreakers began with *American II: Unchained.* And those guys are such good musicians who, I'm sure, were locked-in and did their absolute best in a gesture of respect and tribute to their musical friend—another crucial part of the finished product. This was of particular interest to me because my son Michael Papenburg, in addition to providing his dad good tips on music, is a very accomplished guitarist and member of the band Petty Theft, who perform material from the vast and impressive collection that is the Tom Petty songbook. The band-members are (alphabetically) Django Bayless—bass and vocals, Adam Berkowitz—drums; Dan Durkin—lead vocals/acoustic guitar/harmonica; Monroe Grisman—guitar and vocals; and Michael. The current keyboardist is Steven Seydler. Previous keyboardists include Mike Emerson (now with Tommy Castro), and John Varn.

When Rubin first contacted Petty to see if he'd be interested, the first words out of his mouth were, according to Hilburn: "When do we start?" Hilburn described the sessions as follows: "Once Cash and Rubin agreed on a song, they'd play a recording of it for the musicians. Then the musicians would gather in a circle and work for a half hour or so, on an arrangement, with Cash singing along. Then they'd begin recording, usually wrapping up the song within two or three takes." "Those were wonderful sessions," Petty says. "Everything was so loose and natural." And this impressive accomplishment was helped in a big way by Rick Rubin's vision, direction, and most importantly his encouragement as he bore witness to and had a hand in the summing up of a life in song by Johnny Cash.

Getting back to Cash's "The Man Comes Around," it was a song used on a *Blacklist* season finale from the recording *American IV,* and it was one of Johnny's last compositions, which he'd updated from an earlier version. The lyrics contained a number of biblical references concerning the accounting of sins, a matter of concern for many who are near the end of their time, and this was certainly true for Johnny. For the most part, the piece is a recitation with some singing, and Johnny's own words mixed with scripture makes for a very compelling warning about behavior. It added convincingly to the scenes as they unfolded. The song in isolation had dramatic power; that effect was compounded optimally in combination with the action one sees on the TV screen. And probably the most significant fact ensuring the force of its impact, explained by Cash, was the hold the song itself had on Johnny as it developed. Like the Benny Goodman Carnegie Hall concert, the importance of the moment is transmitted to the listener. A provocation to work on the song happened when Johnny was startled awake by vivid imagery in a dream—"you're like a thorn tree in a whirlwind"—which he immediately wrote down. Cash talked about writing the song in the liner notes for the CD: "...for three or four months I recycled that song...my inner playback system always went back to 'The Man Comes Around.'" "I spent more time on this song than any I ever wrote. It's based, loosely, on the book of Revelation, with a couple of lines, or a chorus, from other biblical sources. I must have written three dozen pages of lyrics, then painfully weeded it down to the song you have here."

And Johnny Cash, working with Rick Rubin and musician friends, finished strong in his final efforts, keeping the integrity of his craft to the last minute, inking down and singing out his final words in song, respectfully honoring the muse, and making his mark under the most difficult of circumstances.

According to Raymond Sweeney, the last show of the Country and Western variety happened on January 4, 1969 with Judy Lynn. She joined a long and impressive list of performers: Merle Haggard, Johnny Cash and June Carter, Ernest Tubb, Cottonseed

Clark, Brenda Lee, Lefty Frizzell, Buck Owens, Red Foley, Black Jack Wayne, Jerry Lee Lewis, Ray Price, Wanda Jackson, Buddy Lane, "Little" Jimmie Dickens, George Jones, Gordon Terry, Freddy Hart, and Bob Wills, each of whom sang their songs, played their music and added to the rich history accumulated in this great place we know as the Dream Bowl. This is an incredible gathering of talent responsible for immeasurable amounts of entertainment. Each of their stories calls out to be told, and I regret that it is not possible to do that in one book. Think too, of their influence in helping to turn the wheels of commerce, the sheet music produced, the instruments bought, the recording studios and their technicians, the vinyl pressings required, the road and local crews needed, the food and drinks purchased, the rich material they provided for writers who document their activities. And finally, think of the much-needed joy brought to the souls of all who heard them. Thank goodness for the musicians!

The last two months of the Dream Bowl's music history begins now. As I said earlier, I got lucky because my sister Paula was friends with Sandy Callahan who was involved in its management during its last phase. After a few email exchanges, a meeting was arranged. We sat outside on her patio during a warm summer day and kept refreshed with iced tea. I had recently retired after twenty-one years of landscaping as the owner and sole employee of Grass Roots Gardening, and admired the beautiful layout and well-cared-for appearance of her yard.

Talking about her life during the time they managed the Dream Bowl, she described herself and her then husband as a busy and hard-working couple. Sandy told me that her husband Randy had been approached by a business partner who saw running the Dream Bowl as a promising business opportunity, and a third partner (and Sandy thought there might have been a fourth) was also involved. I got the feeling that the enterprise was something neither Sandy nor Randy had longed to do, but as soon as the deal had been struck, they did everything they could to make it a success. She designed and furnished a band room and made sure the snack bar was stocked with food and beverages. She was an accountant by profession, so she managed the books while also doing promotion and distributing flyers around town with the help of her sisters Pam and Judy. It sounded to me like she did most of the work.

With Sandy's help, I was able to speak by phone with Randy, right on the spot that same day, who told me that he and one of the partners met with Bill Graham at his office above the Fillmore and worked out a deal for hiring bands. He told me that after that initial meeting, hiring arrangements were made by phone. Being a plasterer and a general contractor by profession, he made the scaffolding to which he attached white sheets to accommodate the light-shows that were typically a part of concerts during the 60s which simultaneously saw the explosion of the poster-art that advertised shows.

At one point during our time talking, Sandy went back into her house, and when she returned to the patio, I was delighted when she produced, and let me have, one of the leftover flyers she'd printed for one of the shows, one that she still had in her possession forty-three years later. On the flyer were The Sons of Champlin, Blues Helping, and Rockwell Blues Band for

NEW

DREAM BOWL PRESENTS

3 GREAT BANDS

February 14 & 15

SONS OF CHAMPLIN
BLUES HELPING
ROCKWELL BLUES BAND

8 - 1   Admission $3.00

Napa - Vallejo Highway

shows on Feb 14 and 15, 1969. Rockwell performed at our first class reunion in 1970. Jimmy Lloyd was its lead guitarist, and Bill Leach was its lead singer.

David La Flamme, of whom Sandy spoke highly, was a classically trained violinist, co-founder of It's a Beautiful Day, and one of the lead singers along with Patti Santos. Together, they sang the duet on the beautiful "White Bird," the group's most famous song. On a Youtube video from 1969, Bill Graham, with sentiments echoing Sandy's, introduces them as "...some of the nicest people around." Sandy described La Flame as quite the gentleman, but as for the Grateful Dead, she told me she scolded them because they made such a mess of the band room she had so carefully set up.

As was said, the enterprise did not last very long. I got the impression from Sandy that because there were several people involved--which invariably makes any operation trickier to run—it complicated the bookkeeping process. For various reasons, it became too troublesome to continue. I remain, however, eternally grateful that they kept it going as long as they did. Because of their efforts, the opportunity to see the Grateful Dead and Santana paved the way for countless hours of still ongoing musical enjoyment, the immeasurable benefits of which began that night in February of 1969 when I saw those bands for the first time at the Dream Bowl.

I'd become curious about all the bands that had sprouted up all over the Bay Area in the summer of '67. The Dead were getting some air-play on AM radio back then, and AM was all that I was listening to at that time. If the "underground" FM stations were operating, I had not yet discovered them. Not long after seeing the Dead, I began checking out KMPX, KSAN, and other Bay Area FM stations. While working on the latter portions of this book, I had the pleasure of reading Peter Richardson's informative and insightful book on the Dead, *No Simple Highway*, and would learn according to Richardson that KMPX experimented with the "free-form" format in April of 1967 and "...went to it full-time four months later."

What a delight and privilege it was to be around for the beginnings of this new approach to radio. FM radio involved considerably less interference from chatty DJ's or static, and they were not hampered by long-standing restrictive formats; instead, they allowed whoever was at the helm the freedom to play what they wanted. I still remember how wonderful it was the first time I heard all the way through, for example—on the radio before I had the record—the twenty-five minutes and twenty-two seconds of Quicksilver's live version of Bo Diddley's "Who do you Love," from their second album *Happy Trails*. Many years later I heard from a friend of mine, a fellow high school classmate who went on to college, that he and a couple of buddies were hanging out in their dorm room going nuts because they were so hyped listening to that same recording. I got to see Quicksilver twice, and both were memorable experiences. The first was at the Santa Rosa Fairgrounds in 1969 in a pavilion in which the power went out temporarily. Someone lit a candle on stage and drummer Greg Elmore played a solo until the lights came back on. The next and final time I saw them was in October of 1970 at Winterland, which was the last time the Dead, Jefferson Airplane, and Quicksilver shared a bill. John Cipollina was Quicksilver's extraordinary lead guitarist, who in an interview talked about the sound he sought, saying that what he really liked was what he called "rodent-gnawing" treble which was achieved powerfully with a grouping of six treble horns that were part of his amplification system. I never saw anyone else use such a set up and this unique on-stage gear made its way to the Rock and Roll Hall of Fame. Quicksilver had, I thought, the best one-two guitar punch of any of the Bay Area bands, as Gary Duncan was not only a very good soloist but a great rhythm-guitarist as well. I find his work on the opening portion of "Who do You Love," to be one of the best examples of rhythm guitar as it adds so much to all else going on and really drives this strong opening of exemplary playing after which is included, later in the piece, some of the most creative audience participation you're apt to find: a right-on-it sustained run of polyrhythmic clapping, as the band lays out, that reaches an unbearable pitch as those gathered anticipate the thunderous return of the guitars. If you've never heard it, I highly recommend adding the twenty six minutes of its duration to your bucket list. It will take you for a grand ride if you just climb aboard.

Pride of place is a satisfying experience, and so also a connection to the time during which significant events happened. Those of us, who were in our twenties listening and appreciating the music of the late sixties, had an added pleasure in the fact that the people making it were our contemporaries; an affinity that remains strong, in any era, for a lifetime.

The Grateful Dead

"They swing."

—Dizzy Gillespie

As was said earlier, with the Swing bands of the thirties and forties, recordings lacked quality and fidelity but live performances were excellent. In that in-between 1950s stage of Rock and Roll, the recordings were better than the live renditions. In fairness to those bands from the fifties, amplification systems had a long way to go before live productions were more able to showcase the music in a better light. It needs to be acknowledged, however, that those musicians playing in Swing bands were of high-caliber, so it was not by accident that their live performances were good. It would become a challenge to match what was later done in the studio through improved P.A. systems, and that challenge would bring about as much creativity in that realm, as in the music itself.

There is a demarcation point somewhere in the sixties where what was referred to as Rock and Roll changed to Rock. It can be seen in an ongoing oscillation in which the musicians are searching for new sounds, and as a result, instruments and amplifiers are designed so that their range and function are continuously expanded in an attempt to keep pace with the imaginations of their users; at the same time, recording equipment was enhanced to the point where it was as important an element of the musical process as the instruments, thereby creating a need for more imaginative advances in onstage equipment in an accelerative cycle of innovation. Much was done in this energetic vortex, by companies with names like Alembic, out of which came systems that remain fixtures in modern sound reproduction, both for studio and live performance.

Important changes are seldom pin-points in history, but near 1965, there was a moment when more young, talented, we might even say serious, musicians wanted to play guitar in a Rock band, than a horn in a Jazz band. This fact signals an undeniable need to take seriously the developments that follow from this very significant period of reference. With regard to musicianship, there was the desire to catch up technically with what had been achieved by Jazz and classical musicians who were obviously way ahead in historical depth and virtuosity. However, despite these developments, it needs to be said there was justifiable resentment among many Jazz musicians who, struggling to survive, saw tons of money bestowed on Rock bands and to musicians not nearly as talented as they themselves. In those *down beat* magazines I began reading while in high school in 1964 a decision was made in the early 70s to include Rock in reviews, feature articles, and criticisms because of its popularity, bringing to an end Jazz as *down beat's* exclusive domain. Most of the veteran writers associated with the magazine were not happy about these developments, but at least Rock had a seat at the table. I remember a rather resentful prologue by regular contributor Martin Williams grudgingly admitting the new direction of the magazine. Alan Heineman began a regular column (*Rock's in my Head*), and also reviewed records with a focus on Rock.

For Rock musicians, whether they were more linked to earlier styles or decidedly experimental, the challenge remained to improve technique. I found myself pulling for Rock groups when they showed signs of increased technical proficiency, and assumed that emerging progressive Rock musicians wanted to get to the point where they could demonstrate to that condescending Jazz critic—through a dazzling performance or recording—that they, too, had developed hard-earned virtuosity.

Put simply, what went on inside the Dream Bowl from beginning to end is reflected by the musical interests that found their way into the amalgamated style that was the Grateful Dead. There were singers in most of the Big Bands, but the focus seemed to be on the instrumental arrangements, solos, and beautiful melodies for all those dancers. With the Country bands, the focus had always been, and I think still is, on the song itself. The Dead were influenced by both of these musical approaches and that remained the case throughout their career.

Ralph Gleason, on a KQED documentary called "West Pole," about Bay Area bands, described the Dead as a "core group…an absolutely indispensable element of the San Francisco sound," and called the City a "spawning ground" for new bands, and with other observers on the scene, came to think of and refer to San Francisco as the American Liverpool. According to one source (Musician's Switchboard), in the summer of '68, there were 500 bands in the Bay Area. When I saw them for the first time it was a learning experience, as I had been to only one concert previous to that night at the Dream Bowl. Involving thirty-one bands, it had been a two-day event atop Mt. Tamalpais, on June 10-11 of '67, which might have been more celebrated had it not been eclipsed by the Monterey Pop Festival which took place just one week later, and because of its tremendous impact was the sole focus of attention and commentary, but it remains the very first Pop-Music festival ever to take place. The Fantasy Fair and Magic Mountain Music Festival, as it was dubbed by its promoters, provided, like the festival in Monterey, a broad sampling of various groups, most famously (and for me, most memorably) the Doors, whose popularity had exploded with the success of "Light My Fire," and who were on the verge of releasing their second album. In fact, they opened their set with "When the Music's Over" from *Strange Days*, which wouldn't come out until September that same year, and it proved to be a very powerful opening number. Like "The End" from their self-named first album, "When the Music's Over" is the last cut on the album, and also like "The End," it serves as the magnum opus for the second album. A good friend of mine, Mike Hohm, organized a group to go to the Festival together and offered his San Rafael apartment as overnight lodging for the two-day event. A very fun time was had by all. Mike had been the person who encouraged me to also join him in going to see The Band's first live performance at Winterland. Two highly significant events, as it turned out, and I'm so glad I went. Thanks, Mike.

Some of the other bands I enjoyed that weekend were Jefferson Airplane, Steve Miller Blues Band, Country Joe and the Fish, from the Bay area, The Grass Roots, Kaleidoscope, and The Seeds, who, like the Doors, were from Los Angeles. Also performing at the Festival were more-mainstream artists The 5th Dimension and great vocalist Dionne Warwick. Seeing the Dead at the Dream Bowl however, allowed me to come in for closer observation and a more thorough one, too, as the Dead were famous for long concerts, the running time of which was not possible in a festival setting with so many bands lined up to play. I remember there being a good turnout, but not so crowded that people were shoulder to shoulder. Considering the huge following the band would generate over time, I can say we didn't know how good we had it, and I never again got as close to the stage as I did that night. I think we stood for most or all of it. I was young enough (twenty-two) that weary feet or stiffened knees were not an issue, which the captivating power of the music I heard that night would have overcome in any event—a circumstance still possible even with the arthritic annoyances I've accumulated beyond middle age. The music was loud, to be sure, but not overpoweringly so. In all the subsequent years of seeing them in performance, it was never the case that it was uncomfortably loud, even when they had their wondrous and gigantic sound system, the "Wall of Sound" which, to transport, required two 27 foot trailers; the one Bob Weir said had the ability to "…part your hair at fifty paces…"

I wasn't familiar with the Dead's material. The one song I recognized was Bobby "Blue" Bland's "Turn on Your Lovelight," which on this night, and many thereafter, was the finale for the evening. The song had been a successful R&B hit for Bobby Bland in 1961, and I dug his version of it something fierce, it having been a surprise hit not often experienced by a Blues singer.

It had a driving beat backed by a horn section, that was accentuated by jabbing chords from the pianist and guitarist, who thereafter added a tasty lead line behind the fervent vocals by Bland. It also had a killer tenor sax solo and before the solo, perhaps the longest drum/vocal segment on record and it always got my attention. With the rest of the band laying out, the drummer keeps the up-tempo rhythm going, adding a bit more emphasis on the cymbals as Bobby shouts out the vocals as they play out the unusual duet up to the solo break. Great stuff! Bland delivered what became a long-standing invocation in song: to lift me up higher with your love, and he screams, more than once, "a little bit higher," and he squeezed in all the aforementioned in less than three minutes as the song clocks in at a running time of 2:49. It was not a surprise then, that the Dead were fond of playing this spirited song, a perfect vehicle for their own Blues specialist, Ron McKernan, who was described by Garcia reflecting back on the history of the band (from a You Tube interview "The History of Rock 'N Roll" 52:44) as their "powerhouse guy...who had no wish to be a performer, but we kind of forced him into it because we knew he could do it."

McKernan's father had been a DJ in Palo Alto whose radio show featured Rhythm and Blues, so his son was steeped in that genre, something quite evident in his genuinely-soulful renderings as a vocalist, organist, and harmonica player. Some of the band's best jamming, in my opinion, is on display on many of the R&B covers that they enjoyed doing, with McKernan usually on lead vocal. "Lovelight" would be *the* night-ending rallying cry, convincingly delivered by the earthy McKernan persuading people to depart the concert in pairs, and it typically involved one of "Pigpen's" patented on-the-fly poetry-slam raps about hooking up with your neighbor. And unlike the tightly-formatted version by Bobby Bland, the one I heard this night went on for 22 minutes and 12 seconds. I have the benefit of being able to refer to the Internet Archives site which (and I was astonished to discover this) has the concert in its entirety, and shows song titles, order, and length, but only memory reports how I responded, and they gave me plenty to remember.

When I saw them at the Dream Bowl, the group had been performing for four years, but they were new to me. I had heard "The Golden Road" ("to Unlimited Devotion") from their first album which was among the songs getting AM airplay, but as bassist Phil Lesh would say, the Grateful Dead really begins with their second album, *Anthem of the Sun*. Their self-named first album contained some original material, and several covers, but on *Anthem*, all of the music is by them and the way it was put together—the combination of material and method—is exceedingly unique. It was the first time that anyone had blended live material with in-studio recordings. When I checked the album for song-writing credit, it simply said: "All songs by the Grateful Dead." This is the only album of theirs on which it was so indicated.

A documentary film, *Anthem to Beauty*, chronicles the band's development from the experimental days of the *Anthem* period, to the scaled-back and song-form focused efforts that are the hallmark of *Workingman's Dead*, and *American Beauty*. Lyricist Robert Hunter, knowing he was going to be interviewed for the film, said he "listened to *Anthem* for the first time in 20 or 25 years." The squeezing together of various tracks brought about sections of sufficient sonic density that Hunter thought there might be dust adding to the mash-up. He tells the filmmakers and us that he actually used "Windex" to clean the record in an effort to thin out the information stream, but did so to no avail. He then abruptly and excitedly observed: "That was a daring record!"

The music is continuous so it doesn't have the normal separation of songs, although there are titles provided for the various movements. It opens with "That's it for The Other One," which as Lesh tells us in the documentary, "…starts out behaving like a regular song…" but becomes a vehicle within which, on this recording and in live performance, there is a barrage of furious playing that leads to vocals by Bob Weir which offers more of the story and maintains the intensity. The opening theme is reprised by Garcia in a moment of calm before a dramatic conclusion, and by this point it is clear that they've left the initial suggestion of a "…regular song…" pretty far behind. While doing research, I came across the following description: "Rhythm is all-important, melody less so; the few tunes in this section…are fragmentary, narrow-range motives that repeat obsessively. Ostinato techniques and increasing thickness of texture take place of traditional development." When I read that description, I thought it surprisingly apt for what was going on in "The Other One." It was a description of Stravinsky's "Rite of Spring," by USC Professor Richard J. Wingell from his book *Writing About Music*.

"The Other One" served as the centerpiece of the set list on this Saturday night, the 22nd of February, 1969. The composition became a signature one, as it represented an important and never-relinquished element of the band, one that endlessly probed and experimented with sound in the pursuit of unique improvisations on every performance. This is evidenced by the fact that "The Other One" is in the top five of most-played songs according to the Grateful Dead Song Graph Chart of "Dr. Beechwood," played a whopping 597 times; only "Playin' in the Band" has been played more often, taking the cake at 602. In a combination of constancy and longevity though, "The Other One" is number one. Of the songs that remained a part of their repertoire until Jerry Garcia's death in August of '95, only "Dark Star" precedes it in origin of performance, but there were long stretches when "Dark Star" was not played, and that was never the case with "The Other One."

When they performed it this night, it knocked me up against the wall. I just hadn't heard anything remotely like it at that point, on the radio or at that first outdoor concert, in terms of group power in a live performance setting. In football terminology, their approach on "The Other One" was an all-out, go-for-broke blitz, bringing all linebackers and both cornerbacks. The double drummers led the charge with propulsive power that established a rhythmic foundation both strong and malleable. Readily apparent in listening to or witnessing a performance by the Dead is the fact that they have utterly abandoned the notion that certain instruments fill traditionally prescribed roles. As suggested in the all-out blitz comparison, no one's role is subordinate. The drummers are as much the lead instruments as are the guitars, and at this early stage in the development of Rock, when good drummers were hard to come by, the Dead were blessed with two very good drummers in Bill Kreutzmann and Mickey Hart.

I became interested in drums in 5th grade, playing with fellow students at school, but I never got further than sticks (ones I still have), and a practice pad. I stopped after a new music teacher came in the following year, one who was not interested in drums, a development that these days I rationalize as being just as well, considering the flamboyant personality-requirements typically assigned or voluntarily provided by drummers in Rock bands. This small exposure to drumming, however, at least brought about more awareness and sympathy for the often-overlooked importance drummers represented, and I was always eager, therefore, to see what a drummer was doing and paid extra attention. I cannot think of a pair of drummers that remained a team as long as these two did while in the Dead, and they still play together when G.D. band members reconvene. They had different styles, as Hart seemed to involve his entire body, leaning in or to a side and moving his head as the intensity grew. Kreutzmann, conversely, kept his back straight and stayed centered that way, but his wrists, hands, and feet were very active, showing great economy of motion. I really liked what he was doing. He struck me as a very musical drummer who emphasized the back beat with a style as unique as the band itself. The percussive sentences that he stated were of long construction, and this effect is made more recognizable, as it is showcased during Bob Weir's vocals on "Cryptical Envelopment," by revolving his sound from one channel to the other in a full circle.

The two drummers blended together exceedingly well, never getting in each other's way. This unified percussive force was developed over countless hours of jamming together, and involved practice exercises in which they sat beside one another with two of their hands tied together as they drummed with their remaining hands so as to be able to lock in to the rhythmic center and be of one mind. While the drummers are constructing a solid percussive force, the rest of the six piece group (and sometimes seven with the addition of keyboardist Tom Constanten) were adding on. Phil Lesh, their bass player, was incredible. His multi-note, unrelenting attack propelled the music in intense fashion, and he would at times play chords on the bass which produces this huge, majestic sound. There just isn't anything quite like chords played on an electric bass through a capable amplifier.

Jumping forward for a moment to focus on the bass, on March 23, 1974, I was lucky to be in attendance, going by myself, when the band unveiled for the first time, their 26,400-watt, 641-speaker "Wall of Sound" system. Capable amplification was no longer an issue. The concert, in Daly City at the Cow Palace, was called "Sound Test," and the evening provided material for a writing project for an English Composition class taken that same year. The two tallest towers of speakers in the Wall of Sound, in an effort to replicate the physicality of the 32-foot expanse of lower frequency sound waves, belonged to Phil Lesh's bass guitar—eighteen speakers per stack. Yow! A few years later, my wife and I drove to a theater in nearby Concord that was one of the few places where *The Grateful Dead Movie* was playing. The theater had a great sound system which they cranked to the max for the occasion, and it was very much like being at an actual concert; the footage had been from a concert at Winterland in which they used the Wall of Sound. The segment with Phil sound-testing his bass before the concert, where his chords boomed out with thunderous reverberations in the empty hall where it had been filmed and also the one we were currently in, was truly awesome, especially when experienced that first time.

One more jump forward to 1986 after Garcia's recovery following his collapse into a diabetic coma, which happened in

July of that same year. With the help of friend and musical cohort Merl Saunders, Jerry re-learned how to play music because much of his muscle memory was not readily available during his recovery, and had to be re-ingrained; it was quite a struggle. His first performance in front of people had been October 4th at the Stone in S.F., a bit of a warm-up, as it were, at the small club where he frequently played with his own bands. It served as a relatively comfortable venue before the December 15th return by the Dead to play at a more pressurized packed house at what is now Oracle Arena, and Sylvia and I were fortunate to be on hand.

With his near-death experience still fresh in most everyone's mind there that night, lyrics from songs like "Black Peter," about a dying man, and "Candyman," took on more emotional weight. One could hear through the course of the first set that Jerry was rusty, lagging behind a bit with his chops. Then something remarkable happened—as if Odysseus had grasped his bow upon his return—during the concluding song of the first set, Bob Weir's "Weather Report Suite." The song contains many required guitar parts from Jerry that are difficult because they call for rapid execution, and all of a sudden he was back to form, pulling them off as the arrangement demanded. I've never seen anything in print that entertains the following scenario, but I saw what happened like this, and knowing the wicked sense of humor that was their standard of exchange, I would expect as much from this rough and tumble brotherhood, who decided: let's throw him in the deep end and see how he does. They knew he had it in him, and they were all right there to help draw it out. I should imagine that the comradery earned by slugging it out for twenty-plus years as bandmates was heightened to an exceptional degree following this exhilarating exchange, and felt very good during that much deserved break. I'm so glad we were there to witness it.

One of my clear memories from that first evening at the Dream Bowl was the serious look on Bob Weir's face when they were deep into their playing. They were all young men bursting with energy and purpose, and although they might have been perceived as crazies—and often enthusiastically promoted that perception—I could not detect, that evening, one shred of frivolity while they played. I should stress that I didn't go there that night like a booster on a mission to cherry-pick good copy. I was not a devotee in any way, and didn't know much about the band at all. I was simply curious. Also needing to be stressed, is that this is before the "Deadhead" phenomenon which began officially after the October 1971 release of a live *Grateful Dead* album (the Skull & Roses self-named double album) on the inside of which they announced in large print: "DEAD FREAKS UNITE—Who are you? Where are you? How are you?" A symbiosis began, grew, and did so essentially under the radar. It wasn't until the 80s that the media began talking about it, and when the Dead scored a major hit, their very first, on their 1987 release of *In the Dark* with the song "Touch of Grey," the Deadheads then became a trending topic.

In addition to their music, part of the reason they lasted as long as they did and earned widespread appeal was, I'm convinced, the fact that they were the band least likely to take themselves too seriously. Reported often is the fact that the band members placed a high priority on keeping themselves in stitches. In a nod to the grass roots, home-grown support the band had always generated, Bob Weir on *Europe '72* introduces "Truckin'" by saying: "This next one rose straight to the top of the charts in Turlock, CA; numero uno for a week or two. They love us in Turlock and we love them for that," so here's to Turlock and hamlets everywhere, for their support of the Grateful Dead.

The so-called "Summer of Love" had occurred in 1967, but the music that had burst forth from that summer was still rippling out, and bands were continuing to put out creative works. Another of my clear memories from the evening was hearing for the first time the song "Greasy Heart" by the Jefferson Airplane as it boomed out over the PA during a break, and thinking how great it sounded with the gargantuan bass lines of Jack Casady that carry the song, which made as lasting an impression as the music I was hearing live that night. The song, I would learn later, was from *Crown of Creation* (the band's fourth album) which had been released only a few months before, in September of 1968. The Woodstock Festival wouldn't happen until August of '69, and the Dead would release *Live Dead* in November of '69. It showcased some of the same material I'd heard for the first time that night at the Dream Bowl. In fact, it was five days later (2/27/69) that they performed the magnificent version of "Dark Star" at the Fillmore West that was the opening track on *Live Dead*.

The night I went, they also played: "Death Don't Have No Mercy," a Blues lament written by Rev. Gary Davis, "St. Stephen" (from *Aoxomoxoa* and also on *Live Dead*), "The Eleven," and "Lovelight;" other versions of which would round out *Live Dead*, a double album. The other songs I heard that night, were "Dupree's Diamond Blues," "Doin' That Rag," and "Mountains of the Moon," which would be part of the band's third recording: *Aoxomoxoa*. After the demanding, time-consuming, and expensive recording project that *Anthem of the Sun* had been, they were decidedly more focused on song-writing for *Aoxomoxoa*. It was at this point that the superb lyricist Robert Hunter became a permanent part of the Grateful Dead family, teaming mostly with Garcia, but collaborating occasionally with everyone else in the band while doing solo projects as well.

Getting back to the band members themselves, it was not difficult to conclude from what went on that night that they were a pretty bright bunch of guys. As I said, I didn't know anything about them, but because I became so keenly interested in their music, I actively sought out any literature available that talked about the band, what they were up to, and what their personal histories had been. That the individual members were intelligent was verified in the discoveries subsequently made as my interest in them continued. I wasn't alone.

My favorite article about the band was a cover story from the December 1979 issue of *New West Magazine*, to which I subscribed. The magazine's editor, Jon Carroll, would later contribute a regular column to the *SF Chronicle* that was always full of wit and wisdom. By that time, during the decade after having first seen them, I'd read many a magazine article about the band, but this one stood out. At roughly the same time, they were also a cover story for *Musician Magazine*, it having very nearly the same photograph on its cover. The *New West* article "New Life for the Grateful Dead," was written by Charlie Haas. Talking about how his thoroughly engaging 2009 novel *The Enthusiast* came about, he said, "Jon Carroll, the editor, was in the habit of assigning me subjects I knew little about. (He didn't have much choice; I was young.)" Not being a Deadhead at the time, he had a fresh approach to the topic—that and the fact that he is someone who can write with great skill about any topic.

His account was full of insights, and included the following description of the band's approach: "The sound of the Dead is not blues nor metal nor disco, but a loose and sometimes sloppy tumbling along, centered around the guitar of Garcia, whose solos are mercury-bright mutations of the western Swing cadences of Bob Wills...." Oh, how I wanted to claim the phrase "mercury-bright mutations" for my own, because I'd never read or heard anything that sounded so right, sufficiently captured Garcia's beautiful guitar tone, and rolled so nicely off the tongue as well. And I thought the comparison to Bob Wills was significant, too, because on certain levels there was a musical connection, but the more direct comparison was that each of those men had a remarkably similar effect on their respective audiences, namely that they epitomized maximum enjoyment of music in the moment of its occurrence. For any fan eager to see them perform, it was just so damn much fun to watch those two guys operate, and share in that for a couple of hours.

Careful observers might reasonably doubt the validity of a ticket shown to cost $1.00, but it was for real. KMEL, who along with BAM Magazine (Bay Area Music), sponsored the event. BAM was a free magazine always available in stacks by the door at Tower Record stores during that company's heyday.

When I first went to the Dream Bowl to see the Grateful Dead, the opening act was a band from Napa called Amber Whine, and no, that is not a typo. Owing to the profound impression the events of that evening in Feb. of '69 made on me, that band name stuck firmly in my memory banks; helping in this regard was the fact that I thought they played very well that night. I would see the Grateful Dead many times thereafter, but would not see Amber Whine again. That a casual mentioning of the band's name some thirty eight years later would lead to a meeting with one of the band's original members is beyond the longest of shots, and evidence that the fates, again, want to oblige in the telling of this story.

My sister Lynda worked at the Dream Bowl during the last months of its operation, doing a variety of things that included changing band names on that marquee I'd noticed so many years before. We were talking one day and I mentioned having seen Amber Whine. She told me, to my amazed delight, that not only did she know John Hannaford (who had been the drummer in that band), but that they worked together at the same school. She talked about what a cool guy he was, and that he would have much to offer about his music experiences. "He has lots of stories," she told me, and she was right. With her help, I contacted him shortly thereafter, and we set up a meeting at a school in Napa where they were both employed at that time.

I remember waiting rather anxiously, as his final class of the day was still in session when I arrived; it actually ran a bit past the hour. This added to my impatience, which was already built up by the fact that I was nervously eager to talk with John as I felt him to be an important link connecting the events that unfolded in the last couple of months of the Dream Bowl's existence. At the time of our meeting, I had not yet talked with Sandy Callahan, so it was still true at that point, as indicated earlier, that information about those last days was, with frustrating irony, proving to be the most difficult even though it was nearest to present time. Finally students started emerging from the door.

When I walked in John's classroom, I could see that music was an essential part of whatever it was he hoped to impart to these young men and women, because the room was filled with percussion instruments and playback equipment. My initial reaction to John after we shook hands and began talking, was that he was a calm and patient man.

He told me that he "had always been interested in music and art, and began to learn to play the drums while in elementary school." An experience while visiting relatives took place in the late 1950s when he was "seven or eight years old," in Southern California's Hermosa Beach, in a house very near the water, "...along the strand..." he told me. "Exploring," one day, he came across an artist community in a warehouse nearby. He recalled that the entrance had something like "Swinging bar doors," which he was small enough to see under, "so I went in." Inside were several artists, working on various projects, and he was struck by the size of the canvases on which the artists worked. Although young, he picked up on the energy of the individuals absorbed in their work. He told me that this experience was "an epiphany" and that he talked with the artists, who gave him a set of bongo drums which he kept "and treasured for nearly forty years."

So often, it seems, life-changing experiences take place somewhere away from one's local surroundings. We needn't have much imagination to conjure a scene in which several painters and sculptors notice a young person boldly walking into their midst, and to see them lending encouragement to a potential artist for activities that typically are starved for followers. In John's case though, he told me he knew after this experience which was "of profound importance," like the one had by Horace Silver, that he wanted to pursue art in a serious way, and it became clear to him in that moment that he would answer the call.

After his meeting with the artists from Hermosa Beach, he returned to Napa and began taking drum lessons while still in elementary school. In Junior High, he got a drum set and, with friends, played surfer music, a fairly common and early starting point for a lot of bands who went on to more challenging musical forms. At age fifteen, he helped form the band Natural Selection, which played locally and opened for Quicksilver Messenger Service and the Jefferson Airplane. He later enrolled at Cal State—Sacramento Art School in 1968 and earned a Master's Degree in Fine Arts. Eventually, he decided to focus his efforts on teaching and other art projects. He stopped his musical pursuits thinking he could not do all those activities at once. Throughout his career as an artist, John's paintings have been exhibited in various museums including the San Francisco Museum of Modern Art's Gallery at Fort Mason. He told me that in 1990 he got serious again as a percussionist, and studied congas and "percussion in all forms," re-thinking his decision to focus on art exclusively, and deciding that "it would be alright to sacrifice a bit of each in order to do both."

After his time in Natural Selection, Amber Whine was formed, and a when a relative of one of the business partners from the Dream Bowl had seen them perform at another venue in Napa, she suggested to them that they should try to get hired. They auditioned with six other bands, were in fact hired, and played there on several occasions with, among others, The Grateful Dead, Dancing Food and Entertainment, The Sons of Champlin, and Rose. The musicians in Amber Whine, the night I saw them, were: John Hannaford (Drums), Carl Altamura (Bass), Greg Miller (Guitar-Lead Vocals), and John Pramuk (Guitar-Vocals).

John told me that the in-house P.A. system was good for the time, and that the "staging and sound team were wonderful," but bands still had to have plenty of their own equipment. His recollection was that they were paid well (payment was guaranteed when they were hired), and that they received "a thick wad of cash," probably from small bills received at the gate.

He enjoyed playing at the Dream Bowl, enjoyed hearing the other bands when they performed, and remembered the "...open and friendly exchange with them"—including time together in Sandy Callahan's "green room" with the Dead, when Jerry Garcia showed them an old Martin guitar he had recently purchased, which John recalled by saying, "It was wonderful to hear him play and sing solo acoustically." How uplifting it must have felt to be in the company of fellow musicians in a private moment there in that small room while at the same time sensing a partnership with all that was happening musically in the innovative swirl worldwide.

I did not see them at the Dream Bowl, but I did get to see The Sons of Champlin a couple of months later at Winterland as part of the bill with The Band (their first live performance following the release of *Music From Big Pink*). There, I learned firsthand that The Sons had great songs and a host of very talented musicians who could really deliver in a live performance setting. They had a horn-section, rare among Rock bands, led by Tim Cain that delivered unique arrangements; another rare circumstance was the presence of vibes expertly played by all-purpose musician Geoff Palmer. And if that wasn't enough there was Bill Champlin himself, a great lead singer and songwriter who played organ and guitar. Providing an exclamation point for most of the Son's history was lead guitarist Terry Haggerty, one of my all-time favorites. For many of the early years as a member of the Son's, he preferred a hollow-body electric which was also a rarity among lead guitarists. He had great technique (his father taught guitar) that combined an understanding of the blues, tremendous speed in execution and psychedelic expansiveness. A tall man, Haggerty seemed to grow taller by tilting his head up and back, and raising his eyebrows above his glasses while he played. The music he created always struck me as though it was spilling out of his guitar. About those glasses: a stereotype I was aware of growing up was that anyone who wore glasses was considered a square. Haggerty helped, along with fellow musicians Jerry Garcia, Phil Lesh, and the Airplane's Paul Kantner, to put that notion to rest forever. And many of the ladies coming to concerts wore granny glasses whether they needed them or not.

Bands that were together during what was then a relatively new phenomenon will tell you they were lucky to be a part of it. In Dave Marsh's book *Louie Louie*, mentioned earlier, he talked about the significance of Ron Holden and the Playboys, who in addition to their regional hit "Love You So," were also the group who, in live shows "…introduced the dormant 'Louie Louie' to the Pacific Northwest," where it was later re-recorded, famously, by the Portland, Oregon band, The Kingsmen. The song had been originally recorded and performed by its composer, Richard Berry, a black musician who was active in the L.A. music scene in the 1950s. Berry sold the rights to his song, which was released in 1957 and later went on to become one of the biggest-selling singles of all time, so he could afford a nice wedding ring. Marsh also talked about the "Seattle/Tacoma…intra-city battles of the bands," about which he said: "But the bands thrown into competition (by promoters)…failed to feud." Ron Holden is quoted as saying those groups "became a fraternity that will last until we die because we went through so much together as budding Rock 'n rollers." Amber Whine was just such a band, who, in keeping with what was happening in that creative moment, "performed their original music" and shared experiences at the Dream Bowl that make them a part of a unique and exciting moment in time.

And as a final and encouraging note, John told me he is "still making and performing music" and has done so with "various groups, such as Akanthos, Cosmos Percussion Orchestra, Drum Party, Grass Child, and Jealous Zelig," at a variety of venues including Napa's BottleRock, and we had the pleasure of seeing Grass Child put in a strong performance opening the show shown below.

Getting back to the Grateful Dead, I don't think it's possible to appreciate fully the minds at work in the band without going beyond casual observation. Yes, they liked to get high and have a good time, but there was a lot more to it than that. Herb Caen, in one of his columns long ago, touched on the condescension prevalent in the early days for hippies, when anyone with the guts to let his hair grow caught a lot of flak. Caen was attending some soiree in San Francisco and Jerry Garcia was there, perhaps as part of the entertainment, and he and Caen, who were friends, were chatting. Their conversation over, Jerry moved on. From nearby, a snooty socialite, who had been observing, sidled over to Herb and said, "It talks." Perhaps she resented and feared the apparent intelligence in someone so different from her, because as a matter of fact, *he* spoke very well, and was one of the most articulate people I have ever encountered. The best means I've discovered for dealing with an opinion that finds such a lifestyle objectionable comes from the Introduction to the book, *Garcia—A Signpost to New Space*. In this interview conducted by Jann Wenner (co-founder of the *Rolling Stone*) and author Charles Reich, Reich offers up an alternate course for Garcia instead of the one he took and the one we know, something more traditional, like a high school music teacher: "The whole senior class wants to thank Mr. Garcia for his help with our production of *Carousel*." Sorry, that just won't do.

I clearly remember an occasion when he was being interviewed on the radio. Initially I wasn't making an effort to listen, but there was a compelling element to his discourse, a blend of intelligence and ease which eventually caused me to listen more carefully, that day and thereafter. I remember him talking about the band's recent efforts at the time of the interview, saying that the music "...had come to fruition." Considering the time period during which I probably heard this, he was most likely talking about the songwriting growth he felt he and his writing partner Robert Hunter had achieved together on *Workingman's Dead*. His conversation was always enriched with vocabulary grace notes that came off the top of his head easily and naturally, and there was never a time when it sounded like he was trying to impress or show off. The only way someone pulls this off, in the natural fashion he did, is if that person has penetrative interest in words and has spent a ton of time looking at them on the pages of a book and in dictionaries. This he did. Later, I learned that he was a part of early educational experiments at the Jr. High level in Palo Alto, that took the brightest students and put them in situations of accelerated studies at higher levels; Garcia mentioned a couple of exceptional teachers who saw his potential and suggested challenging literature they thought appropriate for him that aroused interest and sent him on his way. Also, the fact that Garcia was a self-taught musician, a performer who was involved constantly with improvisation, aided his ability as a quick thinking conversationalist.

Philosopher Alan Watts would often say in his lectures "...people who are interesting, are people who are interested." Jerry was a person who was endlessly interested. That creative personality was on display and pronounced in his work as a guitarist as well. In a long interview done in 1995 at the Grateful Dead Office in San Rafael, he talked about the circumstances during his teenage years in the late fifties in which he learned guitar, saying: "There was enough time to develop the skills that you needed. It wasn't developed in a frenzy. It was developed out of love, my own personal love." In an extensive interview in an Oct. 1978 issue of *Guitar Player* magazine, he addressed the technical aspects of his playing and talked about how, in an effort to enunciate clearly the chosen notes, he used his fingers on the fretboard:

> I've somehow trained myself to come straight down on top of the string. Generally I like to pick every note, but I do tend to pull-off, say, a real fast triplet—intervals that are heading up the scale. I do it almost without thinking about it. I seldom hammer-on, because it seems to have a certain inexactitude for me. My preference is for the well-spoken tone, and I think coming straight down on the strings with high knuckles makes it. So my little groups of pull-offs are really well-articulated; it's something I worked on a lot.

The notion of clear enunciation brings me back to the making of *Anthem of the Sun.* The overriding challenge for many bands in this era was to do something "far out," something that expanded boundaries. The Scottish Philosopher Thomas Reid said in 1764,

"For innovations in language, like those in religion and government," [and we can add music] "are always suspected and disliked by the many, till use hath made them familiar, and prescription hath given them a title." Alex Ross, from his book *The Rest is Noise—Listening to the Twentieth Century*, says, "Musicians and listeners had long agreed that certain intervals, or pairs of notes, were 'clear,' and that others were 'unclear.' The quoted words can be found on a cuneiform tablet from the Sumerian city of Ur."

Gregorian chant, for example, was designed to reflect the divine and therefore used simultaneous voices and monotone to suggest unity and singularity; the oneness of god. When harmony and counter melody came to be accepted, those earlier restrictions were replaced with others. With Stravinsky's debut of his Rite of Spring in 1913, there famously broke out a great commotion in the theater described as a "near-riot." In 1956 Carl Perkins at a rehearsal played his song "Honey Don't" (covered later by the Beatles with Ringo singing lead), which would be the flip-side to "Blue Suede Shoes." During the recording, his brother Jay protested. I remember Carl Perkins talking about that very incident on *Fresh Air with Terry Gross*. He had used an unusual chord change (from the key of E to C), and his brother said, "You can't do that." So there is always going to be a force of unacceptability that challenges innovation, a word that in the sixteenth and seventeenth centuries was most-often used in conjunction with the word "rash."

That "far out" challenge for Rock bands extended to all aspects of the finished product: the music, the lyrics, song titles, group names too, and the art-work on the album. Speaking of that last item, I recall that when compact discs first hit the market, they were hailed as a great leap forward in recording technology, but in the ensuing years, many are saying it isn't so; it has become almost fashionable to praise vinyl as having a "warmer" sound. I've read technical accounts on why this is the case, and my ears tell me it might be so, but I've entered a stage in my life where I am no longer sure I can rely on my hearing to make an informed decision on the continuing debate regarding the subtle matters of recorded sound. In the comparison of CD to vinyl though, one thing is certain: it is not possible to package in a jewel-case the delightful surprises and often compelling art-work that an album could provide. *Anthem of the Sun* is a case in point. The cover art is a painting by Bill Walker. It is reported as a spontaneous development, a process that was an essential part of so much of what went on in the Bay Area music scene in the 60s. Phil Lesh would later say in the documentary *Anthem to Beauty*, "...we needed some cover art and I knew an artist." It was as simple as that, and Walker happened to be around at the time it was needed.

The figure Walker painted is a mandala-like creation of a hydra-headed being that has each band member extending out from the unifying central figure. The colors are striking, and the mesmerizing form is a blend of symmetry and differentiation. I was astonished when, in an interview, I heard Walker himself say that he painted one half with his left hand and the remaining half with his other hand. The portraits have enough realistic depiction so that each person can be identified, including, Walker reported, the condition he sensed of Pigpen's diminishing life-force (from too much drinking) indicated by the unshakeable image he had of McKernan's closed eyes. A model of unity is powerfully conveyed in the front cover art, and reinforced on the back with the fisheye color photo by Thomas Weir which captures the band standing firmly in its solidarity, suggesting the longevity that would, against the odds, take place. The band-members are gathered in the hills where the lush undergrowth is tall enough to cover their boots, as tree branches encircle overhead, while patches of illumination reveal a hand or face here, shimmering leaves there, each bathed in the suffused light that finds its way through the green and blue canopy above. On the back of the album, there is recognition of the beauty and splendor of the natural-world, and the front cover art demonstrates that which is possible in imaginative and/or meditative states, concepts explored by the probing lyrics all through Side One of *Anthem of the Sun*.

The band's next album, *Aoxoamoxoa*, had individual songs—as opposed to the continuous approach used on *Anthem*—but this was also an opportunity to use a newly made 16-track Ampex unit, so this recording was also highly experimental. With the advent of better recording equipment, the studio came to be thought of as an additional instrument, the recording landscape changed forever by the Beatles 1967 release of *Sgt. Pepper*, and the mixing process became a performance component just as the instrumental, percussive, and vocal tracks had been, and was considered significantly important. That approach began in earnest with the making of *Anthem of the Sun*. *Aoxoamoxoa* was a recording that, over the years, I did not listen to very often, but it yielded material, live versions of which became songs I coveted the most, plus it had the mysterious and beautiful "Mountains of the Moon."

In an interview somewhere, I remember Hunter saying he was not totally satisfied with one of the verses, in "Mountains," and in *A Box of Rain-Collected Lyrics of Robert Hunter*, an alternate set of lyrics for the second verse is shown with a footnote indicating the lyrics used on *Aoxoamoxoa*. Either way, it struck me as an example of how richly evocative his poetry can be. This album, too, has incredible artwork on its cover, this time by well-known Bay Area poster artist Rick Griffin, and yet another group photo, a down-home one, on the back of the album taken again by Thomas Weir. It was like the one on *Anthem*, out in the woods, but this time, the photo included wives, girl-friends, regular friends, kids, dogs, and a horse. Perhaps because of the vivid colors used by Rick Griffin, a black and white photo was used to bring in contrast. It has a grainy, noir feel to it, and because of its globe-like rendering (in both of Thomas Weir's photographs), I was reminded of that dramatic, first time earth-rise perspective from space, and imagined coming closer and closer to our world until it focused finally on this group of friends, linked like the earth-rooted trees that surround and join them as part of nature's family.

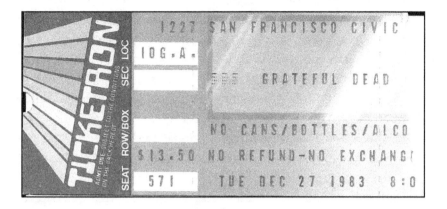

Executives at Warner Brothers were finally made happy with the release (in Feb. and Nov. of 1970) of *Workingman's Dead*, and the follow-up *American Beauty*, because those records proved to be commercially more viable. This was so, not because the band had capitulated to the demands of the label, but because they had taken what they felt to be the next natural step in the genuine development of their craft. It's probably safe to say though, that economic realities were not lost on them and they didn't, at that point, want to pile up another huge debt to Warner Brothers. Before signing a deal with Warner Brothers, the Grateful Dead (and they were not alone in this regard) flatly did not care if they had a recording contract or not; they were content to earn a living playing to live audiences comprised in large part by a loyal following of local supporters who filled ballrooms and other venues that thrived in the Bay Area during the late sixties and early seventies. Nevertheless, the record companies saw gold in the hills of San Francisco, and eagerly sought to (and eventually did) land the bands who resided there, as well as others nearby: Country Joe and the Fish (Vanguard) and Creedence Clearwater Revival (Fantasy) from Berkeley; The Sons of Champlin and Quicksilver Messenger Service (both on Capitol) from Marin County; Jefferson Airplane (RCA), the Dead (Warner Bros.), Santana, and Big Brother and the Holding Company (both on Columbia) from San Francisco.

The Dead were not desperate to ink a deal, and therefore they were able to influence its outcome and gain a measure of control that exceeded typical arrangements, and that allowed them, for example, unlimited studio time for the purpose of recording which, according to Garcia was "...unheard of at the time." Warner Brothers Hollywood studio head Joe Smith described the situation as "...kids in a candy store," and I don't think any of the band members would disagree. Garcia said later that their "strategy" was to pay for an education so as to learn how to use all that recording equipment, and while the time that they were granted in the studio was "unlimited," it was not free of charge; they ran up a huge debt to Warner Brothers that took a long time to pay off. They did benefit from the hands-on experience, and ultimately crafted a carefully engineered mix, the clear enunciation of which found its way to the master tapes, but, Garcia says, they "neglected" to educate themselves about the final transfer-to-vinyl process, because they thought they had done all that was necessary to ensure the quality of the final product. They were dismayed to discover, upon hearing the finished recording, that it was "muddy" and that a substantial amount of the detail and nuance they had carefully committed to the master tapes, "didn't make it across," a lament I've heard from a variety of musicians many times.

Have you heard about the 1945 discoveries at Nag Hammadi, Egypt? Two brothers are digging for fertilizer. The son of the brother named Muhammad Ali uncovers an earthenware vessel which contained documents (the most famous of which was the Thomas Gospel), that were buried for their protection because they did not represent what was the established orthodoxy of the day, and deemed heretical would have been destroyed if discovered. It was an incredible time-capsule find of immense historical importance. They took home these imponderably priceless writings from antiquity, and what I read next, seeing the story for the first time, was one of the most groan-inducing, no; primal-scream-inducing moments as can be imagined. The elderly mother takes several of the leather-wrapped papyrus writings, and burns them. One explanation says she feared the documents might bring trouble, another that she was simply cold. What superb kindling that dry papyrus must have been, huh? Important details, essential information for humanity that needs all it can get, up in smoke. Thankful we must be though, that the miracle of its discovery happened at all, and that most of what was found in that vessel was preserved. Getting back to *Anthem*, with regard to information lost because of the inadequacies or restrictions of what was considered the "industry standard," all I can say is that the musical gods are still fuming about that one.

Nevertheless, despite the fact that we didn't receive it in its fullest expression, the recording remains for me a quintessential example of what bands were up to in those adventurous days. It was a sound collage like no other, that used acoustic guitar blended effectively with the electric and live portions carefully strung together throughout side one. It involved physical (not digital) tampering, and tedious cutting-and-splicing fraught with primitive peril that produced however, effects not possible with the more advanced technologies of today. For anyone interested in finding out what 60s bands from the Bay Area were all about, this should be required listening.

There was a reissue of the recording with a new mix done by Phil Lesh—an exciting prospect at the time—and when I learned of its availability, made sure I tracked it down. I wish now that I had had the foresight back then to have purchased a pair so as to preserve a fresh pressing. An added bonus was that the background for Bill Walker's painting on the reissues was done in white, and I won't say that it's better than the magenta tones used on the original cover, but it does highlight the painting with a different perspective, and it is rare, as not many of the re-mixed editions were produced, and for that reason it is probably the most valuable record I possess. I've no plans to sell it. Alas, that one copy I did buy got played too much, and has lost its sonic luster. No matter how careful one is, even with an expensive turntable and a high-quality stylus, it remained after all, sharp metal scratching plastic; not exactly a design for long life.

On both recordings, there is a transitional segment near mid-point on side one of *Anthem*. Keyboardist Tom Constanten, still in the Air Force (having been granted time off as airman-of-the-week) took part in various Grateful Dead projects as time would permit. He "prepared" the piano, according to him, a la John Cage, by inserting coins over and under strings and created other disturbances in order to come up with a swirling "collage" of unusual sounds achieved in part by activating the piano strings, harp-like, directly with his hands. These manipulations served as a bridge to the opening moments of the section entitled "New Potato Caboose." Another maneuver he dreamed up was the incorporation of a gyro-top that he gave an ambitious spin before placing it inside the piano against the soundboard, the effect of which set off a memorable moment in Grateful Dead lore. As the spinning decreased, so did the pitch of the jarring snarl it produced, sounding for all-the-world like a chain saw which, when listened to on headphones, traverses from the left side of one's head to the right, thanks to deft handling during the mixing process. Constanten said later that it was reported to him that beleaguered producer Dave Hassinger, near his wits end having had to deal with all the craziness, when listening for the first time to the playback of this explosive onslaught, cleared the chair by a full foot and a half. Equally famous in the tale of this recording project is that Hassinger, already near the edge, was sent over it when Bob Weir asked for "the sound of thick air," which Phil Lesh described in the documentary as "The straw that broke the camel's back." Hassinger rose from the chair (again), repeated Weir's request a few times as he exited the studio, never to return. Lesh and Weir retold this with particular glee, which affirms, I think, their mind-set from the outset back then: that if they were annoying enough, they would succeed in getting the Warner Brothers engineers out of their hair. That's how it played out, with the boys working alone for the remainder of their time in Hollywood studios. Other recording and mixing work was done in several New York studios, as well as one in Miami and one in San Francisco. While the activities of the band, in their relationship with Warner Brothers, were in keeping with the "prankster" attitude, it was ultimately in service to the music.

Conventional outlook might suggest that the manipulations to the piano by Constanten could not work in a musical fashion, but it functions very effectively within the contexts of the two movements on Side One of *Anthem*, bridging one to the other. The "Other One" ends in calamitous fashion with the last line of the chorus repeated several times building up the tension, which is followed by a very dense interweaving of live tracks from four different performances in three different locations. The wave of energy gradually diminishes, the entwined guitar-leads spiral out of audible range, and Constanten's connecting segment begins with strident shrieks and the chain-saw sound that rumbles eventually to quiet. You can almost see the dust and debris. Then things begin to settle down with a few outgoing shrieks reminding us, one last time, of what we left behind. A shift in mood and outlook is under way. To accomplish this transition, Constanten, interviewed in the film *Anthem to Beauty*, gave an explanation: "The devices I used…were borrowed shamelessly or not, from the prepared piano devices of John Cage." Cage was an important figure in the world of experimental music; a consideration certainly on the minds of the Grateful Dead and many other bands from the 1960s.

Talking about the desire of various composers to break away from traditional classical approaches, Alex Ross tells us in is book *The Rest Is Noise* that, "Also, Cage loved noise. In a 1940 manifesto he declared, 'I believe that the use of noise to make music will continue and increase until we reach a music produced through the aid of electrical instruments which will make available for musical purposes any and all sounds that can be heard.'" American composer Charles Ives and French born composer Edgard Varese had already used sounds in unique ways in their compositions before extensive use of electronic manipulation was possible. But the use of electronics did grow so John Cage's prediction in 1940 was surprisingly true, but as boldly prophetic as it was, it was equally surprising that it was short of the mark.

In 1993, Frank Zappa, who claimed Varese as an influence, released *Jazz from Hell* which had eight songs, only one of which involved his band at the time. The remaining seven compositions were done entirely on the Synclavier. Most known, probably, for his efforts to shock people with his lyrics and slay sacred cows, Zappa was a person of all-encompassing scope and grand one-of-a-kind vision, who was interested in classical music. He saw early on however, little opportunity for recognition in its pursuit, because new works did not attract financial support, and it was the works of composers long gone—and not needing to be paid—which continued to prevail. So he instead pursued Rock music, seeing it as an entry point and a means by which he could be recognized as a musician, and as such would then have the opportunity to showcase his more ambitious efforts as an orchestral composer, an aspiration he never abandoned. His orchestrations and guitar playing were extraordinary.

In a long and revealing interview with Mary Travers (from Peter, Paul, and Mary) on her nationally syndicated radio program, the "Mary Travers & Friend" show (so named because she always had one guest only), she was surprised to hear Frank say, when asked, that he had not had any formal music education. But he went on to say that he went to the library and made use of instruction books that talked about music in ways that matched up with what he thought would be useful in helping to bring his ideas to formulation. And Frank Zappa was not your typical person checking out a library book. He had extraordinary powers of information processing and retention, readily apparent to anyone who listened to him long enough. In interviews, he was often abrupt, even mean—one of those folks of whom it is said, "they do not suffer fools gladly;" but if the questions were good ones, his responses were loaded with far-reaching information and were carefully delivered.

Recalling the theme of musicians and bands coming up with their own musical ideas (forced sometimes by isolation), such was the case in which Zappa's initial endeavors were indelibly and uniquely stamped. A remarkable manifestation of such individuality and the things Cage spoke of with regard to electronically produced sounds, was *Jazz from Hell*. The Synclavier afforded the user the possibility of making any sound, so what Zappa did on this recording goes beyond Cage's reference in his above statement: "...all sounds that could be heard," to the expanded realm of "all sounds that could be *imagined*." Frank's son Dweezil said that the music on *Jazz from Hell* is "indescribable." The liner notes with the CD are brief: "All compositions executed by Frank Zappa on the Synclavier DMS with the exception of 'St. Etienne.'" "Executed," meant Frank in front of a monitor, tapping keys and entering information borne of invention, which sculpted and ordered the sounds he wanted to use. I recall from a documentary, comments by Frank's dedicated archivists who said they would hear that tapping going on for hours and hours. In the interest of full disclosure, I warn that as the title suggests, the compositions are anything but easy listening. Unconventional doesn't even come close to describing what one hears, and Frank himself found it baffling that the title song won a Grammy Award for Best Rock Instrumental in 1988. When asked on a TV interview if receiving the award had any "special" meaning for him, Frank, living up to his name, was frank as usual, saying he thought it was, "…living proof the process was a fraud… I'm convinced nobody's ever heard it." "I don't know why they gave me a Grammy for this song."

Although the Dead embraced the spirit of musical experimentation and employed it in their music all throughout their career, their vehicle for the broadest exploration "Dark Star," is not as far from the classical tradition as one might suppose. The first night-class I ever took was a Music Appreciation class, circa 1967. The instructor in that class was the distinguished violinist from Napa, Karl Kultti, and the major focus of the class was Dvorak's *New World Symphony*. We learned that symphonies had an introduction, a main theme, and sometimes secondary themes. There was the middle section, of longest duration, in which there was development of the theme or themes. Then there was recapitulation and conclusion. All those elements are easily found in the "Dark Star" version that took up Side One on the *Live Dead* album. The five-minute introduction shows, in my opinion, the Dead at their collective best, each musician contributing to the whole but in such a way that each part deserves singular attention. It is a unique demonstration by Phil Lesh of what is possible if a bass player is not hindered by notions of what a bass player traditionally does.

With that freedom, however, you need to have something to say, and Phil Lesh had plenty to say. I would encourage people to get an inside look at the working of a great musical mind (whose captivation happened at a young age), by listening to his interview on YouTube that runs 19:40 with Matt O'Donnell. It is an excellent interview, one in which he describes enthusiastically the work of American composer Charles Ives (named in the interview as one of his two heroes in music, the other: John Coltrane), who was an important connection to a tradition of experimentation and innovation. Ives credits his father, a musician himself, with starting him down his unique-composing path. On holidays in Redding, Connecticut, George Ives would organize and conduct ensembles that brought together local musicians and lay singers from various counties and spread them throughout town in small groups: placing them by church steeples, in meadows, on roofs of buildings. The music and song would progressively roll down the streets to every sector of the community; a parade of notes. What a great idea—one that found its way into son Charles' compositions, who would say of art that it cannot, if it is to be real and vital, be isolated or "exclusive." He was emphatic that it be from the heart; from life and experience. George and Charles Ives, with music, did much to enrich America. Phil Lesh continued that tradition and helped carry the torch, like the music through town, further on up the road. If you do watch the video, you can readily see that the influence of Ives has seeped into his soul. A good thing.

I felt for a long time that Phil Lesh was an unrecognized pioneer in turning the role around for the bass (true also for Jack Casady of the Jefferson Airplane), and that the band itself was, as demonstrated in their collective improvisations, an early, though seldom recognized, developer of fusion . On Dark Star, Weir plays some wonderful counter-point throughout and gets the whole thing underway with lush chords following the quietly interwoven lines at the beginning when the rhythm comes into play, after which Jerry introduces the melody and Tom Constanten adds ascending notes on organ echoing the theme. Garcia's graceful lead-guitar line is enhanced by subtle touches creating a cello-like sound and adding down or upturns at the end of notes. The music builds up momentum in grand fashion then Jerry states the theme in all its glory. Things get very quiet to add drama, the gong comes in and Jerry sings the first verse, and in very effective manner, Garcia sounds like he's off in the distance, appropriate for a song which in part refers to a happening in deep space. Mickey Hart continues to coax hypnotic waves from the gong that grow in volume while Garcia brings forth gong-like sounds from his guitar as TC builds tension with simmering notes from his organ, and it whips into a concentrated moment with sounds from each musician chaotically entwining, and then bang! Magically they all coalesce landing on an exact point of genesis, then they're off to the long development that follows. This is incredible stuff and if you allow yourself to surrender comfortably to it, just the introduction leaves you with the impression of having gone to quite a number of places on a long voyage. The elapsed time, because of the ideas crammed into it, is distorted beneficially, compressing and enriching the payoff to the listener, way beyond the time of investment.

Bob Matthews and Betty Cantor-Jackson had much to do with how well this and other live performances sounded. From an article in *The Music Box*, John Metzger writes "...the well-respected recording team known simply as Bob & Betty...recorded countless hours of concert material and produced the classic albums *Live/Dead* and *Workingman's Dead*." Matthews, a tight friend of Bob Weir, had first witnessed the recording process in a friend's home studio and admitted he'd been mesmerized by the reeling tapes and "red lights flickering," and "I became obsessed, and I knew it was what I wanted to do." Furthermore, with specific regard to the Grateful Dead, Matthews expressed his opinion that in order to righteously capture the band's live performances, it would require someone on the inside with the passionate commitment of a family member, as it were. He achieved his goal because of his vision, dedication, and determination, along with encouragement by Weir, who even though in a position of influence could not, on his own, bring about the position Matthews hoped for. Weir therefore told him, with regard to what Matthews saw as an essential necessity, "If you think that, if that's your vision, then the only reason that doesn't happen is because you don't pursue it, and you don't believe it enough. So, it's up to you." Matthews then proceeded to convince the band that his efforts would be worthwhile and his important involvement thus came into being, and this strikes me as a beautiful behind-the-scenes detail, one of many which enrich the Grateful Dead story in a significant and emblematic manner.

As for working with Cantor-Jackson, Matthews said, "When Betty is being my counterpart on stage—dealing with the microphones and where they go, interfacing with the band, and addressing the other technical activities that occur simultaneously with regard to the PA and the equipment—she knows how to do it. That's what we did together, and she took care of that really well. I could always count on her if something needed to be done, regardless of the challenge." Lest it sound like Cantor-Jackson was just a helpmate to Bob Matthews, I want to add comments by Nicholas Meriwether, who wrote the liner notes for the May 2017 release of the 3-CD live recording from Cornell University in May of 1977 (a thoughtful gift from my daughter Carol). Meriwether refers to "the release of a spectacular cache of soundboard recordings, taped by Betty Cantor-Jackson," ones she's engineered on her own, that were nicknamed the "Betty boards."

Matthews' live-recording philosophy was straightforward. He avoided mixing and tampering with levels, feeling that while recording is underway, whoever's at the helm: "...shouldn't be dealing with technical, artistic decisions. You should just be documenting it—getting it down, making sure that there is enough level and that the microphones are placed in the correct positions. That's it." Adjustments and tweaking, if necessary, could be done later. That approach proved to be very beneficial, and in particular, *Live Dead* is a wonderful achievement of live recording, which was in fact the very first 16-track live recording ever done. Not only are the individual instruments all heard, but the sound of the room comes through as well, giving the listener the sense of what it felt like to be in the audience—something that was a stated objective by Cantor-Jackson, who said "I want you to be inside the music," so as to recreate, as much as possible, the experience of being there. That important element, in my opinion, can get lost with too much attempted tweaking of individual parts of the mix—and an exact demonstration exists of that phenomenon in the re-mixed version available in the box-set The Golden Road. They took the various tracks, isolated them, and spiffed them up a bit, altering levels and tinkering, and then they pieced everything back together. It provides a worthwhile alternative perspective, sonically, to the listener, but something was lost in the process: the cohesion, the integrity, the reality.

Adding to the John Cage-inspired reshaping of sound that enhanced "The Other One," I have to give thanks also to the enlivening stories of Jules Verne, author of *20,000 Leagues Under the Sea*, and particularly *Journey to the Center of the Earth*, whose images were evoked by the music. I was forced to recognize, as an adult when I saw those movies again, that they were not great, but as a seven and twelve year old respectively when I first saw them, they made a lasting impression. I loved to draw, and testing in Junior High suggested the appropriate career for me would be in animation, a reasonable conclusion as I had spent many hours pouring over and carrying out the instructions in Walter T. Foster books on how to draw portraits, cartoon characters, horses, and other animals, and was helped (as were my sisters), in this enterprise by our Aunt Evelyn, a nurse in Petaluma, who brought home yellow-orange paper used to protect x-rays, that after being used would have just been discarded. I remember that my cousin Gary, knowing I liked to draw, came to me with a very thick and heavy stack of this weird-looking paper, handed it to me and said, "Now you can draw till your heart's content." So when I saw the giant squid attacking the Nautilus, it was inspiration for drawing that scene many times. The adventures under the earth in *Journey* were equally vivid. When I heard the bridge section on *Anthem*, the sounds, added by Constanten and the others– the hissings, and gurgles—reminded me of the damp and dark enclosure from which the James Mason-led crew is trying to emerge. Similarly evoked is the "Allegory of the Cave" as the musical bridge conveys and the movie shows the difficulty, uncertainty, and struggle with things unfamiliar; stalactites and stalagmites facing us at every turn, each step taken with trepidation, wending our way with baby-steps to the bright light of new experience. "You have come out of Plato's Cave of Images," says Irish poet and philosopher John O'Donohue, "into the sunlight and the mystery of color and imagination…when your soul awakens, you begin to truly inherit your life."

Both Tom Constanten and Phil Lesh had extensive knowledge of the Classical tradition and together studied under renown composer Luciano Berio. As for the transitional moment in The Other One, Constanten describes the technique as an oft-used motif in Classical works, "the calm after the storm" that leads into "the delicious sounds of 'New Potato Caboose'… in the sun-shiny key of D." Inexperienced as we might be, we nevertheless find ourselves, the lyrics tell us, on "bare earth where green was born," and where "sun comes up blood-red," and where "wind yells among the stone," with the gift of conscious realization that, "all graceful instruments are known."

For the longest time, the Dead didn't make much of a profit, didn't care that much about it really, and what money they did make, they used to make the concert experience a better one through invention and equipment upgrade. Most importantly, they honored the music respectfully and with integrity, and continued to do all they could to ensure a quality product as they saw it.

Because of their focus on the product, as it were, they ultimately triumphed in traditional manner as a business. In one of the more delightful ironies of the free enterprise system, the Grateful Dead operation was taken seriously in the corporate world as a model, albeit an unusual one, of how to run a business successfully. Evidence that this was happening, and that they could cover their studio-time debt to Warner Brothers, came from the success of the (Skull & Roses) *Grateful Dead*, the band's first gold album.

The self-named *Grateful Dead* double live album was the band's seventh release from Warner Brothers. It followed *Workingman's Dead* and *American Beauty* but coincides with that period of creative output, and is an excellent display of how they sounded in concert back then. It is also a grand tour of song selection that effectively sums up the band's history to that point, and even though none of the songs from either *Workingman's Dead* or *American Beauty* are used, it still represents the different styles that both the group and its individual members were drawn to. Moreover, it is an example of the great live work that, in general, Bay Area bands were doing in 1970-71 when, in my opinion, those bands had all grown musically because of their time together. This was evident in the still intense yet collective ease of their interplay, which came at a time when Rock journalism was writing the period off as stagnant. And proof that bands were still making great music, was a film produced by Ralph J. Gleason and later televised on KQED: *A Night at the Family Dog*. I was rather disappointed when, in an otherwise very thorough and engaging treatment of the Dead, Dennis McNalley gave only one inch of page length to account for the occasion in his book *A Long Strange Trip*. Within that one inch, however, he described the event as a "high quality show."

The concert took place Feb. 4, 1970, and was later shown on KQED; I watched the (then) one-time airing when it happened Dec. 13, 1970. I set up my Roberts 1600 reel to reel tape recorder, using the very good microphone which had been a generous replacement and upgrade for the defective lesser model which I'd

156

originally received—along with the recorder—as a graduation gift from my mother and stepfather George. It was a wonderful gift. With the quality inherent in the ¼-inch reel to reel format, and that much-better new microphone, I was able to make good quality recordings. I learned that an advantageous angle was achieved by propping the microphone up in a shoe, and with the heel facing the TV, located the sweet spot on our living room floor which yielded good results even as the sounds came forth from TV speakers that at best in those days, were so-so.

I wish the show could have run ninety minutes instead of one hour, at least so viewers could have seen and heard the rest of that (cut-short) final jam that was really heading somewhere special. I know that what went into the film were selections from a regular set (say 45mins.) done by each band that night. Hmmm, might the rest of those performances be "in a can" somewhere?

The show opened with Santana, who played two songs; they were terrific, showing the same kind of intensity that had earned them a rousing reception at Woodstock a few months earlier, and that I had witnessed first-hand at the Dreambowl. The songs likewise included Carlos' incandescent guitar work and another dramatic drum solo by Mike Shrieve. Solid up-tempo assaults with their awesome percussion line of lightning-quick drummer, Michael Shrieve and exceptional percussionists Jose Chepito Areas and Mike Carabello provide razor-sharp renditions on both "Incident at Neshabur" and "Soul Sacrifice." At one point, just after they've begun "Soul Sacrifice," you can see keyboardist Gregg Rollie mouth the word "fast" to nearby Mike Carabello, as they both react with a smile to the challenging tempo in which they find themselves trapped. It's well-known that Steely Dan used the bass line from Horace Silver's "Song For My Father" to begin "Rikki Don't Lose That Number." Not as well-known, is that Silver found his way into Santana as well. After Greg Rollie's organ solo on "Incident at Neshabur," the bass line intro just before Carlos' solo is a direct lift from Silver's "Senor Blues."

Greg Rollie always provided solid soloing and support that was an important element of Santana's overall sound. In addition to the percussionists and Rollie, the rest of the band members were Carlos himself, bassist Dave Brown, and the neglected Alberto Gianquinto. What a great band! Gianquinto, whose name was not included among band member's names in the rolling credits at the film's conclusion, added some extraordinarily beautiful lines on acoustic piano as the music slows way down during a solo by Carlos. This was followed by his own solo, the camera not even focusing on him until near the end on "Incident at Neshabur," a song he co-wrote with Carlos.

The Dead were next, opening with the funkiest groove you're likely to hear on Otis Redding's "Hard to Handle," with Pigpen in top form on vocals, and great solo work by Jerry. They concluded with a highly energetic version of "China/Rider," with Weir playing a great solo, as they speed along on cruise control, the locked-in level of which is conveyed by the gleaming grin of drummer Mickey Hart as he looks over to his bandmates as the jam winds down.

The Jefferson Airplane followed with two songs: "The Ballad of You And Me And Pooneil," and "Eskimo Blue Day." On the first, Jack Casady plays a monster bass solo, the best I've ever heard, followed by an equally impressive effort on guitar by Jorma Kaukonen. Jack Casady had a unique approach to bass, and the tone he was able to achieve was a real thing of beauty.

One of the important aspects of instrument identification for the listener is the "attack." In Levitin's *This is Your Brain on Music*, we are told that the "attack," "...is the sound of the initial hit, strum, bowing or blowing that causes the instrument to make sound." Levitin continues, "This middle part of a musical tone is referred to as the steady state." In experiments done in the 1950s, composer Pierre Schaeffer literally cut away from tape recordings the "attack" portion of various tones produced by instruments. After doing so, Schaeffer found, "...that it was nearly impossible for most people to identify the instrument that was playing." More bewildering still was the "…ambiguous hybrid…" if the "attack" from one instrument was put with the "steady state" of another. I mention this because I think that Jack Casady's manner of striking the strings with his fingers (he did not play with a pick) was unusual and has much to do with why he sounds the way he does. Sly Stone's famous bassist Larry Graham (who later formed his own band Graham Central Station) is known for coming up with the "tap and slap," technique which he used initially to try and replicate bass drum and cymbal sounds because a drummer failed to show up for a gig. This technique produces a distinct sound that has been extremely influential in scores of funk bands and its use became widespread. I think that the way Jack Casady "attacks" the strings with his fingers, lies somewhere between the way Larry Graham uses his thumb, and the normal plucking of strings by most bass players. The only modern bass player that I know of, whose sound is similar to Casady's, is Flea from the Chili Peppers. From a book entitled *The Superstars in Their Own Words*, by Douglas Kent Hall and Sue C. Clark, there are a number of interesting interviews, which according to its preface, were conducted "…between September and December, 1969, in New York and San Francisco." Commenting on Jack Casady, Phil Lesh said the following:

> I think Jack Casady is the world's greatest electric bass player. Jack plays all over the instrument; he plays music on it instead of just bass lines. Like a lot of bass players will just play bass lines over and over again, but Jack will play along with the guitar player or along with the drummer, and he'll make a whole musical line out of his bass line. And not only that, he gets the quintessence of the Fender bass kind of sound. He's the most evolved product of Rock and roll bass playing.

From the same book, David Crosby described his playing this way: "Casady plays a sort of French horn lead line that's just stupendous. Unbelievable." A remarkable demonstration of what Crosby is talking about can be found on Jefferson Airplane bandmate Paul Kantner's *Blows Against the Empire*, in Grace Slick's song "Sunrise," which introduced a suite that began side two on the original album. After vocals shared by Slick and Kantner, Casady begins layering several bass lines of colossal proportion, a mighty chorus of amplified bass guitar tones resounding like a thousand French horns. If you listen to this, by all means turn up the volume and allow yourself to be bathed in its low frequency majesty.

In *A Night at the Family Dog*, the evening concludes with a long jam featuring members from each group, Gary Duncan from Quicksilver, and others. Seen digging the music, dancing, and blending in with everyone else are Janis Joplin and David Crosby, as Jim Marshall, my favorite photographer covering Rock, moves around adding to his impressive photographic history of the music scene in his inimitable way.

Good lord how I enjoyed that homemade tape, until I lost it in the shuffle somewhere down the line. In the years that followed, I never heard anything about a re-telecast, but after more than two decades beyond its initial showing, I miraculously noticed a small article in the "Datebook" section of the *Chronicle*, which said that it would be part of the SF Jazz Festival's film series, and would be shown at the Kabuki Theater. Halleluiah! That the film was a surprising choice for the occasion would have been the expected reaction, and I too was surprised, but at the same time I didn't think it inappropriate, because I had long held, even while stylistic differences remained, that the improvisation engaged in by these bands was compatible philosophically, with what Jazz musicians were doing. This was validated when later in their career, the Dead, in particular, played with Branford Marsalis, (who did some great things with the Dead and described the band members as having "big ears"), Ornette Coleman, and David Murray. So stoked was I by the good luck that allowed me to notice the event in the paper, and the opportunity to see the film again, that I contacted my daughter Jennifer, who'd become a fan of the Dead on her own without any prodding from me. I was eager for her to get a glimpse of what all the excitement was about from that lively period.

She was interested, so, the night of the show, I picked her up and off to the Kabuki we went. Unfortunately, about a third of the way through the movie, the projector started acting up, and the video portion became a snow-blizzard. The soundtrack was fine, but difficult to enjoy under the circumstances. Jennie and I had an enjoyable time together, but I was sorry she didn't receive the complete impression of what had transpired.

The theater issued refunds to everyone, a decent gesture, but not enough certainly, to offset the fear that had already began to form in my mind: that a rare opportunity had not been realized. Sure enough, as I discovered shortly thereafter with written inquiries, there were no plans to show the film again. Because of this, I began a one-man campaign to convince involved parties not to let this valuable time-capsule start another twenty-plus years of dust accumulation. One of the people to whom I wrote was Ralph J. Gleason's son Toby. In that letter, I appealed to the notion that I was sure his father had not documented this creative moment so that it could be, from that day forward, utterly ignored. He did respond and told me he was at work on a website in which his father's catalogue, the "Jazz Casual" series, and some of his other productions would be available to purchase. Great news, I thought at the time, but when I checked back periodically, the site was always "under construction," so I eventually gave up.

Then one afternoon, fate smiled upon yours truly. I was at a shopping mall in Fairfield, I don't remember why, and stopped into a video store that was going out of business. I saw several tantalizing DVD's of concerts, and bought, perhaps, two or three. The next day, while making my landscaping rounds, I couldn't shake the idea that I had not seized the moment to its fullest that previous day. I was sufficiently disturbed that I did a rare thing: I cut my work day short, notified everyone, and rolled over the remainder of my schedule to the next day so that I could drive back to Fairfield, because I also knew that it was the last day the store would be open. When I got back to the store, I started grabbing up the other DVDs that had aroused interest, and lo and behold, what did I see that was not there the day before in the same section I'd poured over, but a DVD of *A Night At The Family Dog*. I couldn't believe it. So, at last the show was available, and Toby Gleason had in fact seen his plan through. It is now available at www.eagleRockent.com, www.Jazzcasual.com, and on Amazon. At that point, I was extremely glad I had gone with my gut feeling earlier in the day.

As you might imagine, I had a most enjoyable evening at home, right up to the closing moments of the film during what was described as "A Super Jam!" in which the joyous participants, players and audience alike, were treated to one of those Garcia moments on a "Dark Star" jam when gorgeous guitar lines just come pouring out. Underscoring this is a moment when Carlos, who was also playing at the time, is moved by a cluster of notes played by Jerry, his body reeling back a bit in response. Near the end of the film, the music trails off into the realm of the innumerable possibilities of the unseen, available only to those there that night, but possible for you or me on another night. What I did see and hear in the comfort of my home that night was a source of contentment several decades of waiting had enriched immeasurably. Another source of contentment is that those "still fuming" musical gods talked about earlier were kept from wreaking havoc on inhabitants of the nether regions who saved themselves by making available this important historical document from a highly energized moment of collective creativity. Let's hear it for pleasant surprises.

Getting back to the Dead's double-live Skull and Roses album (from several 1971 concerts engagements), which, Garcia would say, shows them as "…the prototype Grateful Dead basic unit. Each one of those tracks is a total picture, a good example of what the Grateful Dead is musically. The new album is enough of an overview so people can see that we're a regular shoot-em-up saloon band. They're hot!" For someone unfamiliar with the band, this recording might serve as its best introduction. The songs are:

"Bertha"—A report from the sometimes magical insularity from a world of one's own creation. Ken Kesey often said: "Always stay in your own movie." This song functions as the trailer for that very movie. It has great guitar work by Weir, who carries the load on this arrangement, and effectively weaves rhythm, chords, and lead lines in support of the vocals, as Jerry demonstrates towards the end of the song, his ability to sing and add tasty guitar lines at the same time.

"Mama Tried"—A spirited rendition showing their love for Country and Western and also their respect for the great songwriting of Merle Haggard, who claimed this song among his many compositions as his personal favorite, and who, at another time, said he liked what the Grateful Dead were doing, which was received as very satisfying praise by the band. The bass line by Phil Lesh is perfectly appropriate and carries things along so smoothly that I just can't say enough about it. It's as comforting and satisfying as the sound of coffee brewing in the cool of early morning in a quiet kitchen.

"Big Railroad Blues"—If the Grateful Dead didn't actually go to Gus Cannon's porch as had Johnny Cash, they certainly traveled mentally across time to the traditions set forth by Cannon's Jug Stompers, and then brought something back. They brought back "Minglewood Blues" and "Viola Lee Blues," both on the Dead's first album and written by Noah Lewis, one of the Stompers who sang and played harmonica, as well as the song here, "Big Railroad Blues" which echoes Haggard's theme from the previous song: sitting in jail regretting that you didn't take mother's advice.

"Playing in the Band"—A Mickey Hart, Bob Weir, and Robert Hunter collaboration. A pretty composition used often, but not here, as a piece on which they stretch out. Tandem guitar lines by Garcia and Weir sound great, as does the (added) organ work by Merle Saunders.

"The Other One"—Just letting people know that their psychedelic adventurism is still alive and well. As Weir liked to say, from time to time: "Hang on to your hats." The Other One has a compositional framework, always observed, that serves as linkage points-of-return within which occur free-form forays into a wide range of interior states of mind that are intimately and starkly revealed. They cover a wide spectrum of impressions, all of which are conveyed in the music, and you know it when you hear it: A difficult time in your life, the dread of thinking you may not come out of it, then a settling out succeeded by the comfort of the familiar, and finally the increasing momentum as you sense a measure of control headed your way along with the good old light at the end of the tunnel. Out of context, a cross-section snipped from one of these developed movements may sound downright unmusical, but the logic is clear if one sticks around for the development from beginning to end, and so too, the payoff. The Grateful Dead was one of the best at tapping into these areas of the psyche, turning them inside out in powerful and sometimes uncomfortable ways in a manner similar to classical music in its attempts to convey the entire range of human emotion.

"Me and My Uncle"—Well, if there was ever a song that a "shoot-em-up saloon band," must play, this would certainly be it.

"Big Boss Man"—Pigpen gets his turn, nice harmonica work, convincing vocals, and backed by a solo by Garcia, who always exhibited a very nice feel for the idiom every time they played a Blues, and here he maintains the relaxed delivery set forth in this version of the Jimmy Reed classic—nothing forced, nothing overplayed, and just right.

"Me & Bobby McGee"—As everyone knew, it was done so well by Janis Joplin and so identified with her, that this was a tribute to her as her death had occurred less than six months before this performance. It is definitely heart-felt. Everyone in the band loved her dearly, and for that reason the song, co/written by Kris Kristopherson and Fred Foster, was added to their repertoire.

"Johnny B. Goode"—A rousing version of the Chuck Berry classic, from Winterland. It's the only performance from the album that takes place in San Francisco.

"Wharf Rat"—One of my favorites (more in a moment).

"Not Fade Away/ Goin' Down The Road Feeling Bad"—As tight as a band can be. Even though the band always had a formidable sound system, it came through as a clean sound, without resorting to effects and distortion to enlarge their sound further. They did have their sound-tinkering moments and later in their career used sampled sound, but by and large they maintained that clean delivery, the fullness of their group-sound achieved through the non-colliding intricacy of their improvisations. Phil Lesh, whose playing, on more than one occasion, has been described as contrapuntal, shows why on this performance. He lays down the traditional bottom, as he also seems equal part lead instrument, and shows time and again that he has the ability to pick just the right note, or succession of them, which achieves the best embellishment possible to all else going on. Weir shows here why Garcia called him "…the best rhythm player on wheels…," mixing, as he always has, lead lines with chords, shifting emphasis rhythmically, and adding color and harmony to great effect. Bob Weir has single-handedly done much to keep the activity of rhythm-guitar alive, in spite of its being an overlooked and undervalued tradition. In the Netflix documentary on Weir, *The Other One,* he talked about his guitar playing within the band: "The traditional role of a rhythm guitarist is somewhat limited. I got to where I was feeling hemmed in by what I was doing…I was listening to a lot of Jazz…I was listening to the piano players, Bill Evans, McCoy Tyner, and I listened to the way they chorded. Particularly McCoy Tyner, the way he chorded underneath John Coltrane and supplying John Coltrane with all kinds of harmonic counterpoint to what he was doing. That appealed to me greatly so I started trying to do that on the guitar for Jerry." In a separate interview, Garcia talked about Weir's playing: "With Weir, he's an extraordinarily original player, you know, in a world full of people who sound like each other. I mean really, he has really got a style that's totally unique as far as I know. I don't know anybody else that plays the guitar the way he docs. That in itself is, I think, really a score considering how derivative almost all electric guitar playing is." And Phil Lesh adds: "Bob arguably has the most unique guitar style of anybody playing in music. And I've loved it forever."

With respect to the percussion provided by Bill Kreutzmann, the performances on this recording came during a time when Mickey Hart was apart from the band. I loved the double drum setup, and loved Hart's playing, but with just four of them playing here (Pigpen comes in on the vocals near the end) one is quite able to hear everything that's going on in the four-way conversation, and Garcia has said that when they were forming the band one of the things he thought important and that they all agreed was worth striving for was a situation, musically, in which the "…instruments talk to one another." David Crosby alludes to this approach when he described the group's interplay as "electronic Dixieland." I think Kreutzmann really shines during their discussion. He is able, with sufficient force, to drive the band, but not in an intrusive way, placing his rhythmic emphasis in spaces not yet filled, enhancing the overall effect as he, at the same time, allows the intricacy among the guitars an uncluttered continuation.

Keeping in mind the notion of conversation, in one part of his six-hour television PBS series, *The Brain with David Eagleman*, the neuroscientist demonstrates how regions of the brain work together as a coordinated ensemble by using a group of drummers who are initially pounding away, each in their separate world, and creating cacophony. Then they begin to listen to each other, with more accord, working toward what he called a "sweet spot," reflective of the inherent harmony of brain networking.

I remember an article in which one of the band-members talked about them spending a lot of time together—a necessity for any band, and something you enjoy and are more apt to do when you're young--and out of all that hanging-out time came instances in which they all started behaving like Donald Duck's nephews, Huey, Dewey, and Louie who delivered sentences progressively, each speaking one-third of its length, picking up where a brother left off, one-mindedly; a brand of triplet telepathy. As you might suspect, this phenomenon found its way into their music as well. And that is the ideal state, is it not, when any band gets in a groove and really starts going somewhere remarkable. People can feel it, that "sweet spot," and perhaps the reason it feels so good is that it resonates with the cooperative operation of the brain in its best moments.

Wharf Rat

In May of 2008, Malcolm Gladwell writing in the *New Yorker* about the "Annals of Innovation," did a piece entitled "In the Air" which investigated simultaneous innovation. The focus of the article was scientific invention, but I think the phenomenon applies to literature and music as well. Gladwell writes about instances in which different scientists were focusing on the same type of developments coincidentally, while not aware of the other person's work. According to research compiled by William Ogburn and Dorothy Thomas in 1922, such simultaneous occurrences were not unusual, but unaware of the frequency, people would assume, when hearing about an individual case, that

167

something suspicious was going on. The conclusion of their study was that the unfolding of these developments by more than one person at the same time suggests that they were as much a result of something imminent in the culture as they were a singular idea from the mind of an individual—a possibility with which many are not comfortable, according to Gladwell, because we want to believe it was totally from that perhaps-overrated region between the ears. Joseph Campbell, in a cautionary statement, told Bill Moyers that the brain might be more appropriately understood as "… a secondary organ that thinks it's in charge."

The ideas from Gladwell's thought-provoking article seemed apropos to what follows: The Grateful Dead's "Wharf Rat" and Jethro Tull's "Aqualung" both surfaced in 1971. One would be hard-pressed to find a pair of bands more dissimilar. I did find, and took delight in, a bit of a connection between the two bands from a 1973 interview in *Guitar Player* magazine with Glenn Cornick, who provided very strong bass playing on Jethro Tull's first three albums. The questioner in the interview mentions Jerry Garcia, and Cornick responds: "He's such a heavy trip, I think he's my favorite lead player. And Phil Lesh is undoubtedly one of my favorite bass players. He's got such an unusual style, he just cruises along and never comes over as though he's trying to take the limelight. He really amazes me." Throwing in another connection, both Lesh and Cornick liked to play chords on the bass, which Cornick used to great affect in concluding his bass solo on Bourée, a composition by Bach. And Phil Lesh himself said his "style of bass playing is essentially modeled on Bach."

There exists in both bands a connection to the folk traditions of their respective countries; they both occasionally did a Blues piece; the Blues was a significant part in their early developments; and they have Jazz influences apparent in their improvisations. Nevertheless, they sound completely different. It's so trite to say, but the Dead, for the most part, had a very loose and open approach in the way they delivered most (but not all) of their arrangements, and Jethro Tull was very sharp and precise in their execution of songs while avoiding duplicate repetitions. I always suspected that their nearness, both geographically and historically, to the classical tradition, influenced many of those British Rockers: Moody Blues, Emerson-Lake-Palmer, Procol Harem, and Yes. Their music struck me as being noticeably more structured and formal than their American counterparts.

I bumped into a friend of a friend once in the late 60s. We talked about music, and I remember him telling me he had gone to a concert where both Country Joe and the Fish and Led Zeppelin had been on the bill. His opinion of the evening had been that Zeppelin had just wiped out Country Joe. I don't mean to pick on Country Joe. I loved their very trippy first album *Electric Music For the Mind and Body*; if you put that album on, you can smell pot burning. But I knew what that person was talking about in terms of the musicianship that comes out in live performance. Now, in that comparison, who would you choose as being closer to the classical tradition, the ones who did "Not So Sweet, Martha Lorraine," or the ones who did "Kashmir?"

I heard *about* Jethro Tull before actually hearing their music. My first recollection is of one co-worker talking about another co-worker who would, without fail (according to co-worker number one) "take a day off," whenever Tull was performing in the area. I went to that person, who in front of his work-bench right on the spot gave such an animated description ("they were all smoking cigarettes, and looked like a pack of demons") of what they were like, reeling about and reenacting leader Ian Anderson's movements in excited fashion with fire in his eyes, that I thought, man, there must be something going on there. I've got to check that out.

I started getting familiar with the music, and soon after went to see them live at one of my favorite venues, the Berkeley Community Theater, in June of 1971. This was the *Aqualung* tour, and I paid attention to the band for a long time thereafter. Seven years later I would be looking at one of those *Saturday Reviews* I subscribed to, when I did something that I absolutely had never done before, I swear. I looked at their ads in the back of the magazine, and among the other obscurities, saw to my great surprise an ad for a book on Jethro Tull. So I ordered *To Be The Play*, by Brian Meyers, said to be, according to the front cover of its 140 pages, "A timely meditation on the creations and performances of Jethro Tull." At the time, I paid maybe twenty bucks; I was amused to discover that in mid-2016, a used copy of this out-of-print book was available through Amazon for a mere $269.00.

It was an engaging book that was set up as a dialogue (a useful writing trick that frees one to say anything) between a middle-aged professor of British Literature and a fellow tenant who'd been writing about Tull. The professor could hear "...the sound of his typewriter beating the night long next door."

The two eventually start meeting regularly and the obsessed young man plays Tull's music for his guest and explains his theories about the importance of Ian Anderson with regard to Dionysus, mythologies, and his place among "major English poets," which was the professor's area of specialization. The book was a bit over the top, but it was a serious discussion of the band, which to my mind gave it inherent value, as I knew of no other books on Tull in 1978 when it came out, and for that reason, I enjoyed it and found it to be informative.

In the book, Meyers describes the beginning of a concert saying that the band members "...were not at all the same." That was true. For the Aqualung tour, Barrie Barlow was the new drummer, original drummer Clive Bunker having left to have more time with his family, and the new bass player was Jeffrey Hammond-Hammond. Meyers tells us the band opened with a song, which could have been "Wind Up," but more likely was "My God," and his description matched what I experienced at my own first Tull concert: "A figure in a white suit came out to a piano on the stage. A spotlight found him in the darkness. He played a pleasing bit of keys before the entire hall erupted, tore loose, exploded like nothing I had ever seen." That was the scene exactly at the Berkeley Community Theater, with Ian Anderson instead stalking out on stage through a trailing plume of cigarette smoke exaggerated by the spotlight, holding the neck of his acoustic guitar with both hands, brandishing it really, and announcing to the throng: "Welcome to the Andy Williams Hour." He begins "My God" and sings, slowly and quietly, the first verse while sitting on a stool, the rest of the stage still dark. With tension mounting unbearably, Anderson comes to the last line of the first verse, and sings: "So lean upon him gently—and don't call on him to save." **BHA—BHA!** Now the house lights come on full force, and the entire band is raging; an onslaught to the senses, just an incredible performance.

It was a spectacle, and this represents an early instance among Rock bands in which the presentation is given more consideration. Although bad, non-musical things happened because of this trend, Jethro Tull, who like Jimmy Lunceford before him willingly added theater to their shows, never let it interfere with the quality of the music. They were funny as hell to boot and, it could be seen, relished adding a bit of madcap Monty Python to go along with the music. For their 20 year anniversary tour in 1988, when the band is introduced, Ian Anderson and longtime lead guitarist Martin Barre are brought to the stage in wheelchairs, and at the end of the concert, attendants in white coats whisk them away flat on their backs on hospital gurneys, the two waving to the crowd as they depart.

I've already mentioned how much pleasure I derived from seeing bands I liked really nail it in live performance, so it must have been all the more pleasurable for those musicians who were actually getting it done. And lordy lordy did Jethro Tull get it done! They were absolutely exceptional in live performance.

Simultaneously from the Grateful Dead and Jethro Tull came similar songs about a bedraggled old soul living on the street. After considering it, I thought that a mash-up of the two songs would prove quite interesting. The various verses interchange effectively and both songs have a reflective, quieter section in the middle. The storyteller's relationship to the characters they tell us about is a sympathetic one in both songs. It remains for me a fascinating coincidence, from these two very different bands.

A footnote to these experiences from two bands that meant so much to me begins with the musings described in the song "Mother Goose," from Tull's classic album *Aqualung*, in which a foreigner is wondering about the zoo population in Piccadilly Circus. So it was with particular and added delight during our 2016 trip to London, that Sylvia and I, two foreigners, hung out one night with fellow animals gathered at Piccadilly Circus beneath the statue of Eros, after an enjoyable evening of music at another sought-after local landmark, Ronnie Scott's Jazz Club. Earlier, that same day, Sylvia had taken a photo of me, "As I was walking 'round Grosvenor Square," the opening line from the Dead's "Scarlet Begonias," a spot I had to see, since the song had been the source for so much enjoyment from the many versions I'd heard over the years.

The Grateful Dead's "Wharf Rat" demonstrates the essential elements I find so captivating—music and intriguing lyrics coming together to make a compelling whole—and they need each other. I'm reminded of the fact that one of Willie Dixon's last musical efforts, before he died on Jan. 29, 1992, was with Bob Weir and bassist Rob Wasserman. Their collaboration came as quite a surprise to me, and I was so pleased that it happened. It came about because Weir had gone to see Dixon perform at the original

Sweetwater in Mill Valley, a venerable watering hole with a small stage where many a great musical night had taken place. The Sweetwater had a family atmosphere, warm and inviting, that served as a second home and personal playground for the many musicians who famously resided in that community. Weir set-in with him during the show, and after, hung out with him. During that time together, a plan was hatched to work together on some new music. They collaborated on the song "Eternity" which the Dead began working on in practice sessions, some of which survived on tape. The song had great potential, and it was a shame it didn't get worked up fully in the studio before Jerry's passing in August of 1995.

Dixon had written many Blues classics, quite a number of them in collaboration with Howlin' Wolf, and there were so many Rock bands and Blues performers who covered his songs, that they are too numerous to name. A few of the more famous are as follows: from Mose Allison Sings, "The Seventh Son"' from the Doors first album, "Back Door Man" from *Led Zeppelin II*, "Bring it on Home"' from Jeff Beck's first album *Truth* (with Rod Stewart on vocals) "I Aint Superstitious"' from *The Rolling Stones, Now!* "Little Red Rooster"' from *Wheels of Fire* by Cream, the song "Spoonful"' and from Howlin' Wolf, my favorite Dixon song, "Wang Dang Doodle."

Wang Dang Doodle; rolls of the tongue doesn't it? It's fun to say, more fun to sing. The man knew how to put words to song; words that worked, words that fit and words that sang well. Seeing a TV documentary on him, I learned he never went anywhere without pad and pen, so he could always get down an idea he thought worthwhile should one spring up. It was not long into the documentary before it could be seen that Dixon was a shrewd observer of the human spectacle and a very wise man. I would encourage people to check out the lyrics to "Wang Dang Doodle" on-line. I so wanted to print the words Dixon used in the first verse, but copyright permission, especially regarding music, can be a very costly enterprise. If you do take a look, you'll see just how clever he was.

As for their collaboration on "Eternity," Bob Weir was mainly responsible for the melody and chord structure etc., and I remember him recalling that Dixon had suggested "nothing too fancy." When the music for the song had been worked out, Dixon did his part and gave Weir his completed lyrics to the song, written, appropriately enough, on a scrap of paper. When Weir looked at them he didn't think they amounted to much, but, out of respect for Dixon, said nothing. The first time they rehearsed the lyrics set to the music, Weir was bowled over by how well they worked. In an interview with "Deadhead Hour" host David Gans, Weir talked about the experience:

> And so we started working this thing up, and he liked it, and he started writing stuff. And by the time we had sort of fluffed up a verse and a chorus, musically, he handed me a sheet of paper. "Now, you go ahead and sing this." And I was reading it, and it was so simple, and I was thinking to myself, this is awful simple, this is really pretty simple-minded stuff. And it's really a great honor to be working with the legendary Willie Dixon and stuff like that, but you know, maybe he's gettin' old or something like that. Maybe he doesn't have the grip that he used to have, the edge he used to have. And he was sitting back there, saying, "Go ahead and sing it now. You know, you play it and sing it, too." And so I figured, well, I gotta do that, you know. We're working with him. And so we started playin' it. And I read the lyrics off the page, and when I was done, I was transported somewhere else. I was speechless at what had just happened. Just the elegance of the statement that had just come through my lips. And he'd been watching me. You know, he's an old guy, he's seen me go through all these changes, he'd been watching me. And so, I'm sitting there with my mouth open and my eyes just sort of wide open, and he's just crackin' up. He said, "Now you see, now that's the wisdom of the Blues."

This same phenomenon happened in the way the music and lyrics came together in "Wharf Rat." That performance, too, has the reward that only chance-takers receive, as demonstrated when the group hits upon something rare in their search for a transcendent moment as they bring the song to its beautiful conclusion.

The song, as performed on the album, had long been an enigma to me and I finally was able to figure out a few things by which I'd been puzzled. According to liner notes from S.F. record store proprietors, Paul Nichols & Hale Milgrim, the version used on the album was from a performance at Fillmore East in New York on 4/26/71. Nichols and Milgrim are given credit for the liner notes (new ones) in the booklet that was part of a box-set with all the Warner Brothers recordings (including several re-mixes and bonus tracks throughout) from 1965-1973. The original album and subsequent CD's all mention Merle Saunders playing organ on the opening track "Bertha," as well as "Playing in the Band," and "Wharf Rat." Since Saunders did not travel with the band (although he and Garcia frequently played together live apart from the Dead), his contributions had to have been added on in the studio. There is nothing mysterious about that, but the "Wharf Rat" recording always sounded to me like it had the cleanliness of something done entirely in the studio, and I could not detect a live presence as you can on all the other tracks, including audience response and the spatial effects of the venue. Also, during the "I'll get up and fly away…" vocal segment, it doesn't sound like Weir harmonizing with Jerry, which, in live performance, was usually the case; it sounds like Jerry's voice doubled up, something they certainly could not do live. The last part of the mystery is the acoustic piano on "Wharf Rat," which is heard from beginning to end. In all recorded formats, no one is ever listed as playing piano.

I wanted to know more, and from two live performance sites on-line found the date in question. After listening for a while, it became clear that the vocals had been touched up in the studio (and the simultaneous voice by Jerry added), but the shimmering instrumental work at the end of the song is exactly what took place in real time. As for Garcia's vocals, even with a little tweaking for the final cut, it's still a very soulful rendition, and I can't imagine anyone else singing this song, and giving it its proper due. Also important is the fact that this is early enough in Jerry's career that his voice still has a youthful purity to it before the ravages of Camel cigarettes and other abuses took effect. I know that he would sometimes be off-key, but on the right night his vocals could be very effective, making a strong connection emotionally with the listener. The impact of Jerry's voice in this earlier period would be as if tone controls were set at mid-range, and then you cranked the treble knob way up to enhance clarity. Such was the natural quality his voice had back then and his approach to singing was in keeping with his attitude towards his guitar playing where he found a technique to clearly enunciate notes. A careful listening will reveal an effort to sound out every vowel and consonant and not short-change a single syllable, something evident in his normal speaking voice as well.

"Wharf Rat" is an admirable showcase of the wonderful things the band can do. Like "Bertha," most of the guitar work during the course of the song is by Weir while Garcia plays a bit of the melody at first, then quietly strums chords underneath his vocals until he comes in more forcefully at the end (on the right channel). The song, slow paced, lopes along with a swaying, shifting rhythm that doesn't call for a steady pulse, asking instead that the drummer add color, something that Kreutzmann could do quite well; similarly, Phil Lesh does not lay down a typical bass line, but adds accents and commentary. The song's structure is somewhat repetitious, but this is not noticed if attention is given to the scene-capturing perfection of Robert Hunter's lyrics. The apt dialogue places one within earshot right there on the lonely and littered corridor of (dare I say), the dead-end street of life.

The "old man" introduced in the opening verse is San Francisco's version of Aqualung: August West. During the song's confessional middle section this fallen man ponders his predicament, thinking out loud in an act of contrition, and promises—("the good Lord willing")—to "live the life I should."

That sort of drunken sentiment; a moment of regret, perhaps even a genuine one, conjured by Hunter, is exactly the sort of thing one would likely hear if around an old man "...way down down, down by the docks of the city." The music slows down for the bridge while the organ of Merle Saunders brings a hymn-like quality to the proceedings, a nice touch that added significantly to the mood in that confessional moment. Before getting "...a new start..." however, August West tells us, "I'll get up and fly away," just one more time before putting his house in order. The power of delusion, you might say, brings about a fleeting moment of positive energy that is reflected in the soaring uplift in the music and vocals as he boldly makes his declaration. Things then begin to settle down, and sad realities return. "Pearly's been true—true to me—true to my dying day he said—I said to him: I said to him—I'm sure she's been." The narrator, having listened to "...his story..." wanders off and we learn more about him in the final verses. I hope you'll listen to it (on Youtube, running time 8:32) to hear the full effect of the ending.

In reading a review of this record long ago, I remember a comment (and this was a song that, by then, I'd listened to many times), that described Garcia's vocals during the middle section, when August West says "But I'll get back on my feet someday." Of that line, the reviewer says that the way Garcia sings the word "feet," conveys the exhausted and world weary state of this defeated man. I'd heard it, but didn't notice it. The observation of that nuanced moment, now brought to my attention, was added to the many compelling aspects of the song, the highlight of which, for me, is the instrumental play-out after the verses are completed.

The guys begin searching for a groove in which they can conclude in dramatic fashion, and it takes quite a while for them to come together. Jerry's probing guitar struggles, but gradually climbs out of the morass and you can hear it when they finally hit their collective stride. And unlike the failure sure to happen for the subject of the lyrics, the band members in this live setting can, and do, actually rise to the occasion. They do that and more; the conclusion is defiantly triumphant and exhilarating. A sublime feeling is generated as Garcia's up-the-scale crescendo at the climax of the solo is the perfect moment after which, the music, with carefully placed patches of tonal color, diminishes in exquisite fashion. For the life of me, I don't see how anyone could not see the beauty in the interplay between all the musicians: the bass line and two guitar lines are molten gold, crisscrossing lava-like as they flow down and cool from the uppermost regions.

Alright, so as a band, you've scaled the heights and through group improvisation arrived at a rare and special moment; now what do you do? Here's another demonstration of the closeness of the ensemble, as they ponder what they've just done, which in real time they had to do because neither the concert nor even the song was over. There follows a close-knit conversation one would expect from a team of mountain-climbers in that moment of exaltation after having reached the summit: there would be a toning down of the conversation and the party would quietly reflect on its collective achievement. And as one hears this conversation between the band members, it effectively leaves the added impression, with perfect touches, as it trails out completely, of both the music and the Grateful Dead walking gracefully into the infinite.

I want to stay with the notion of rising above circumstance to achieve something wondrous in any activity, but especially with music. I am certainly fascinated by and have read about the phenomenon often enough that I would enjoy writing about it, but since I am not a musician, I'd rather have someone who has had the experience first-hand do the talking. I asked my son Michael if he could say something about those instances in which he was sick or emotionally down, or upset because of some less-than-ideal situation with a venue, the club owners, the sound guy, or all-of-the above, and then go on to play very well. Other than that, I did not coax Michael to talk about certain things so that they would fit in with what I'd done or planned to do in the book, which was nearly complete when I received his response. I was very moved by how well it resonated with ideas touched on throughout the book. See if you don't think so too. Here's Michael, and it is his title as well:

RISING ABOVE: IMPROVISATION IN MUSIC
by Michael Papenburg

"Becoming a musician is a multifaceted endeavor. Like any language, there is the business of learning the mechanics. Scales, chords, melodies, songs—they all come together as one beautifully mathematical whole. It can take years to learn and even more time to fully comprehend the connectivity of everything. If that wasn't enough, I have often felt that music itself is the purest manifestation of emotion in sound. I believe that this is why music has been a part of the human race since the dawn of its existence.

It would be great if being a musician was merely a technical exercise. If I knew that practicing guitar x hours per day would result in a fantastic, emotional performance every time, I would sign up for that program immediately. In reality, it is practice and technique combined with intuition and emotion that brings about the best performances but one cannot count on it. A day filled with happiness could lead to a joyous performance or a completely lackluster gig. A difficult emotional time could lead to inspiration or writers block. It is this seemingly random element that leads people to credit divine intervention as often as hard work and dedication. There are classical musicians who dedicate years of their life to

179

perfecting their technique and seem to be able to move concert halls with the smallest gesture of their bow. Others come across as technical robots that play all the right notes but never seem to convey an ounce of emotion. Lastly, there are the purely intuitive who may not even know the name of a single chord but can evoke the sound of heaven as easily as they breathe. It's a mystery worthy of lifetime pursuit.

In my early 20s, I was dating a young woman who was a true free spirit. It was made clear from the beginning that the word "commitment" was not part of our relationship vocabulary. Things were fantastic in the beginning. Over time, though, everything began to unravel. This all came to a head when I invited her and a friend to a weekend party and jam session in rural northern California. The drive there was pleasant enough but things fell apart once we reached the party. She quickly connected with some random guy she had just met. I freaked out about it and confronted her. Her response was to break up with me within a few hours of our arrival. I was in complete shock. I don't think I had ever felt so upset in my life. I was about to wander off to lick my wounds when I heard the words, "Hey, the jam session is about to start. We all need to meet up in the barn."

I barely remember walking to the barn. It was a multi-level structure that sat by itself in a large field near the owners sprawling ranch home. Upon entering, I climbed a ladder to the second floor in order to join my band mates and 20 or 30 audience members. In a daze, I strapped on my guitar and proceeded to experience the purest form of improvisation I had ever encountered. It was as if I could predict every note the bassist planned to play and every beat the drummer could imagine. Chords, melodies and songs flowed from me like never before. It was clear from the comments in the room that everyone felt the connectivity. This went on for several hours until it felt like every emotion that needed to be expressed was spoken. I drove home the next morning in a devastated state and spent the day with a close friend talking through the experience.

Since that day, I have experienced small windows of enlightened playing but nothing as pure or as extended. I started teaching guitar again a few years ago and have found that it has really helped to improve my improvisational abilities. There is something about revisiting the building blocks of music every day that seems to make it easier to reach that place where your fingers are moving but it's unclear if it's of their own volition or if they are being directed by my mind or some other force. Is it purely technique, intuition, emotion, divine intervention or a combination of all of the above? Perhaps my last day on earth will end with answers to the musical mysteries of the world. One can only hope."

Thank you, Michael.

The joy I experience when writing about music was undoubtedly the main reason for beginning this project, but there were other important reasons why I was encouraged to do it. One of the things that struck me about music is that it has value on a practical level, and that the ideas put forth in song lyrics tell us about ourselves in ways that more formal means of education and other modes of expression cannot. I'm thinking how those torch songs by Sinatra I heard when I was a teenager let me in on what was happening in the adult world in a way that no psych., lit., or history class could. The limited length of a song forces the writer to get to essential points quickly. This in no way ensures the quality of a song, but for a skilled lyricist, this means that words are chosen carefully for their greater currency... that and the fact of the pure entertainment value of clever lyricism, even when there are no weighty advisory messages involved.

Getting back to another thing that made me want to do the book was the work of Nick Tosches. I first read something by him in a collection by Greil Marcus, *Stranded—Rock and Roll for a Desert Island*, first published in 1979. The book presented essays by people who, in Marcus' view, were doing the best writing on Rock and Roll. The one by Tosches put you in the car with friends of his youth, let you in on a caper gone wrong, and ultimately focused on the Rolling Stones, one of the groups whose music came out of that car radio and made its mark. While telling his story, one of the details he included parenthetically was a description of a friend's no-nonsense boss, "a man who, it is said, listed 'Gum' as his hobby on a job application." No matter the great commentary he made on the Stones throughout the article; seeing that detail made me a fan for life and it still slays me whenever I recall it.

Later I read *Where Dead Voices Gather,* an investigation into the life of singer Emmett Miller, which demonstrates how one should do biography. Tosches acknowledged that he'd had help collecting facts for the book, but I got the impression he would have done it all himself, if necessary. My dear wife Sylvia replaced my loaned-out or lost paperback version with a hardback edition. If I remember right, in his introductory remarks (not included in the hardback), Tosches talked about being obsessed with trying to put together Miller's deeply-buried story, causing him to put aside all the other tasks that were calling to him. Also, the paperback edition had several examples of various praise-loaded blurbs my favorite of which was one that simply said "Whew!" His extrapolations are far-reaching, he is a research demon, and if you commit to the detailed long haul, essential riches await. *Voices* gives us the life of Emmett Miller—not a famous musician, but one whose unique singing style served as evidence and was representative of important combinations learned and absorbed in his lifetime that would also be influential for the music that developed beyond his time. Where others would have given Miller footnote status or overlooked him entirely, Tosches looked more carefully. The way he, as they say, "ran with," the subject of Emmet Miller, made the task of telling the Dream Bowl story, with so many famous (and information-rich) individuals, seem easily possible. As regards writers doing biographies on musicians, I know of no one doing better work. Nick Tosches is one hell of a writer.

Another thing that made me think this book was worth doing was a fact I noticed being pointed out on several occasions: that there were very few reports from or about the audience. From *First Fusion*, talked about earlier in this book, editor Nicholas Meriwether says, "Deadhead scholars must smile when they read remarks like that of pioneering Rock sociologist R. Serge Denisoff, when he stated in 1975 that, 'Perhaps the most impoverished area of popular music studies is that dealing with the audience.'"

Backing up Denisoff's observation were comments from author Poe Ballantine, another writer whose work I greatly admire. The February 2014 issue of *The Sun* magazine had, inside the cover as they always do for contributors to the magazine, a nutshell-bio of him that says, "...after years of having stumbled down long corridors of philosophical mystery, he has learned that spaghetti can make you happy." Towards the end of an interview in which he talked about his profession, he said this: "I would recommend to other writers whatever life comes naturally to them. Honesty is your most powerful and persuasive tool. I grew up in a working-class neighborhood [as I did] and still live among working-class people..." [as I do]. "Though the working-class constitute the vast majority of the population, we are woefully underrepresented in literature and the arts..."

And finally, after committing to the project, I kept the following in mind: In the documentary *Make a Noise* about his life as a filmmaker, Mel Brooks tells us he asked Warner Brothers Producer John Calley if (for a scene in the comedy *Blazing Saddles*) he could beat up an old lady. Calley's response was: "Mel, if you're going to go up to the bell; ring it." Brooks added: "I never forgot it."

Philosophers Speak

We humans have been talking about music for a long time. From the earliest moments in the philosophical tradition to the present, it has been a topic of great interest and it stands as a mysterious yet essential part of the human story. And it is likely, many say, that before we could talk about music, we were making it. In Daniel Levitin's *This Is You Brain on Music,* he adds the following observations after talking about the oldest found musical instrument, a 50,000 year old bone flute:

> Music predates agriculture in the history of our species. We can say, conservatively, that there is no tangible evidence that language preceded music. In fact, the physical evidence suggests the contrary. The archaeological record shows an uninterrupted record of music making everywhere we find humans, and in every era. And, of course, singing most probably predated flutes as well.

A bit later, Levitin says, "Mother-infant interactions involving music almost always entail both singing and rhythmic movement, such as Rocking or caressing. This appears to be culturally universal." And from a book by Elena Mannes entitled *The Power of Music* (made into a TV special), she talks about Sandra Trehub, a psychologist, "...who specializes in studying infant response to musical intervals at her Toronto lab, [and] points to 'motherese'- the way mothers vocalize to their babies—as a great example of the link between music and language. 'Motherese' is that kind of singsong musical speech that communicates emotion to babies and can put them into a trancelike state and it exists across cultures."

In a confessional story by Lynn Davis in *The Sun* magazine, she comes clean as much as is humanly possible about relationships and the pursuit of happiness, and in the process we (with sympathy) see why she used a pseudonym. Davis quotes Douglas Hofstader who, she explained, had written a book entitled *An Eternal Golden Braid*, in which he says, "In general, the Zen attitude is that words and truth are incompatible, or at least that no words can capture the truth." The title of Davis's beautifully written story is *And So On*, itself a quote from Kurt Vonnegut's *Breakfast of Champions*; it is a phrase he uses often to bypass the mindnumbing effects a full disclosure would entail, and an indication that lying (on the book page) has commenced, an illustration Davis uses "…to acknowledge that literature lies," and even when true, that words frequently fail to provide what we need from them.

With regard to the insufficiency of words, an important appeal of music is that when played on an instrument, particularly if improvised, it conveys something pure and direct. In what struck me as an ideal setting for a beautiful spontaneous moment, I read an account in the book *Jade Visions*, by Helene LaFaro-Fernandez, of an after-hours get-together of musicians and friends in "someone's" apartment. Pianist Bill Evans was there, as was his bassist at the time Scott LaFaro and vocalist Morgana King. During their time together in 1961, The Bill Evans Trio, with LaFaro and drummer Paul Motian, were creating a new standard for the way trios performed. Theirs was a conversational arrangement rather than the typical soloist-with-rhythm-section-support, and they were putting in remarkable performances. LaFaro's girlfriend Gloria Gabriel tells the story to the author Helene, Scott's sister:

> Bill started out playing light stuff, Scotty started playing on the bass. Then they played classical stuff. Morgana started doing things with her voice, like an instrument. When it was over, I remember how quietly, carefully, Scotty put away his bass and walked out of the room. He was in tears. There are things that happen once in a lifetime. Bill didn't even move.

And then there is a segment which concluded side-one of Pink Floyd's superb 1973 album *Dark Side of the Moon*, called "The

Great Gig in the Sky," the performance of which similarly falls between notes played instrumentally and lyrics that are sung. This unique and powerful contribution to this extraordinary example of performing and recording excellence was done by Clare Torry, a well-known vocalist at the time in the UK. It is her remarkable voice that is the instrument here, and in an interview about the session, Torry indeed did say that after a couple of false starts—since neither Torry nor the band members knew exactly what to do—she told herself that "I have to pretend to be an instrument, and that gave me an avenue to explore." Her imploring vocalizations are deeply expressive, seeming to have more meaning than words, and this middle ground between instrumentation and lyrics affects us—perhaps because its spontaneous articulation is tapping into earlier human exchanges like "Motherese" before language came into being. In the documentary about the making of *Dark Side of the Moon*, bassist and singer/songwriter Roger Waters says that what Clare Torry did was "incredibly moving," and of Richard Wright's piano and Torry's vocals in combination, Waters said they were, "...both absolutely brilliant."

In another instance, we have vocalizations given us by singer Donna Godchaux from the *Closing of Winterland*, filmed and televised December 31, 1978 when she and her husband, pianist Keith Godchaux, were in the Grateful Dead. After the band sang the verses to "Scarlet Begonias," there is an interlude during which Donna does her version of voice-as-instrument before the jam gets fully underway. This is one of my favorite "Scarlet Begonias" to "Fire on the Mountain" transitions by the band. There was a very palpable sense of heightened expectation that night (as there always was at a Grateful Dead New Year's Eve show), which demonstrated itself in a rousing set-opening version of Sugar Magnolia, done in honor of host Bill Graham because it was his favorite Dead song, which marked the beginning of this historic evening. This was during the period when the Dead and the Saturday Night Live crew were interacting with one another, so the Blues Brothers were the opening act and Dan Ackroyd did the New Year's Eve count-down.

Some years back, I had written about this performance and described Donna's vocals as cooing. Jerry lays-out during her smoothly-delivered voicings, as the rest of the band supports her tastefully and quietly, and one can hear the music breathe, the rapt audience savoring the unforced flow of the sounds they were hearing and pleased in the certainty that more would come their way. Her solo worked beautifully, setting the stage and inspiring the oh-so-subtle jam that would follow.

Considering these two examples, it occurred to me that each situation asked for a unique range of expression: Donna Godchaux's effort was soothing introduction on a New Year's Eve night of celebration, a totally different musical environment than the one Clare Torry was in. Torry's effort was emotional conclusion to themes on the album that dealt with the troubling aspects of life, namely, the hanging on in quiet desperation that often characterizes the English people. I can't imagine a male voice giving what was needed in either of those significant musical moments. I checked the running time for each of their performances: Torry's total = 3:23, Godchaux's total = 1:34; under five minutes when tallied together. The value in each of these efforts goes way beyond whatever might be conveyed using minutes and seconds. Duration doesn't tell us enough about the impact of what they did. With accuracy, then, we *can* say that what they did was beyond measure. Their value? Incalculable.

In E. L. Doctorow's superb novel, *City of God*, he speculates beautifully on ancestral mothers who give birth to new life and then bring song into their infant's world:

> Perhaps the first songs were lullabies. Perhaps mothers were the first singers. Perhaps they learned to soothe their squirming simian babes by imitating the sounds of moving water, the gurgles, cascades, plashes, puddlings, flows, floods, spurts, spills, gushes, laps, and sucks. Perhaps they knew their babies were born from water. And rhythm was the gentle

Rock of the water hammock slung between the pelvic trees.
And melody was the sound the water made when the baby
stirred its limbs.

I have to pause to say that the impact of Doctorow's elegant
stylings had maximum effect because, when those words sang off
the page to me, Sylvia and I were, by good fortune, in Florence,
Italy. Each time we were done exploring the city for the day, we'd
return to our room at Hotel Pensione Pendini and I would station
a comfy chair by the (second-story) window where, looking up
and out from time to time, I could see the constant activity
happening in Piazza della Repubblica directly below, and beyond
that, just a short walk away, the Duomo and the rest of the city's
panorama looking north and east. More than the other places we
visited in Italy—Milan (briefly), Venice, Rome, the Cinque Terre,
and Bellagio—Florence embodied the Renaissance more than
those other cities and towns. The artistically conceived city-
planning becomes impressively evident when walking and
surveying this beautiful city. We would learn on our tour (and
climb to the top) of the Duomo that the technology had not yet
been developed to construct the dome that would span the great
distance of the cathedral as designed. They didn't know how they
were going to do it. It is, then, the ultimate demonstration
befitting a monument to faith, and an achievement that enshrines
also the artistic spirit of the age.

The Duomo's dedication in 1436, with the Pope in attendance,
was accompanied by a commissioned work [a motet—"a short
piece of sacred choral music"], by composer Guillaume Dufay.
USC Professor Richard J. Wingell talks about this piece of music
as an example of the importance of historical context when
analyzing any musical work. He suggests that its form could be
analyzed in isolation, as it were, but its impact is more fully
revealed and appreciated, if it is known that its structure was
proportionally constructed, musically, for two tenor voices, in a
way that mathematically was related to the arrangement of the
dome.

The genesis of a language we were inching toward—with which, eventually, we would analyze music—those initial sounds made long ago, were utterances of feeling. It is not possible, at this remove, for humans to experience the novel purity of the sound of a voice, but something of its importance must remain within us. A reverence for the sound of our voices survives and with it the fascination with all sound. When the breath of life takes hold at birth, our first accomplishment is to make a sound, and we do.

The spoken word, more complicated, would inherently require more time to develop, and that reality is demonstrated by every newborn whose vocal chords function normally. It will be a stunning achievement of our species, when a baby emerging from the womb says: "Hey, keep your hands to yourself," rather than the piercing "Waahh!" with which we're so familiar.

Pushing ahead to a time when we have learned language and number, we then see the development of a formal structure that organizes the variety of tones produced by instruments both natural and devised. I don't know what math classes involve these days by way of study, but I'm assuming that Pythagoras (from the 5th Century BCE) is still lurking in the hallways, and with him a musical notation system which likewise is not going away any time soon. Whether or not Pythagoras deserves credit for all the systems ascribed to him, we cannot say, but we can say for certain that discussion of music among philosophers goes back to its earliest beginnings; it has been suggested that he might have been the first to refer to himself as a philosopher. Pythagoras, so it was said, used music while giving his patients medicine, feeling it to be essential to correcting the body's system whose rational balance was out of harmony. A few years ago, such a technique would have been considered holistically rendered, and cutting edge. What's that old expression?—"There's nothing new under the Sun."

Part of the lore surrounding Pythagoras was that he heard the music of the spheres. It's quiet in deep space, but if Pythagoras himself or someone from the Pythagorean School *sensed* the underpinning framework of relationships exhibited in the heavens—an harmonic arrangement—it was not so misleading to have said he *heard* it. Whatever the applied terminology, we see that it was an understanding, a vision that inspired the development of a musical system still with us today.

Music, Mysticism and Magic, edited by Joscelyn Godwin, is a collection of writings on those connected topics from the time of Plato to the twentieth century. Godwin introduces us to the writings of Iranian philosopher Suhrawardi (1153-91); the form which these writings took was of introductory remarks given by Shirazi, a commentator, and then statements from Suhrawardi himself. Together, they offer a lofty account of Pythagoras' insights. As a preface to his explanations, Suhrawardi began by talking about the mystery of dream. "How can the brain, or one of its cavities," he asked, "contain the mountains and oceans seen in a dream, whether the dream be true or false, no matter how one conceives of, or explains this capacity?" Well, that's a very good question. Suhrawardi and Shirazi were paving the way for the notion that there are other realms of understanding beyond the range of consciousness normally experienced on earth, and I present their account as a more poetic, albeit over-the-top explanation, of how Pythagoras became aware of the music of the spheres.

Continuing with ideas regarding brain function, Suhrawardi said, "We cannot say that the tremendous terrifying sounds heard by the visionary mystics are caused by an undulation of air in the brain." Shirazi summed up Suhrawardi's beliefs which were that Pythagoras had visions of (and astral-traveled to) heavenly cities because of the "...purity of his being and to the divinatory power of his heart...afterwards he returned to his material body. As a result of what he heard ("voices of their angels," in those heavenly cities) he determined the musical relationships and perfected the science of music."

Godwin also presented the writings of Simplicius, whom he describes as being from the School of Athens and belonging to the last phase of Neoplatonism. In contrast, Simplicius, writing five centuries earlier than Suhrawardi in the first half of the sixth century CE, sensibly puts things in perspective by telling us: "Pythagoras, however seems to have said that he heard the celestial harmony, as understanding the harmonic proportions in numbers, of the heavenly bodies, and that which is audible in them."

What struck me in Godwin's book was the similarity of tone (a reverential one) from earliest writings to more current ones. This is testimony to the compelling nature music holds for humans, making it all the more alarming to learn from Oliver Sacks's 2007 book *Musicophilia* that: "The first formal music therapy program was set up in 1944 at Michigan State University, and the National Association for Music Therapy was formed in 1950. But music therapy remained, for the next quarter of a century, scarcely recognized." To that alarming revelation, I add something I heard in 2014 on "What d'ya think?" which is a Mon.-Fri. morning quiz segment on Vacaville's radio station KUIC: "that 90% of males said they do this (?) to keep their sanity." The answer was "Listen to music."

From Daniel Levitin's *This is Your Brain on Music* we learn that in 2006 there were "…about 250 people, world-wide who study music perception and cognition as a primary research focus…" a very small number it seemed to me, but, thankfully, general interest and scholarly studies have increased since then. And finally, in David Byrne's beautiful book *How Music Works*, a portion of which was used in his essay for the October, 2012 *Smithsonian Magazine* issue on "Sound," he refers to both Levitin and Sacks, as he'd also done in his book, saying: "Oliver Sacks wrote about a brain-damaged man who discovered that he could sing his way through his mundane daily routines, and only by doing so could he remember how to complete simple tasks like getting dressed. Melodic intonation therapy is the name for a group of therapeutic techniques that were based on this discovery."

Continuing with music's important place in philosophy, we have the ideas and opinions of Plato, which—unlike those of Pythagoras—were recorded and passed down to us, and whose writings are foundational in the tradition of Western Thought. In the dialogues of *The Republic*, Plato said: "Education in music is most sovereign, because more than anything else rhythm and harmony find their way to the inmost soul and take strongest hold upon it, bringing with them and imparting grace, if one is rightly trained…"

In a lecture on Thomas Reid by Professor of Philosophy Daniel Robinson from his five-volume series *The Great Ideas of Philosophy*, he said a respected and learned friend of his had told him that if he wanted to read two-hundred pages of "…luminous prose…" he should read Thomas Reid's 1764 book *An Inquiry into the Human Mind on the Principles of Common Sense*. If we are to engage fully our ability to appreciate music, the *Inquiry* serves ideally as a fundamental training course and prerequisite to that end. It was and is a beautifully written book that dives into the operation of our senses in such a thorough manner that I was made to feel more alive than ever because of its unique and revealing descriptions of who we are and how we function. The amazing operation of these senses is taken for granted and vastly underappreciated unless we are not only initially taught, but also thereafter reminded and encouraged, to do otherwise. The *Inquiry* is a document which does just that. It addresses the importance of initially making the individual aware of the miraculous function of these tools of perception and does so in reverent fashion, and in the process adds valuable perspectives that cause the reader to see the world anew.

In my experience, there was scant education in this regard in the home or at school. I stumbled into the classroom, you might say, by hearing Philosopher Alan Watts on the radio, and I grumbled initially because I was expecting to hear music. Needless to say, I was not in a receptive mood in those first moments, but luckily for me, I did not reach for the dial nor turn off the radio. It turned out to be an experience similar to the one with Jerry Garcia, in that at first I wasn't paying much attention, but was then overtaken by the ideas and the skill with which they had been expressed. What Watts, whose 7:00 AM Sunday lectures I started listening to regularly, was talking about was Buddhism, calling it the "lowdown" on life—and he indeed did say that you would not be shown this lesson in school. It was truly a revelation, a beacon of truth and logic the likes of which I'd been closed off from entirely in my experience. I almost want to describe it as the "miracle" of Eastern thought because of the positive effect it had on me with its emphasis on "seeing" the world with a reverential attitude. It is grand understatement to say that hearing these ideas was a refreshment from what in fact we had been taught, which for the most part, was that our allotted time here was one in which we slogged through life, on an earth which we were told was inherently corrupt, pending judgment after having been pronounced condemned at birth.

Watts had been my first introduction to philosophy and served as a springboard to other philosophers the way that Ray Charles had been my starting point to other musicians. In both of those endeavors, the same operations occur in the search for that which speaks to you. You begin to find out by whom someone was influenced and who they in turn influenced, and on and on you delightfully go.

Watts emphasized a down-to-earth approach, asking that we respectfully listen and look at the world without being in a hurry to put names on our experiences. After initially hearing all this, I didn't suddenly feel an urge to travel to the East, join a monastery, and abandon all traditions of the West, but I nevertheless saw these new perspectives as important, practical, and useful lessons that rang true, and I took them seriously.

Getting back to Thomas Reid, it needs to be said however, that he was no proponent of Eastern thought, as translations of Sanskrit and other teachings were not yet available; had they been, he would not have been an advocate considering the fact that he had been Minister in the Church of Scotland for twenty years before taking a regency at King's College, Aberdeen. He took this position because he felt that the more pressing need, in service to the church, was to work on the *Inquiry* whose purpose, he stated, was to refute the skepticism of David Hume, a contemporary and fellow Scot whose philosophical writings were seen as a challenge to religious doctrine. Hume's ideas had affected Immanuel Kant in the same fashion. However, and this is a *crucial* point, if you strip away the dogma of either of those different philosophies, East or West, and stay with what Reid focuses on in the *Inquiry*, they both deal essentially with matters of attention. Attentiveness, it has been said, is the natural prayer of the soul.

In his fascinating book *Geek Sublime*, Vikram Chandra, a novelist and writer of computer-code, talks about the connections he finds in the two activities and what constitutes beauty in each of those disciplines. What he presents to us effectively leads into what Thomas Reid said about language. And with respect to Sanskrit, I recall scholar and mythologist Joseph Campbell saying he was of the opinion that it was the most ideally designed (best-equipped you might say) language to deal with and convey spiritual meaning. The Upanishads were quite influential for Arthur Schopenhauer, the first person within Western philosophy to incorporate them into a work when translations became available in the first decade of the 19th Century. Worth mentioning is the opinion of noted philologist Max Muller who described those first translations (into Latin) by Anquetil Duperron as "...written in so utterly unintelligible a style, that it required the lynxlike perspicacity of an intrepid philosopher, such as Schopenhauer, to discover a thread through such a labyrinth."

Vikram Chandra had this to say about the Rig Veda, which was "The earliest available text in Sanskrit, dating—according to current scholarly consensus—from around 2000—1700 BCE. The Rig Veda, and the other Vedas that followed…were considered to be eternal, uncreated, 'not of human agency,' and 'directly revealed' to the seers…distinguishing them from all other religious texts…" the word for which was "…*devavani*—'the language of the gods.'" "The truths that the Vedas embodied lay not only in the sense, the verbal meaning, but also in the sounds, the pitch, the tonality, the meter." "The pitch, the tonality, the meter"— these are essential components of music and demonstration of its all-encompassing significance and importance to humanity.

Thomas Reid said that as we first begin to learn language and reasoning, we are incapable, in that early stage of development, to document the process. He explains to us that "…it is extremely difficult for the mind to return upon its own footsteps, and trace back those operations which employed it since it first began to think and to act…reflection, the only instrument by which we can discern the powers of the mind, comes too late to observe the progress of nature, in raising them from their infancy to perfection." Reid added: "Could we obtain a distinct and full history of all that hath passed in the mind of a child, from the beginning of life…to the use of reason; this would be a treasure of natural history."   Indeed it would. Ever since reading that passage, I try to honor Reid in a small way, during the daydreaming flow of ideas when I get to a point of: "How did I get started down this trail of thought?" I then attempt to trace the trail back to its origin. I can't always do it, but when I do, it brings a bit of warm satisfaction.

As regards the purposes of this book and the search for ways to more fully appreciate this life, the passage from Reid that really grabbed me, one which seems to have fresh applications to our modern age, was this:

> May we not hence conclude, that the knowledge of the human faculties is but in its infancy? That we have not yet learned to attend to those operations of the mind, of which we are conscious every hour of our lives? That there are habits of

inattention acquired very early, which are as hard to be overcome as other habits? For I think it is probable, that the novelty of this sensation will procure some attention to it in children at first; but…as soon as it becomes familiar, it is overlooked, and the attention turned solely to that which it signifies. Thus, when one is learning a language, he attends to the sounds; but when he is master of it, he attends only the sense of what he would express. If this is the case, we must become as little children again, if we will be philosophers: we must overcome this habit of inattention which has been gathering strength ever since we began to think.

Reid underscores what he obviously believes to be an important idea by recalling the words of Jesus himself ("as little children") and bringing to them additional meaning. In the seldom-recognized Thomas Gospel, as translated by Marvin Meyer, Jesus is reported to have said "…the kingdom of the Father is spread out on the earth, but people do not see it." The failure of vision, I think, that Jesus was talking about according to the Thomas Gospel was of the sort that Reid was at pains to drive home in the *Inquiry*.

A very similar outlook with regard to the learning process was put forth by Rousseau two years earlier in his 1762 book *Emile*, and in an article by Ryan Patrick Hanley from the April 2012 issue of the Johns Hopkins *Journal of the History of Philosophy* quarterly, he demonstrates how important these matters were to Rousseau: "Rousseau is remarkably insistent on the indispensability of such sensory training to our later development; indeed he hardly misses an opportunity to remind us not only that this education is today 'completely ignored' and the 'most neglected,' but also that we need 'to learn, so to speak, to *sense* [italics mine]; for we know how to touch, see, and hear only as we have learned.'"

As regards the importance of receiving instruction so as to appreciate these gifts, I think Diane Ackerman's book *The Natural History of the Senses*, (also made into a TV special) should absolutely be required reading in high school. This totally enjoyable book would certainly be on the list of top five things I would recommend as a cure for depression. The book informs us about how our senses function, their importance in general, and is full of delightful passages of explanation such as the following account which talks about a dinner out with friends after wine has been poured: "…whose apricot blush we behold, whose bouquet we inhale, whose savory fruitiness we taste. Then, wishing each other well, we clink our glasses together because sound is the only sense missing from our full enjoyment of the wine." There are other reasons for the origin of this tradition, but none as charming as the one Ackerman provides. So here's to learning new things about ourselves. Clink!

Perhaps the most exasperating of truisms is "familiarity breeds contempt." I've yet to find a philosopher who, if looked at long enough, didn't reveal some distasteful characteristic of disturbing measure and Arthur Schopenhauer was no exception. He feuded with his mother, who was the first woman to make a living as an author writing what today would be called popular novels, and they had long periods when they did not speak to one another. She said of his works that they would collect dust in libraries unread, and he said of hers that her pages would line the bottom of bird cages. There was an element of truth in both charges. His rancor, so one explanation goes, was brought about in part because his father had committed suicide, and Arthur thought his mother responsible for his father's depressed state that led to the tragedy. So despite his wisdom demonstrated elsewhere, Schopenhauer's works unfortunately contain bitter attacks on women, and cantankerous cynicism leaps forth from both the page and any photo. He nevertheless wrote about music with surprising warmth and sensitivity because it held for him a very significant place in his philosophy, resulting in some of his most inspired passages, believing as he did that among all the arts, music afforded the most expressive showcase for the telling of the world story.

Immanuel Kant was one of the most influential figures in all of philosophy, and for Schopenhauer, Plato and Kant were the two most important thinkers in the shaping of his opinions. According to Kant, our knowledge of the objective world could be, at best, an approximation. We could never know the "noumena," the "thing-in-itself," completely. According to Schopenhauer, the one exception to this rule is self-knowledge. We have direct self-knowledge which is our window and link to the world, and this reciprocal arrangement Schopenhauer calls the "will." Schopenhauer says:

> We have to regard art as the greater enhancement, the more perfect development, of all this; for essentially it achieves just the same thing as is achieved by the visible world itself, only with greater concentration, perfection, intention, and intelligence; and therefore, in the full sense of the word, it may be called the flower of life.

Shopenhauer went on to say that compared to the other arts, music "...stands quite apart from all the others." "We must attribute to music a far more serious and profound significance that refers to the innermost being of the world and of our own self." The music Schopenhauer had foremost in mind when explaining its importance was classical music. With regard to his contention that music constituted the most direct link, among all the arts, to our "innermost being," a logical extension of that idea would involve the development of improvised music which never had widespread use in composed and arranged symphonies and was therefore not a significant part of the music heritage available in his time. Had it been available, I like to think that Schopenhauer would have been similarly moved as was a famous composer in the following account by Alex Ross in *The Rest is Noise*:

> When Charlie Parker came to Paris in 1949, he marked the occasion by incorporating the first notes of the *Rite of Spring* into his solo on 'Salt Peanuts.' Two years later, playing Birdland in New York, the Bebop master spotted Stravinsky at one of the tables and immediately incorporated a motif

from *Firebird* into 'Koko,' causing the composer to spill his scotch in ecstasy.

Given that I hold for music a profound standing and considering the fact that it finds a place, uniquely significant, in Schopenhauer's philosophy, it is of particular importance to say that the spontaneous element that improvisation brings to the making of music—the very centerpiece of his theory—optimizes that level of directness in the creative moment, which Schopenhauer emphatically thought of as "the voice of the world."

In an important moment in David Byrne's book *How Music Works*, he says, "...it is the music and the lyrics that trigger the emotions within us, rather than the other way around. We don't make music—it makes *us*. Which is maybe the point of this whole book." And it was Schopenhauer's ultimate wish, expressed in the third section of his most important book *The World As Will and Representation*, that "...the importance and high value of art, seldom sufficiently recognized, are realized."

Another very helpful book regarding aesthetics and the appreciation of art is John Dewey's 1934 book *Art As Experience*. A 1958 edition had a cover price that I'm looking at of $1.95, for which I paid the typical 50 cents/inch rate at a Vallejo Library book sale which at 7/8 of an inch thick, brought the price to 44 cents. What a bargain! Within the chapter entitled "The Natural History of Form," Dewey tells us:

> We say with truth that a painting strikes us. There is an impact that precedes all definite recognition of what it is about. As the painter Delacroix said about this first and pre-analytic phase "before knowing what the picture represents you are seized by its magical accord." This effect is particularly conspicuous for most persons in music. The impression

directly made by an harmonious ensemble in any art is often described as the musical quality of that art.

Furthering this idea, Dewey says: "In music, form…develops with the hearing of the music. A melody is set by the tonic note, to which an expectancy of return is set up as a tension of attention. Moreover, any section of the music and any cross-section of it has precisely the balance and symmetry, in chords and harmonies, as a painting, statue, or building." And he then concludes with this most beautiful description: "A melody is a chord deployed in time." Those comments by Dewey made me recall the supremely illustrative observation by Goethe, who described architecture as "frozen music."

In a way that helps explain our sensitivity to music, Dewey puts in perspective the tremendous importance the ability to hear has had in our survival, calling attention to the fact that: "Sound stimulates directly to immediate change because it reports a change. A foot-fall, the breaking of a twig, the rustling of underbrush may signify attack or even death from hostile animal or man. Its import is measured by the care animal and savage take to make no noise as they move. Sound is the conveyor of what impends…it is sounds that make us jump."

There was a Seinfeld episode in which Elaine compared male and female form, and with that devastating bluntness only she could bring said the female body was a thing of beauty while the male body was more for utility, "…like a jeep." Well, it is true enough, and I think the ear comes under the same utilitarian account. It's not often you hear someone delivering poetry or prose about beautiful ears, as in Haruki Murakami's engaging 17-page fetishistic plunge in *Wild Sheep Chase*, but when considering design complexity, the ears put other body parts to shame. With all those complicated curves and swirling shapes, inner and outer, the ear has the elegance of a nautilus, and what wondrous and beautiful experiences lay possible within its function.

With these physical gifts, all of us have the potential for an enriching aesthetic experience. In summing up with language that properly elevates this human-only opportunity, Dewey says "A work of art elicits and accentuates this quality of being a whole and of belonging to the larger, all-inclusive, whole which is the universe in which we live. We are carried out beyond ourselves to find ourselves...the work of art operates to deepen and to raise to great clarity that sense of an enveloping undefined whole that accompanies every normal experience. This whole is then felt as an expansion of ourselves."

Hypnosis and Trance

"And isn't the whole point of things—beautiful things—that they connect you to some larger beauty? Those first images that crack your heart wide open and you spend the rest of your life chasing, or trying to recapture, in one or another?"

- Donna Tartt (*The Goldfinch*) -

I had nothing to do with our music-therapist neighbor randomly showing up at our house after hearing my mother playing the piano, and then demonstrating to me (without intention) the power of music to change lives. Neither was I involved with hypnotist Arthur Ellen's decision to visit Napa, although his demonstration there, at Ridgeview Jr. High, profoundly affected me; nor did I ask in advance that as a listener I be entranced by the music I happened to put on the record player on a particular afternoon. Still, I remember and was affected by them all.

Arthur Ellen was a show-biz hypnotist who had been known to help people when traditional treatments had failed. He had worked with celebrities, among them Tony Curtis, Johnny Mathis, Eddie Albert, Pamela Mason, and baseball stars Jackie Jensen and Maury Wills.

There were different groups of volunteers who were given the opportunity beforehand to mention something with which they might like help. At my father's behest, I asked for help to improve my study habits in school. When it was our group's turn (we were seated in chairs on a stage), Mr. Ellen looked me in the eye, and tugged on my arm a bit to put me under. His first attempt failed. I apologetically shrugged my shoulders and a moment later he stepped back over to me after working with another person, and repeated the steps. This time it took. Now Mr. Ellen stood me up. My eyes were closed, but I could feel and hear what was going on. He ran his hands down my sides as if to stiffen my frame. He spread out two chairs and with help, he and someone else placed my head on one chair and my heels on the other, my back facing the floor. Mr. Ellen then had my 200 pound father, sit on the stomach of his 120 pound son. I felt my stomach muscles strain just a little, but otherwise had no trouble supporting his weight. As I returned to my seat and became a spectator for the remainder of the evening, I did feel different. A sense of calm seemed to envelop the room, and the normally ignored space between objects had a more noticeable presence, something like a barely perceptible fog.

I would learn later that what Ellen did with me was not an unusual thing for a hypnotist to do, and that in fact he had done it on the Jack Paar Show with comedian Buddy Hackett as his subject. Nevertheless, it remains a remarkable thing to have experienced, and it certainly reveals untapped powers of mind, and the fact that humans can do more than they think they can.

Some time after that experience was another entrancing moment, at sixteen or so, when an experience took place that was a blend of external forces and their interpretations by an observer who realized that there was something significant about their combined state of affairs. It was not a dramatic occurrence in spectacular setting, just a significant moment of sufficient privacy during which I was introduced properly to the universe for the first time, as it was to me in a moment of respect and wonder.

Talking about the "routine of the daily mind," in an essay entitled *The Question Holds The Lantern*, the poet John O'Donohue proclaims: "Only seldom does the haze lift, and we glimpse for a second the amazing plenitude of being here." I had that experience visiting my aunt and uncle's home on the southern outskirts of St. Helena. It was a beautiful old home right off Hwy.

29 (now the Sutter Home Family Winery) with vineyard and countryside surroundings that stretched towards the setting sun.

There was a gravel road to the few residences nearby that soon dissolved into undeveloped areas that didn't seem to belong to anyone. One day, without plan, I followed that gravel road west into the wilderness and to *the* place of privacy. The half mile or so of ground I covered was mostly flat and open pasture with oaks here and there that turned into steeper inclines of dense forest further west. I was "by myself" more keenly than ever before, and this feeling slipped into the all-encompassing awareness of everything else. I wasn't dramatically that far from people, but had achieved a critical distance which brought about, in essence, a sense of utter isolation, but in a good way. For a few moments, I had the earth all to myself and more importantly, I was somehow open mentally for that ideal combination of forces that would follow.

I'd had inklings earlier, I think, laying in my bed when home sick from elementary school, in the solitude of my bedroom hearing what struck me as a lonely airplane going by overhead in the quiet and unusual afternoon which helped to provide a vague sense that there was this bigger experience happening about (as if in a neighboring realm) whose possible discovery offered itself but briefly and whose connection was fleeting and illusive. I see these now as natural occurrences that happened long before I'd read anything in a book that talked about such matters, and they served as adumbrations, understood in time and equal in value, to the explanations given in philosophical works and other experiences, that came later in life.

During my sophomore year of high school, I would be entranced in yet another way. In the relatively care-free state that is the mind-set of a teenager, I had an experience take place because I was comfortable in the moment and comfortable in the privacy (again) of my room, the combination of which made me very receptive. And who among us didn't enjoy the refuge and sanctity of that space? People as far from one another in every respect as Virginia Woolf and The Beach Boys unite in their testimony as to the importance of one's own room and it involves more than just the physical space, does it not?

However, the privacy of one's room brought about by itself, it can be said, a mildly hypnotic effect different certainly from one's state of mind everywhere else. It was all these factors that ushered in what I think is best described as a trance-state that came over me for a short time while listening to saxophonist John Coltrane, whose music was the most important element of the various factors of which I was a part that day. The experience never struck me as so strange as to be a matter of concern, but I still kept it to myself and never uttered a word about it to anyone.

What I can say about it is that at that time, I experienced images that were of a dream-like nature, but it was not a dream. It was not alcohol, drug, nor fever-induced. With hindsight, I think it might (now) be best-described as a meditative state, because I had surrendered completely to Coltrane's music, but I did so naturally, because I was in no way seeking such an outcome, probably a necessary condition for that which came about. I was transported, albeit briefly, to a place in my psyche that was utterly new. It was not at all scary. Afterward, I was nonplused by what had happened to me, but at the same time invigorated, because it struck me as being so singular an experience it seemed to involve some measure of privilege as if I'd been let in on a secret. In the aftermath, I did not dwell on it, but the experience was sufficiently impactful that it never escaped my mind.

Coltrane was seriously interested in the music of India, had sought out and discussed music with sitarist Ravi Shankar, after whom he had named a son, and let me pause briefly to say that one of the many joys of going to concerts is the fact that I've been doing it long enough, to have been able to witness the second generation of great musicians, and the attendant lift and encouragement to the soul such an experience provides. And so it was in January of 2010 when Sylvia and I went to a wonderful performance at Yoshi's in Oakland and saw Ravi Coltrane playing with his late father's renown pianist and band-mate McCoy Tyner, along with another of the next generation, bassist/vocalist Esperanza Spalding.

In Indian ragas, the emotional quality and coloration given each note by the musician is more important than a melodic arrangement of those notes, akin to the "modal" approach taken on Miles Davis' well-known and huge-selling 1959 record *Kind of Blue* on which Coltrane performed. After forming his own quartet, Coltrane famously used soprano sax on his 1961 recording of *My Favorite Things*, a very successful album that effectively put soprano saxophone on the map, and which underscored his continuing interest in making use of an Indian approach to his playing. New Orleans born Sidney Bechet, a contemporary of Louis Armstrong, was the first musician of note to use the instrument, picking it up in the twenties and using it throughout his career until the late fifties. The very talented Steve Lacy played soprano sax before Coltrane, using the instrument on pianist Cecil Taylor's debut album *Jazz Advance*, in 1956, and in a YouTube profile described the soprano sax "...as being in a state of limbo." "I was all alone; the soprano had been abandoned by the older players and not taken up by the newer players." Lacy however, continued to use the soprano for forty-eight more years during his life as a musician, but the widespread use of the instrument didn't happen until Coltrane began using it in 1961.

While working on this portion of the book, I was made to recall a wise-crack comment from famous drummer Buddy Rich in a "Blindfold Test" from *down beat*, a regular feature of the magazine which had a guest musician listen (without information) to a piece of music, and then the listener would comment, and rate the record. I dug through my stacks and found Rich's remarks from the April 20, 1967 issue. After listening to the quartet's version of "Chim Chim Cheree" from the movie *Mary Poppins*, with Coltrane on soprano sax, Rich, who claimed he didn't know who the musicians were (a puzzling circumstance considering the group's notoriety), had this to say: "I imagine they had great difficulty in keeping that snake in the basket." So while he intended nothing complimentary, it does say something about the success with which Coltrane had incorporated the essence of Indian music. Snake charmers, by the way, in fact use a woodwind instrument called the pungi that is related to the bagpipe. The sound is continuous (a trance-inducing aspect) as the player uses circular breathing to keep the gourd reservoir filled with air from which are channeled two reed-pipes. Putting aside whatever effect the pungi might have, or not, on cobras, it has a high-pitched tone similar to the one produced by a soprano sax; a tone that found its way across time and distance from the East to my own small temple of privacy near the very edge of the West.

As an example of the broad cultural difference between East and West, trance was something encouraged in the East and induced through the music and embraced by the listener; hardly the case here in America. The piece by which I had been entranced was "Your Lady," from *Live at Birdland*, on which Coltrane again plays soprano sax. That recording was made in November of 1963, a bit before the "New Age" flirtation with all things having to do with Eastern Philosophy that swept America. But there were people here whose interest was more than superficial and John Coltrane was certainly among them. The music I listened to that day was expressly conceived for the changing of one's consciousness and just hearing a few notes of "Your Lady," one can clearly hear the influence of India, where the consciousness-changing effects of music was not something new. The transforming power of music was taken seriously in India and had been for centuries, and John Coltrane learned, regarded, and applied it with the reverence with which it had been developed as it fused also with the influence of his grandfathers, who were both ministers. Hence, it was a bona-fide translation of sacred music streamed through Coltrane's experience of America and its music, to my room where it was received by welcoming ears, then sent to my psyche where it secured solidly a place of significance.

Dream of Flight

Religious scholar Houston Smith and drummer Mickey Hart worked together to facilitate and promote a series of performances (for the first time) in the U.S. by Gyuto Monks. Hart had long held an interest in World Music, and had made several recordings with a host of international musicians. Smith, who had traveled extensively all of his adult life studying world religions, learned about the Monks in remarkable fashion on a 1962 trip to Tibet. Not knowing this would happen, while staying near a monastery in the Himalayans, he was drawn to their devotional chants which awakened him at three o'clock in the morning. In introductory remarks to a performance by the monks on radio, Smith talked about the experience. His ears were the first "western ears" to hear the chants. He arose and followed the sound, walking toward the chorus of incredibly deep, chthonic tones, which struck the amazed Smith as "the holiest sound I have ever heard." Hart and Smith, over time, came to realize their mutual interest in the phenomenon and discussed their shared desire to get the Monks to America, which they finally succeeded in doing in 1995. While the two of them were on a talk-show to promote the events, one of the hosts asked Hart, "Well what do you have to do with any of this, you're in the Grateful Dead?" Smith, recalling the moment, said: "Without batting an eye, Mickey answered: 'We're both in the business of transportation.'"

Speaking of which, in more literal fashion, imagine distant ancestors, male and female, leaning comfortably against a warm rock briefly resting their tilted-back heads, before moving on. They see a bird glide by overhead. What an admirable way to get about, they must have thought. In a *Smithsonian Magazine* that talked about their Air and Space Museum, was a little blurb that said the following: "Wilbur Wright saw the desire to fly as a legacy from the ancients, 'who, in their grueling travels over trackless lands…looked enviously on the birds.'"

The flying dream must be an old one. In the ones I've had, I didn't find myself at dizzying heights, but once one overcomes gravity, what does a few feet matter? And in that twilight zone between dream and normal consciousness lodges the fading notion that this ability might carry over. Here's a tale:

There they all were; in the throes of secular entrapment, slugging it out in the here and now. Is this not a more-elevated state of accomplishment than the other-worldly dealings of saints, wizards, angels and holy-men? The wily Akbar had been thinking about this of late. Jinni Akbar, upon his release long ago, acquired and had been moving about atop his many-seasoned magic carpet. Although Akbar was steeped in hallowed tradition that considered frugality wise, he nevertheless broke from tradition in an act considered rebellious, but one he thought instead yielded at long last to the sensible. He could no longer abide by the fanciful standing a thousand and more tales had established and maintained for his magical medium of movement: that colorful rippling material of renown. A second definition of "renown" after fame, (said to be obsolete) was rumor. Akbar no longer cared to perpetuate this rumor as he glided, for the last time, with crossed arms and legs and erect back, into that part of Carson County's Mazda/Chevrolet dealership (his frugality still in place) that showcased "certified pre-owned" models. If he was going to trade in his magic carpet, he need not acquire a brand new vehicle. A convertible caught his eye but he thought again; hadn't he had enough of the open-air experience. A complete severing of ties was in order, besides, that al-fresco stuff was highly overrated. The only area of concern for him, with regard to driving, was the danger factor, but if ordinary people became successful "defensive drivers," it wouldn't be a problem for a wizard. A deal was struck (he was a tough negotiator), and he happily drove away with a year-old Mazda, learning in the process less literal understandings of the terms bells and whistles.

What a delightful up-grade! He was still off the ground, but now in comfortable seats, with backrest, headrest, and form-fitting adjustments. It was smooth, responsive, and fast. It could be as cool or warm as he wished, and quiet too, unless he wanted to take advantage of his newly acquired sound system. A capitol idea, he thought, as he asked his navigation system for directions to the nearest Rasputin's. Once there and inside, he was overwhelmed by the amount of choices. An observant employee sensed Akbar's frugal nature, and led him to the discount bins where used, or should I say "certified pre-owned" vinyl was stored, and recommended for him the Grateful Dead's *Blues for Allah*; "right up your alley," he said. The Jinni stroked his chin whiskers with one hand, and with his other, extended and clutching, beheld the beautifully rendered red folds of the skeleton-fiddler's cape on the album cover. He was intrigued and his interest grew when he removed from the album sleeve a sheet containing lyrics to the title tune written in English, along with Hebrew, Persian, and Arabic translations. "Might you have it in CD," he astutely asked, remembering instruction from the salesman about his playback system. "Right this way, sir." Back in his Mazda, Akbar quickly read his owner's manual, eased down the road, and watched the shiny gold-tinged disc, which he inserted, slip and disappear from his hand. From that disc came the transmutation to glorious sound. Never mind his incredible new method of travel; he had never encountered such magic as this. Informed by the L.E.D. screen, he saw that the title of the first song was, aptly enough, "Help on the Way." Stringed instruments and percussion commenced, the clear voice of the singer emerged from the center as instruments enclosed it from both sides. The lyrics rang out:

> Paradise waits
>> on the crest of a wave
>> her angels in flame

By Jehovah, by Jove, by Allah, by all deemed holy, Jinni Akbar had had a divine experience.

Museum Pieces

In the book review portion of the *SF Sunday Chronicle*, they occasionally have a section called "Special Edition—Bay Area Readers on Their Most Treasured Books." Neal Benezra, the director of SF Museum of Modern Art, cited Orhan Pamuk's *The Museum of Innocence*, as his choice. The book is about a personal museum that contains objects that were part of and represent the creative process that went into the making of the book. Pamuk actually constructed that very museum. If I did such a thing—and aren't we all involved in such a project in the place where we live—it would contain the following:

Coltrane's *Live at Birdland*.

The album was and still is a multi-faceted object d'art that offered excellent examples in several ways. Top billing goes to the music within, which was comprised of five performances; three recorded live at the historic night club in New York City, and two, done in the studio. When one looks at the album for the first time, the front cover color photo (by Joe Alper), captures Coltrane playing soprano sax, in such a way that boundaries are indistinct, and he appears as a blur of energy which was of course, very nearly the case. The photos on the inner sleeve are black and white. They show the as-they-were-playing intensity of each member of the quartet, and they surround the listing of performances within. The album contains the Coltrane composition "Your Lady," by which I had been entranced, and it also had the compelling description and commentary of poet Leroi Jones, who was there in the club when it happened. I was greatly impressed as a high school student by what Jones had written for the album and my feelings have not changed over time, that is to say, that as liner notes go, the ones by Jones for the album were as good as it gets. Jones, who would later change his name to Amiri Baraka, gives an account of his subway trip to the club, and paints a contrast between the less-than-edifying moments that made up most of his life, matched by the "bowels" and the "traffic and failure that does shape the area," to the experience of seeing Coltrane: "...and then finally amidst that noise and glare to hear a man destroy all of it, completely, like Sodom, with just the first few notes from his horn, your 'critical' sense can be erased completely, and that experience can place you somewhere a long way off from anything ugly...and the emotions... [ellipsis his] some of them completely new... [his again] that I experience at each 'objective' rehearing of this music are as valuable as anything else I know about."

Jones described "Your Lady" as "...the sweetest song in the album. And it is a pure song, say, as an accompaniment for some very elegant uptown song and dance man." The coming about of that image may have been helped by the way in which Elvin Jones' drumming dances over the top of everything else that's going on. And the manner in which he plays reveals just how much he is pushing against the boundaries of tradition and that which is physically and mentally possible. It is a demonstration of his one-man-band capability, about which I'll have more to say later. When listening to the piece for the first time, focus on just his drumming, and if you fully lend an ear, the drumming by itself is utterly mesmerizing. Then listen to the musicians in combination. The effect "Your Lady" never fails to have, if I properly surrender to it, is an apparent manipulation of the sense of time so that it seems way longer than the 6:53 it is said to last; a misleading on-the-surface report vastly short of the aesthetic mark.

As an assignment in Mr. Payne's high school public speaking class, we each had to select something, anything we wanted, to read before the class. Jones' liner notes were what I chose. I return to them, with appreciation, from time to time, but not nearly as frequently as I do to the music he describes, and that music is for me as enduringly satisfying as can be imagined.

Eric Dolphy At The Five Spot

I have Dennis Meehan and Phil Wharton to thank for telling me about several great Jazz musicians in my early years of interest, when we were juniors in high school, and that interest has continued to expand to this day. There's so much out there to be enjoyed and appreciated, one lifetime is just not enough. The impact of those first experiences cannot be overstated, and one of those defining first albums was this Eric Dolphy recording from July 16, 1961. It was Dennis who first played it for me. Like the Coltrane album, it had a great photo on its cover by Prestige Art Director, Don Schlitten. Prestige was an important label that had a very impressive stable of great artists from whom many classic albums were the result, and they took special care on the art work and photography so that the albums always had a very cool and recognizable look to them. In this case the photo was done in sepia, and does about as good a job as can be done to seat one at a table right there in the club. Looking at the hazy coloration, you can almost smell the cigarette smoke. The liner notes tell of Schlitten risking life and limb getting in front of people to take the shot, with flash photography no less. Despite the intrusive nature of its inception, it's an intimate portrayal of the moment that also tells you something about the less-than-ideal conditions musicians have always had to deal with in clubs.

Since they're so scrunched together in the photo, I have to assume that the stage was way too small. It's been suggested, in other accounts, that such a physical arrangement lends itself to tight-knit playing by the musicians; maybe so, but I'm sure if the players had their druthers, they'd want more elbow room. Another restriction one discovers when listening to the record, is that the "house" piano is worn out and badly in need of tuning. Trumping all that and functioning as another triumph of the sort Leroi Jones talked about in his liner notes to *Live at Birdland*, is the talent combined here in this quintet co-led by multi-reed player Dolphy and trumpeter Booker Little, with a rhythm section made up of pianist Mal Waldron, drummer Edward Blackwell, and bassist Richard Davis. Years later it would be regarded as an historic occasion, as it was one of Dolphy's earliest instances as a leader of his own group, and the event showcased the new directions in Jazz for which so many musicians had been striving. Adding to the record's significance, unfortunately, was the fact that both Booker Little, only three months after this recording, and Eric Dolphy, three years later, died way too young.

As mentioned earlier, in any musical setting I was always interested in what the drummer was doing, and Ed Blackwell, the drummer here, was unique. He grew up in what I think is one of America's most deeply-entrenched and musically enriched ley lines: New Orleans, Louisiana. He absorbed the music of his home town, much of which was right there on the streets where anyone could see and hear it. He took lessons and eventually participated in parade bands, and that aspect of the marching rhythm, which he loved, remained a part of his versatile and adventurous style. He was also influenced by African drumming. He liked to use mallets which gave his snares and tom-toms a tympani-like resonance, and his sound seemed much more melodic to me than other drummers. It was a barrage of swirling little tunes, and was always ideally supportive to whatever was played.

I recall a travel show on television that probably aired in the late fifties and early sixties before the days of Mutual of Omaha's Wild Kingdom. A husband and wife team (she had striking blonde hair) went to remote places all over the globe. The theme music to the show was African drumming, and I noticed it because it didn't sound like any of the drumming I'd heard in America. I have never forgotten those rhythmic patterns. In those remote enclaves to which they traveled, the villagers did not have modern instrumentation, but percussion instruments of various design and function could be (and were) made, and it was as if the drum was their instrument of choice for the making of music that was an essential element in their recreation, and important also as a communication tool. Not surprisingly then, they were very good at using them, and the group drumming (always the way it was done) had many complexities, which accounts for why they sounded different to my American ears.

From Paul Austerlitz's book *Jazz Consciousness*, the second chapter: "Kente Cloth to Jazz—A Matrix of Sound," has a section entitled "Conversation," in which he tells us:

> After recording Afro-Dominican *palos* drumming [accompaniment to celebratory processions] once during a field trip, I politely asked the lead musician if each player could demonstrate each drum alone; I wanted to record a separate track of each for purposes of transcription and analysis. His answer: "We cannot do that." Thinking that the drummer had misunderstood me, I repeated myself in respectful terms. He again said, "We cannot do that." I later realized that my request was perverse: playing one part alone is antithetical to the way that musicians hear the music. Similarly, ethnomusicologist John Chernoff notes that while Western students of African drumming usually find it easier to play a pattern isolated from its ensemble context, the very idea of playing one part alone is foreign to the African sensibility: Ibrahim Abdulai [Chernoff's drumming teacher] felt that isolated beating was meaningless without a second rhythm…There was no conversation.

And from Mickey Hart's *Drumming at the Edge of Magic*: "When he studied the Venda of South Africa, John Blacking noted that whenever a little kid began banging some object, an adult or older child would instantly add a counterrhythm, transforming the child's spontaneous gesture into polyrhythmic play."

The communicative influence of that percussion heritage is always on display from Blackwell. On side two of the album is the Dolphy composition "The Prophet," which runs the entire length of the second side. The main theme is played slowly and repeated, and then there is a double-time interlude of a few bars with Dolphy soloing before they return to the theme after which a long run of improvisation begins. As the horns state the melody once more before Dolphy's brief but blistering solo, Blackwell's playing becomes more active and pronounced as an appropriate build-up to the increase in tempo just ahead and his playing and support during this stretch, impresses me as a perfect moment of percussion.

Two years after my initial exposure to Dolphy's music and graduating from high school, while an apprentice sheet-metal worker, I became acquainted with a driller. Drillers were available for any trade that needed a hole drilled that they themselves could not do. Part of the job involved waiting until you were needed. As I worked and he waited, we struck up a conversation, and before too long the topic turned to Jazz. I had told him how impressed I'd been with the Dolphy album and it was one with which he was familiar. I had not seen the album available in any regional record stores, but he knew a store near his residence that had the album. He was a black guy, maybe in his mid-thirties, and I think he saw me as a young white kid (I was twenty) who showed genuine interest and respect for both the art form and the people largely responsible for it, and because of that, he voluntarily picked up the album and brought it to me, carefully wrapped. I greatly enjoyed and appreciated the gesture.

Seven years later, in 1973, after having been part of a "reduction in force," I was living and working in Fairfield, California, at a low-paying job in an upholstery shop, after foolishly failing to try to find work in sheet-metal. One day, while reading a *down beat*, to which I still subscribed, I came across a request to readers to support a fund for Ed Blackwell who had been hospitalized, so as to help with his medical bills. I sent a check with a small donation. Time passed, and I'd forgotten I'd done it, but then, one afternoon when I was feeling, as author

John Barth would say, "…chin-high in the shallows," I was going through canceled checks, when I came across the one I'd sent to Blackwell. There in shaky script, as one might expect from someone still recovering from an illness, was the endorsement and the words: "Thank you Mike." It made my day. He played music for nineteen more years.

Coming up another seven years, in 1980 I went to see pianist Mal Waldron at the old Yoshi's in Oakland on Claremont St. before they moved to Jack London Square. Waldron, who had been the pianist on the Five Spot album, and whose improvisational style I loved, was appearing at the intimate club with the brilliant soprano saxophonist Steve Lacy. I'd just heard an engaging interview with Waldron by Bay Area radio personality Art Sato. In that interview, he talked about "…going on a voyage…" whenever he took a solo, and "milking" an idea for all it was worth, aspects very much in evidence on the Five Spot recording. I also learned from the interview that he was a world traveler who spoke several languages, had played during his career with many Jazz giants including Charles Mingus, and had been the last pianist to work with Billie Holiday before her tragic passing.

As the date drew near, I was a bit under the weather, and nearly talked myself out of going, but I did go, and was glad that I had. I was seated at the bar because all the tables had been reserved, and when Waldron came into the club to begin the set he walked right by me heading to the bandstand. I made an effort to give a smile of respect that I hoped would reflect appreciation for all the contributions black musicians had made, without looking too goofy in the process. He smiled back, tapped me on the arm, and said "Hey" as he went by. It was enough. When I later recounted the story to a regular client of mine, an English lady (a Jazz-lover herself) who had moved to California, she responded in her typically witty way with her high-pitched Julia Child-like voice, "You were anointed."

After a mesmerizing evening of duets by these gifted musicians, to my surprise both men came off the bandstand to mingle with those in attendance. Not thinking for a moment that it would really happen, I had still, just for the hell of it, brought along my album on the outside chance that Waldron might sign it, and here was my opportunity. I waited till he had a free moment, approached and told him how much I liked his music, and how inspirational the interview had been. He graciously autographed the album; an imprint which adds perfectly to the already rich combination of human activity and connection the album represents which never fails to provide good feeling whenever I hold it in my hand. It definitely has museum-scale value in terms of its meaning for me. A final note that wraps up this series of events in remarkable fashion is the fact that forty-seven years after the Five Spot album was made, and twenty-eight years after I saw Waldron, I got to see bassist Richard Davis perform with the Barry Harris/Charles McPherson Quartet in Dinkelspiel Auditorium on the Stanford campus in August of 2008. It was a doubly attractive bill for me because of Davis' participation on the Five Spot recording, and because Charles McPherson was responsible for one of the greatest solos I'd ever heard on Charles Mingus' beautiful composition, "Orange Was the Color of Her Dress," from his stunning set at the 1964 Monterey Jazz Festival. I was anxious to see both of them, and was privileged to experience yet again another great night of music while being, as well, a witness to its placement in the rich historical record that Jazz represents with such elegance.

Lunch Break

In 1989, Ace Hardware, where I'd been employed for sixteen years, moved from Benicia to what was for them the greener (and non-union) pastures of Rocklin, CA. Not wishing to find out how much more miserably they would treat employees without a union presence, and not willing to accept what for me (because I received extra pay for driving fork-lift and working graveyard) would have amounted to a 40% reduction in pay, I started my own landscaping business at age forty-two. With great satisfaction and never looking back, I did that for twenty-one years before retiring.

In the opening paragraph of this book, I reported that I repeatedly played Little Richard's "Jenny Jenny" on the malt shop juke-box. That experience would come into play fifty years later during my Grass Roots Gardening life-phase.

It was 2007, and I was brown-bagging it on a lunch break in my trusty truck, listening to "Fresh Air" with Terry Gross on the radio, a thing I tried to do as much as I could. Her guest that day was author Salman Rushdie. I had not read any of his books, but had seen him on TV read from one of his stories at an awards presentation. I had been greatly impressed with his story telling and command of language.

On "Fresh Air" that day, he told Terry that he was born in Bombay, India, and that growing up he and his friends tried to hear as much American Rock and Roll as they could get their hands on—not an easy task, as his parents and everyone else's frowned upon those decadent artifacts from the West. Listening to them had to be done on the sly as if they were dealing in the Black Market. And what singer did Rushdie mention when talking about these activities? Little Richard. A smile of recognition came to my face, because that place in my truck at that precise moment, was a very good place for me to be.

Prior to this, I had read somewhere that Rushdie was born in June of 1947, so we were four months apart in age. I flashed to the fact that here was an example of the great connecting power of music, that while as a ten year old, I'm dropping, the coins right into the slot, Rushdie is on the other side of the world, holed up in his bedroom or at friends listening to and diggin' Little Richard, hoping the parents don't intervene. I took great pleasure in that.

Natural Magicians

Before talking about musical magicians that come in human form, I want to acknowledge Mother Nature as our first musician, or more correctly, our first band. In the prelude to Bernie Krause's eye and ear opening book *The Great Animal Orchestra*, he talks about those early periods of human existence when "The sounds of animal life...dominate the rather modest noises humans generate." He concludes the prelude in the following manner:

> This is the tuning of the great animal orchestra, a revelation of the acoustic harmony of the wild, the planet's deeply connected expression of natural sounds and rhythm. It is the baseline for what we hear in today's remaining wild places, and it is likely that the origins of every piece of music we enjoy and every word we speak come, at some point, from this collective voice. At one time there was no other acoustic inspiration.

That last sentence is one that ought to be contemplated for a few moments. "Musician and naturalist Bernie Krause," so it says from the inside flap of the book cover, "is one of the world's leading experts in natural sound, and he's spent his life discovering and recording nature's rich chorus." His first efforts took place in Muir Woods, an always-invigorating and favorite destination for Sylvia and me, in nearby Mill Valley. He went into those woods, put on head-phones, turned on his sensitive microphone, and was astonished: "the instant I switched on my recorder in resplendent Muir Woods one lovely fall day in 1968, my acoustic sensibilities were transformed by the ambient space that enveloped me." It was, without a shred of exaggeration, a life-changing experience which drove home the understanding that, "Many of us don't distinguish between the acts of listening and hearing. It's one thing to hear passively, but quite another to be able to listen, fully and actively engaged." Krause, like Daniel Leviten, was a professional musician, a "studio guitarist," who worked with Paul Beaver on "electronic music sessions," for sound effects for films, among them the "Apocalypse Now" soundtrack, on which Mickey Hart and Bill Kreutzmann had also worked. Krause suggests we turn the tables when listening to the "*Biophony*," the word he coined for: "the sounds of living organisms." Listen for the highs, lows, and mid-range just as you would for music.

There have been many advancements in sound reproduction, and there exists a dizzying array of electronic gizmos for enhancing, altering, and moving sound. I have no quarrel with the use of these fabulous tools, but I also am comforted by the inextinguishable inclination of musicians to always be drawn back to basics, using acoustic, wooden instruments, and their un-auto-tuned natural voices. In Krause's book, he talks about the work of composer R. Murray Schafer in what struck me as the ultimate example in which a music performance involves nature. This is reminiscent of George Ives' positioning of musicians at various locations. Imagine yourself in the following situation:

> *The Princess of the Stars* has been performed on a lake, usually in Northern Ontario. Instrumentalists from the Toronto Symphony are scattered out of sight of the audience throughout the forest surrounding the lakeshore, while the singers, on illuminated boats, begin their musical narratives along with the changing sky just before daybreak—emerging a little after four a.m. on late summer mornings from small alcoves that encircle the lake. While the audience stands or sits on the shore, the performers are induced into action by the natural soundscape, led by the dawn chorus of bird song.

Bernie Krause's book is full of fascinating details about sounds in nature, how insects each have their own frequency range, ensuring they won't be canceled out by similarly-pitched buzzing but will be able to hear fellow members of their species. There exists clockwork reliability as to when creatures make sounds, and precise temperature conditions that correlate with insect songs. We are privileged to still have the great animal orchestra in those "remaining wild places," and we also have the staggering array of sounds produced by the human orchestra, which leads me to talk about one of its most remarkable and magical exponents.

Coltrane

Much has been written about saxophonist John Coltrane, and it is always mentioned that he worked incredibly hard at his craft. That the quartet consisting of Coltrane, Elvin Jones, McCoy Tyner, and Jimmy Garrison was together four years (1962-1966) seems remarkably brief, considering the extent of the ground they covered. In that time they reached a level of development unmatched in its scope, power, and influence in terms of group achievement. The single-most concentrated gathering of musical geniuses was the Dizzy Gillespie Quintet with Gillespie, Charlie Parker, Max Roach, Charles Mingus and Bud Powell. It would be unreasonable to expect that any member of such a collection of talented musicians would not want to seek an individual course, and it's an easy conclusion that any such gathering is not likely to stay together long enough to fully realize group development. I'm thankful that the quintet was together long enough to have been recorded at Massey Hall in 1953. I am equally thankful that I was lucky enough to see two-fifths of that legendary group by seeing Max Roach at the Berkeley Jazz Festival (twice), and Charles Mingus at the Berkeley Community Theater in 1973. For anyone interested in finding out what Be-Bop was all about, that live recording is a very good place to start. It showcases the leading pioneers responsible for the development of that style, which according to Grover Sales Jr. who wrote the liner notes "...presents a quintet of the most fertile talents in modern Jazz at the height of their creative and emotional powers."

In the case of the John Coltrane Quartet however, "fertile talents" remained together for four years of fervent development. The results of those developments were on display on countless occasions in which it was demonstrated that not only were no words needed beforehand among the players regarding what they intended to play, there were none available to observers immediately afterward, as it is no exaggeration to say that the quartet's intense efforts left people breathless, momentarily bereft of lung function and/or articulation after the fact. I know that in a documentary on Coltrane's life, Elvin Jones talked about how when John stepped up to the mic, he felt like there wasn't anything he couldn't do. He had such amazing control and facility with the instrument that it was true that he could play whatever came to mind because of the virtuosity he had worked tirelessly to attain.

As for the other members of the band, listening to drummer Elvin Jones was like listening to an entire band, and I find myself continually marveling at all the things he did, wondering how in the world just one man was able to do it. Coltrane would say of him: "I especially like his ability to mix and juggle rhythms...I guess you could say he has the ability to be in three places at the same time." He was the perfect man to match the relentless energy set forth by Coltrane himself, and John admitted that there were times when he could not match his drummer's energetic output.

Pianist McCoy Tyner, whom I've seen perform on several occasions, has dazzling technique, and adds incredibly interesting counterpoint with his left hand as if he had been given two brains. With all that, he nevertheless always seems to be pushing himself, in the example of their leader, trying to go beyond whatever it was he had done on his last solo, and according to the liner notes by Leroi Jones on *Live at Birdland*, was "...the polished formalist of the group." Tyner had a way of rolling out, in dramatic fashion, a red carpet which served as conclusion to his own solo while ramping up to the place where John enters with his own. In one of Ashley Kahn's many perceptive analyses in his book, *A Love Supreme/The Story of John Coltrane's Signature Album*, he writes about this aspect of the quartet: "One of Tyner's intuited tricks was to raise the passion of the performance as his improvisation approached its close, so that the transition to Coltrane's solo could take place just as anticipation and energy crested and converged. It was a well-practiced maneuver, requiring an equal degree of fervor both before and after the high-intensity handoff."

Even without the stimulation of a heightened introduction, Coltrane had the ability to start off solos in an intense fashion. Stories abound in support of the idea, that with his all-encompassing dedication to music, if he wasn't playing (a rare thing) he was certainly thinking about what he could be playing so that when he did start a solo, it was as if it had been underway for a while. Kahn tells us that Miles Davis, whose insights always got to the point quickly and effectively, said in his autobiography: "I'd tell him to begin in the middle, because that's the way his head worked anyway." To me, this is further evidence of just how accomplished he was as a player. If we think of a stage production, for example, and its creator dumps too much impact into the opening scenes, raising the bar unwisely high, the audience will be left wanting in Acts III and IV. Such a danger never existed for Coltrane as he routinely set the bar high and went up from there. I remember an account by one of the writers in *down beat* who had seen Coltrane take a solo that he thought "surely would have turned his lips to blubber," and then saw, after the set's conclusion, Coltrane backstage quietly playing scales alone in a corner. My favorite story is from David Crosby who, when seeing the band, was so overwhelmed by its force, he sought refuge in the men's room, only to have Coltrane, while someone else soloed, burst into the bathroom playing his sax. It's easy to imagine how forceful such a scenario would have been in the echoing confines of that small space.

Equally amazing as Coltrane's limitless passion, Tyner's challenging precision, and Elvin Jones's physics-defying drumming, was bassist Jimmy Garrison's ability to keep pace with the maelstrom of musical lines that moved with great force among the musicians. Ashley Kahn also wrote the profile of the band in the booklet that came with the Jazz Icons series that featured Coltrane. Talking about rounding out the quartet, Kahn quotes

McCoy Tyner: "It's amazing how everything fell in line as far as personnel. We went through different bass players, and finally settled on the right combination of people when Jimmy joined that band. I remember when he and Elvin first played together—it was just amazing."

The band was known for playing long stretches at a time. Three of the four were good-sized men and Jones in particular was a muscular powerhouse. Jimmy Garrison, however, was a slightly-built man who probably weighed less than 150 pounds, yet he had the band's most physically demanding job. It seems to me that his forearms must have been screaming after 30 minutes of, say, "Impressions," played at its always-rapid pace, but his stamina and strength never faltered. From Leroi Jones's *Live at Birdland* liner notes, he says of the bass player's contribution: "…Garrison's bass booms so symmetrically and steadily and emotionally, and again, with such strength, that one would guess that he must be able to tear safes open with his fingers." I saw the quartet on Ralph Gleason's *Jazz Casual* in the mid-sixties. Garrison took a solo during one of their numbers, and poured so much of himself into it that witnessing it seemed like an invasion of privacy. To think that he did that night after night is incredible, but if ever there was music of sufficient uplift to make one forget about something as trivial as aches and pains, this was it.

As regards Coltrane's leadership qualities, my assumption is that the other members of the quartet saw early in their association with him that he had the potential to take them to places where few musicians had gone, if they, as it is said in the sports world, "bought in." His reputation as a respected talent within the Jazz community was already well-established at the time of the group's formation. If any of the prospective band members thought at all about the fact that some critics had not been very welcoming to Coltrane's music, it was well-outweighed by the satisfaction they sensed possible on an artistic level that joining the group could bring. Thankfully, as it turned out, the band was a commercial success that earned critical acclaim as well.

A commonly repeated attribute one must have, according to NBA analysts and/or ex-players, in order to be called a "superstar," is the ability to make those teammates around you better, beyond the establishment of impressive individual statistics. Upon an athlete so gifted as a Michael Jordan is conferred the respect of being the best at one's craft, quite apart from what might be added by force of personality, and Jordan was one of those who unquestionably made those around him better. The ultimate example of this, in my opinion, was Dennis Rodman's tenure with Jordan and his team, the Chicago Bulls. To say that Rodman was a "free spirit," would be to put it lightly. He was one of the least controllable people ever to play in the NBA, yet he performed reliably with the Bulls, helped them win three straight championships (1996-98), and the Chicago Bulls fans loved him as if he was one of their tough-minded blue-collar own, his multi-colored hair notwithstanding, doing the pro-basketball equivalent of dirty-work: fighting for rebounds and disrupting the opposition with hounding defense. Something more than athletic ability from a teammate, then, was required to bring that situation about. Although Jordan was not shy about telling people what to do, that in itself would not have been enough to do the job either, but with help from savvy coach Phil Jackson, the combination of the level of respect Jordan had earned because of the grandeur of his excellence, his persuasive personality, his compelling competitiveness, and his "eyes on the prize" mentality, I think he might have been the only NBA player capable of eliciting that sort of cooperation from Rodman during that time in his life.

Coltrane, too, was a person capable of affecting those around him in extraordinary fashion, but in his case it was done more by example than it was through direction; he teamed up with musicians eager to bring the best they had to offer. It would be the cooperative legacy which followed that surpassed even the incredible individual talent on display in the John Coltrane Quartet, because here was the ultimate example of the whole being greater than the sum of its parts, even if those individual parts were extraordinary. Those men honed themselves to razor-sharp preparedness. They had complete confidence knowing that each of the other musicians could respond in near perfect and telepathic fashion, and because of this were able to achieve unhindered momentum to an astonishing degree as they piled up in rapid succession one musical accomplishment after another.

A Love Supreme (December, 1964) was a landmark recording for the quartet. It was Coltrane's masterpiece in terms of composition. In Ashley Kahn's book, he talks about all that went into its creation. According to Kahn, Coltrane, in an upstairs room at their home in the Dix Hill section of Long Island, New York, went to work on the composition and, "For five days he had secluded himself upstairs with pen, paper, and saxophone." Kahn then tell us, "When he finally reappeared, she (Alice Coltrane) noticed that Coltrane—normally deep in thought—was unusually serene." His wife then said, "Tell me everything…He said, 'This is the first time that I have received all of the music for what I want to record, in a suite. This is the first time I have everything, everything ready.'"

What he had was, as he said, a "suite" intended to be done in four parts. It is a spiritual declaration of the highest order. When one listens to it, the continuity and wholeness of its realization is utterly apparent. This is something you would expect from the force of commitment compressed into those five days that account for its diamond-like outcome. The prayer/poem that is the album's title is included inside the album, along with a heartfelt letter of thanks from John to all concerned, making the album's presentation an exceptionally personal offering. Every aspect of album's conception was unique. It did not contain typical liner notes, customary at the time, and record label Impulse broke with their own tradition of an orange colored spine on the side edge, keeping it black and white like the pensive photograph of Coltrane on the front cover. In addition, inside the album is the charcoal drawing by Victor Kalin (done from a photograph), which is an incredibly life-like rendering of Coltrane playing his tenor. At Ace Hardware, in an effort to liven up the place, someone came up with the inspired idea of doing artwork on the several containers in which we put cardboard. And lest anyone think I wasted company time, I only drew during lunch hour and my breaks. Using magic markers, black sharpies, black ball-point pen and pencil, I tried my hand at recreating a life-size image of Coltrane on the 4'x4' plywood.

John Coltrane, drawn by the author

With all that I'd read regarding *A Love Supreme*, it wasn't until I read Kahn's book that I learned that part four, "Psalm," is a musical recitation of the poem itself, each iteration a note played by Coltrane. Maybe someone had written about it and it just didn't sink in, but I couldn't remember that musical situation being mentioned in any of the previous accounts I'd come across. In any case, it strikes me as a highly significant aspect of this creative endeavor. Upon learning this, I immediately listened to it and tried to follow along. It's easy to get lost, but it was certainly worth the effort to put words and music together as John and the rest of the quartet had done so beautifully.

In his foreword to Kahn's book, Elvin Jones wrote, "Everything we were trying to do, everything we were about— McCoy, Jimmy, myself, and of course John—came together on that one album. Four individuals who gravitated together from different parts of the country, different backgrounds, all focusing around the personality of one man—John Coltrane."

Coltrane was able to muster intense focus and attain in private the spiritual intimacy the piece required because of the familiar and comfortable environment he found in that upstairs room where his vision was realized. The grand concept had been thought out and notated, and then the challenge was to convey to vinyl, with his musical brethren, the ideas and sounds generated in his mind; a tall order.

The sound engineer Coltrane wanted to work with, as he had on earlier occasions, was the meticulous Rudy Van Gelder, a master craftsman in his own right. Van Gelder had been the choice of many musicians on the Prestige, Blue Note, and Impulse labels. He had always been able to achieve a very warm sound in his Englewood Cliffs, New Jersey studio, with just a hint of echo. The space in the room came through to you so that the experience was as if the instruments were virtually right in front of you in your own room.

Although the quartet felt at home any time they worked with Van Gelder, it was still going to be, after all, in a recording studio.

Was there a way that the elation generated by the development of his concept, in what for Coltrane turned into a sacred space, could be carried over and into the studio? One thing that was done is talked about by Van Gelder in Kahn's book: "He would call me directly and say, 'I would like to come in Wednesday at 7 p.m. and work for two or three hours.' I would say 'OK.' They would arrive—always on time, I might add." Such sessions would repeat until Coltrane was satisfied that he had enough material for the next album, but for the completion of *A Love Supreme*, the quartet began recording at 8 PM Wednesday, December 9, 1964, and finished just before midnight. McCoy Tyner talked about another aspect of the session: "I remember something very unique about that recording session—Rudy turned the lights down. They were on, but they were low, and I guess he wanted to set a mood, but I never saw him do that (before)."

During my sheet-metal apprenticeship I had to study metallurgy, and learned the subtle nature of metallic combinations and the importance of the elements in alloying that can either degrade or enhance the final material. I enjoyed working with sheet-metal and did it for six years (age 19 to 25), and still find it fascinating that a material of such rigid quality can be coaxed into so many shapes. I was moved, therefore, when in Homer's *Iliad* the blind tragedian goes for several pages describing the metal-making craft. The goddess Thetis comes to Hephaistos, "...the renowned smith..." asking him to forge new armour for Achilleus. He assures Thetis the task will be done: "there shall be fine armour for him, such as another man out of many men shall wonder at, when he looks on it." "First of all," so Homer's account unfolds, "he forged a shield that was huge and heavy...and threw around it a shining triple rim that glittered, and the shield strap was cast of silver. There were five folds composing the shield itself, and upon it he elaborated many things in his skill and craftsmanship."

Sharing a similar structure, the shield and the gong also share long histories. From Mickey Hart's *Drumming at the Edge of Magic*, he tells us, "The Zildjians were the best cymbal makers in the world. They had been in business for at least five hundred years (and had) a secret formula for how to mix the molten sounding-metals from which fine metallophones are almost alchemically made. Supposedly some scientists from MIT had tried to crack the formula using scientific techniques but had failed." The Zildjians had a collection of Chinese Gongs at the factory visited by Hart. Because of his interest in the instrument, a gong could be found on stage near Mickey's drum set at Grateful Dead shows at least as early as 1968, and was always a part of the ever-adventurous "Dark Star." There's nothing quite like the sound of a gong. Fritz Kuttner, a scholar of Chinese music, concluded after fifty years of study that "...metallophone guilds..." had existed for 2000 years, and "...had possessed techniques of metallophone production far superior to anything in the West, even with today's technology," but now, "...these secrets had been lost." "Now only the gongs themselves existed." Hart tells us that a private collector "...brought one to the Metropolitan Museum of Art, a magnificent [and very large] tam/tam gong, where it had been tested by one of the staff technicians, who made the following report of its unique powers:"

> One single gentle tap of pianissimo strength with a soft padded drumstick to the cymbal's rim produces the following sound phenomena. A soft hum issues and remains unchanged for about ten seconds; then a gradual crescendo develops over the next 20 seconds and begins to gain enormously in volume after 30 to 35 seconds. After about 60 seconds, a colossal triple fortissimo is reached, which is truly terrifying and close to unbearable; bystanders witnessing the sounding in the large entrance hall of the museum covered their ears and felt like running away from the tremendous roar.

So, as the composition *A Love Supreme* introduces itself to the world, the first thing the musicians and we hear as that historic session begins is the sound of a Chinese gong being struck by Elvin Jones, its reverberations signaling the shimmering spectrum into which the listener was about to be immersed. Kahn says this "opens the album with an ethereal, exotic splash." John's son Ravi observes, "It's the signal of something different. You don't hear that instrument anywhere else on any other John Coltrane recording." Then another musical device is used to maintain the seriousness the occasion calls for: a fanfare. In poetry it would be an invocation at the beginning of a work, an appeal and an opening up to the muse, and in this context, a call and an invitation to those willing to listen. The rippling series of notes John offers up on his tenor sax on the record's beginning constitute, according to Ashley Kahn, "...a time-honored device with a timeless function. Fanfares demand attention, heralding the importance of the message to follow." One more element was added near the end of the first movement, to further demonstrate the uniqueness of the occasion: the voice of John Coltrane himself, never before heard on record. He sang/chanted the album's title fifteen times after which, Kahn tells us, "...Coltrane's voice drops a whole step from F minor to E flat minor, a carefully planned modulation that the band follows, and which sets up the link to the next section of the suite. He chants the phrase four more times and stops." When I heard it the first time, it was unexpected and it personalized the proceedings even more, and this listener and I'm sure many others were drawn in more closely by this startling and surprising moment.

A Jazz musician—a player very much influenced by Coltrane (as so many had been)—was interviewed on Bay Area radio personality Michael Krasny's show "Forum." His heart was in the right place as he was talking about how the critics had dealt unfairly with Coltrane, as they surely had done earlier in his career, but his contention that *A Love Supreme* received only "...three stars," in *down beat* magazine, was not correct. By the time that particular recording had been made, the critics had either come around genuinely to see the error of their ways and thereafter rightly-acknowledge his achievement or they had altered their expressed sentiment to be more in accord with current and prevailing opinion. To wit: the December 30, 1965 issue of *down beat* announced on its cover the "30th annual Down Beat Readers

Poll Results," and under that, "The Year of John Coltrane—First Place in the Hall of Fame, Tenor Saxophone, Record of the Year, and Jazzman of the Year," and a photo of him that filled out the rest of the cover. And when the soon-to-become "Record of the Year" was reviewed in *down beat*, Editor Don DeMichael gave it five stars, the magazine's highest rating.

It is an earlier period that I like most from this great artist and his quartet, particularly the recordings *Impressions*, *Crescent*, and *Live at Birdland*, which range from 1962 to 1964. Every cut on *Live at Birdland* has something remarkable to offer. The opening track "Afro Blue" is a great display of the power they could generate as a group. The next, "I Want to Talk About You," is a ballad that Coltrane turns inside and out, exploring every possibility the composition could allow in what Baraka in his liner notes refers to as a tenor "lesson." At roughly mid- point, the rest of the band drops out and Coltrane solos unaccompanied. Somewhere near the end, there are three sets of rapidly descending notes played at mind-boggling speed. Every time I hear it, I can't believe I heard it. Coltrane's virtuosic display on this track brought to mind numerous articles which referred to his ease and control of transitions within the upper and lower registers of the tenor saxophone. Adding an exclamation point to Coltrane's skills in these areas was Miles Davis' specific comment in his autobiography, "Trane was the loudest, fastest saxophonist I've ever heard. He could play real fast and real loud at the same time and that's very difficult to do." Beyond the mastery of the mechanics of the horn, as with many innovators, he got things out of the instrument way beyond what it was designed to do. Comparable examples are Michael Hedges and Kaki King for acoustic guitar and Jimi Hendrix for electric guitar.

The next cut on *Live at Birdland*, "The Promise," offers a great solo by McCoy Tyner, in which the flow of ideas unfolds beautifully one to the next—no one could pound out resoundingly huge chords like Tyner—and then Coltrane backs it up with his own searing statement on soprano sax. "Alabama" is a lamentation on the Birmingham church bombing and expresses deep sorrow and a resolve to carry on. And the final song is the spell-binding "Your Lady," an incredible showpiece for the unique percussion magic Elvin Jones consistently provided.

Before the forming of the famous quartet, I greatly enjoyed the 1958 recording *Standard Coltrane* that was later released on CD with additional material as *The Stardust Session*. On the original *Standard* recording were two slow ballads, "Don't Take Your Love From Me," and "Invitation." Both of these songs were beautifully done, and "Invitation," was my go-to musical companion whenever I was feeling down. Written in the early 50s, it was not a song with which I was familiar. It had a haunting melody, and, I would learn later, utterly beguiling lyrics, the spirit of which Coltrane delivered with great empathy. Robert Levin, who wrote the liner notes, describes his playing:

> Coltrane has always been an exceptionally stirring ballad player. Don't Take Your Love From Me and Invitation offer richly melodic and soaringly tender Coltrane solos. They are very **vocal** solos and their special sensuality can be found in all of Coltrane's music. He has made great use of the tonal possibilities he has discovered in the timbres of the human voice, the pitches and nuances of which are what can confirm or belie the ostensible meaning of words, and that is a very important facet of his uniquely urgent sound.

In Ben Ratliff's *Coltrane—The Story of a Sound*, he mentions Babatunde Olatunji (with whom Mickey Hart would collaborate on Planet Drum), who said Coltrane had expressed fascination with the musical qualities of West African speech. Ratliff then comments: "Coltrane's obsession with language—the mechanical and signifying aspects of art—had taken him to this point, and perhaps here Coltrane saw signs of a much larger area to explore, one where the mechanics of music could liquefy and cross over into the mechanics of language." Then Ratliff inserted the recollections of pianist Matthew Shipp, who said: "When I was a teenager, there were times when I'd be totally into a certain Coltrane album for a while, and I'd listen to it over and over.

Sometimes I'd be lying on my bed and falling asleep, and I remember hearing his playing, while I was in a semi-sleep state, decoded into some kind of words." I could certainly relate to that.

In what I feel to be an important example of this phenomenon, worth talking about again, is the vocal contribution by Clare Torry on Pink Floyd's *Dark Side of the Moon* on the instrumental segment "The Great Gig in the Sky," that ends side one of the group's most famous recording. In this case it is the use of the voice as an instrument which reaches the liquified point that Ratliff speaks of, and it strikes me as being at the exact mid-point between word and sound. It is incredibly expressive. Torry accomplishes this with sounds so beseeching and emotion-filled that they come very close to words, but they bring about a response in the listener, as good or better than words could, in that moment. Also worth mentioning in this regard is Harvey Mandel's 1969 album *Cristo Redentor*, which I would say was *the* instrumental guitar album of its time before Jeff Beck's 1975 release of *Blow by Blow*. The spellbinding title track involves minimal guitar colorings by the normally explosive Mandel, a unique and underrated guitarist, that quietly support, along with strings, the heavenly vocals by Jacqueline May Allen. I highly recommend that you do yourself a favor and check it out on Youtube.

The song "Invitation" had an impressive pedigree which involved its composer Bronislaw Kaper, who had also composed the often-played Jazz standard "On Green Dolphin Street." In addition, he had provided musical scores for many Hollywood movies, won an Oscar for the musical *Lili*, and had introduced gamelan orchestras to Western audiences in the soundtrack for the movie *Lord Jim* in 1960.

The lyricist of "Invitation," Paul Francis Webster had collaborated with Duke Ellington in 1941 to write another standard, "I Got It Bad And That Ain't Good," and Webster won three academy awards for "Secret Love," (1953) "Love is a Many-Splendored Thing," (1955) and "The Shadow of Your Smile," (1965). Only Johnny Mercer exceeds him in Oscar nominated songs. I have a strong recollection (I would have been between six and seven years old) from the Uptown Theater in Napa, of seeing and hearing "Secret Love" performed by the crush-inducing voice and shining beautiful face belonging to Doris Day in the movie *Calamity Jane*. It might well have been the first time I saw someone sing a song on the big screen, and a lasting impression was made. Being the willing supplicant I was at such an age, it felt like she meant what she said in that inspiring song.

Tenor sax legend Lester Young had famously emphasized the importance of knowing the lyrics to a song so that an instrumental interpretation of it would be enhanced by that knowledge. I'm assuming that Coltrane had either heard the lyrics to "Invitation," or his always-present musical curiosity led him to find out what they were. After having written that last line, I later came across this comment from Prestige Records chief Bob Weinstock in Ashley Kahn's *A Love Supreme*: "As Weinstock recalls, an almost encyclopedic retention of song structures was a rare talent, peculiar to Coltrane and a few others: 'There were certain musicians who knew every song ever written, almost: Stan Getz, Red Garland, Al Haig, and John Coltrane. You could name any song from any stinking movie of the twenties, thirties, or forties, and they knew it.'" I invite people to poke around on Youtube to hear the lyrics sung. There exists a compelling version of it by Rosemary Clooney, one in which you can understand every clearly sung word, and it would prove ideal if you followed it with the beautiful version by Coltrane himself.

As can be seen, there was a lot operating in the song "Invitation," when I first spun that record on my turntable. The encoded richness established by Webster and Kaper was honored and embellished further by Coltrane's essence-penetrating version of this exceptional example of what can be accomplished with the blending of great talent.

While Coltrane is known primarily for his forceful style, he was, as has been shown, equally adept at softer compositions and more tender renderings in his solos, and I missed this element of his playing which was not as much a part of what he was doing in the latter stages of his career. I'll just say here, if you're not a person who likes far-out Jazz, Coltrane's recording *Ballads* is a great place to start, as he for the most part plays the well-known and well-loved songs straight, honoring the melodies and offering just a bit of the rapid flourishes that were so much a part of his playing. Coltrane did not consider himself to be a very good composer, but I was moved, as were many others, by beautiful pieces like "After the Rain," from *Impressions*, "Wise One" and "Lonnie's Lament" from *Crescent,* and many others. Towards the end though, he just seemed to be screaming, and maybe he was.

George Wein was the producer responsible for starting America's longest running festival, the Newport Jazz Festival. I'll just say, in an unfairly brief manner, that he was a very important promoter of Jazz, and has lived a remarkable life. In his book, *Myself Among Others*, he talked about efforts to help start the New Orleans Jazz Festival. While engaged in meetings about the festival, to which he had been invited because he had been successful at Newport, Wein learned that the City of New Orleans, working with the NFL, scheduled an all-pro game for Christmas Day, 1964. Wein tells us that:

> About ten days before Christmas, the NFL all-pros (both black and white) descended upon New Orleans. But the league's many black players quickly realized that although the laws had changed, the city was not yet socially ready for integration. Famous athletes found themselves stranded on street corners, ignored by taxicabs, rejected for tables at restaurants.

In Coltrane's thank you letter within the album *A Love Supreme*, he referred to a "spiritual awakening," and "...humbly asked to be given the means and privilege to make others happy through music." Near the end of the letter, he adds:

> Our appreciation and thanks to all people of good will and good works the world over, for in the bank of life, is not good

that investment which surely pays the highest and most cherished dividends.

These events in New Orleans took place a week after the completion of *A Love Supreme*, and seven months *after* the passage of the Civil Rights Bill. Reading Coltrane's beliefs, expressed in the letter, one cannot doubt his good will. How frustrating then, to put it mildly, it had to be, to know what was taking place, and it wasn't just in New Orleans where such things were happening. So if there was anger coming forth from many Jazz corners, there were plenty of reasons for it.

I would say also, with regard to Coltrane's particular state of mind (and I don't know if it's ever been suggested elsewhere), that since it is now well known that liver ailments affect mood but do not announce their workings in dramatic fashion, it is possible that subtle though disquieting changes (*dis-ease*), were happening to his disposition near the end of his life, of which he was not fully aware. That seething force within, however, had always been a component of his emotional makeup, brought on by the harsh realities of racism in America, and whatever his state of health might have been, that force contributed to the making of incredibly passionate music.

In theater, we speak of an actor "falling on his sword," and it is acknowledged how draining this can be to the performer who does it repeatedly. Fans of the superb 1968 BBC television series *The Prisoner* may remember episode sixteen in which booming-voiced actor Leo McKern playing #2 is pitted in a psychological battle-to-the-end against #6, played by series creator Patrick McGoohan. Such was the intensity of the 52 minutes of confrontation—the entire episode—involving just the two of them, and its effect on McKern, that it brought about a mental breakdown in the veteran actor.

I struggle to think of any artist who amassed more energized moments of intellectual and emotional output than John Coltrane. Regarding Coltrane's passing, the phrase "he played his heart out" seems insufficient in its quaintness, but I believe that is literally what happened. I think it proper and important that we apply the transcendence which characterized his music to the manner in which he departed this realm. It would be a disservice to the man to think of his death in medical terms only.

One other factor that should be mentioned is one brought to my attention by pianist Mal Waldron who told Art Sato (in the radio interview mentioned earlier) that he was of the opinion that people had an inner sense of how long they would be around, and this was dramatically demonstrated by the gifted bassist Scott LaFaro who predicted several years in advance, his death at age twenty-six, so perhaps John was trying, frantically, to squeeze in all of his constantly-brimming musical ideas while he could, because he would only make it to his fortieth year. And isn't it true that geniuses, George Gershwin, Jimi Hendrix, Frank Zappa, Charlie Parker, and Coltrane accomplished much in a short time?

The John Coltrane Quartet came to an end in 1966. McCoy Tyner felt a calling to do things on his own, and heeded that call in December of 1965. Elvin Jones did not think the double drummer arrangement with the addition of Rashied Ali was working, and went out on his own in January of 1966. John continued with his wife Alice on keyboards, Jimmy Garrison still on bass, Pharaoh Sanders on tenor sax, and Rashied Ali on drums. But throughout 1965, their final year together, as was befitting an accumulation of such steadfast effort, the quartet played some incredible live performances. It was possible to hear during that year all that the band had learned in their time together, and intimations of where Coltrane was headed. From Ben Ratliff's *Coltrane—The Story of a Sound*, comes testimony from saxophonist Joe McPhee as to what was going on at the Village Gate where he saw the group in the Spring of '65: "I thought I was going to die from the emotion," he said. "I'd never experienced anything like that in my life. I thought I was just going to explode right in the place. The energy level kept building up, and I thought, God almighty, I can't take it." Ratliff goes on to talk about (with accurate assessment) Dan Morgenstern, a regular contributor and associate editor to *down beat* magazine, "whose passion runs toward swing and bebop players and who has never been known as much of a Coltrane booster said, 'the intensity that was generated was absolutely unbelievable. I can still *feel* it, and it was unlike any other feeling within the music we call jazz.'"

In August of '65, the quartet was in Belgium, where the Comblain-La-Tour, was captured on film and later released on the very valuable Jazz Icons series. The DVD is superbly educational as it shows rare performances (with Stan Getz and Oscar Peterson) from 1960, 1961, and 1965 making it possible to see examples which cover the entire range of the development of his style. One of the three songs recorded in '65 for the DVD was "Naima," one of those softer compositions I spoke of earlier, which then explodes into a staggering display of ensemble magic and expansive soloing taking us into the territory described by McPhee and Morgenstern above.

My wife and I had joined friends one morning for breakfast: Dave, Leo, and my journalist friend Jeff who knew me to be a Coltrane fan. Sometime before our get-together, Jeff had picked up, from a discount bin, the DVD described above. At one point he told me, "I'd be embarrassed to admit what I paid for it." Initially chagrined that so rich an item was in the discount bin, my mind was somewhat soothed when I discovered later, a small puncture in the case which I hope accounted for its lowered price. After our time together sharing a meal and catching up, the perfect end of the day came when I put in the DVD and experienced it for the first time. With the pleasure of meeting with friends, combined with Jeff's generosity, and my comfortable state of mind, it's difficult to express how thoroughly enjoyable it was to settle in at home, and savor those performances later that evening. It's a valuable source of comfort to know I can return to those performances for as long as I live, but there is nothing like the level of impact you experience when you see and/or hear something for the first time: "virgin beauty," as Ornette Coleman liked to say. Considering the power of the performance and its newness, it had the effect of doubling the impact transmitted by the musicians themselves that was enhanced to the maximum by ideal filming which captured close-up the "safe-tearing" fingers of Garrison at work on his bass strings, and the energy he, Tyner, and Jones generated before John came in with his solo, and I knew that the intensity would continue to build, which it did dramatically as steam rose from each of their heads, halo-like in the chilly evening air of the outdoor concert. It was so incredible! Whew! Thanks Jeff. (Naima-John Coltrane, Belgium 1965, running time 7:28)

In 1964 I saw the equally-probing tenor saxophonist Dewey Redman, a contemporary of Coltrane, at the Both/And (a long gone Jazz club on Divisadero St. in San Francisco) during a Sunday matinee jam session. The performance ran long, so my return-time estimation was way off, and I remember having to go outside the club to a phone-booth nearby to phone my girl-friend's mother to see if we could stay longer. She reluctantly agreed. Good thing because it allowed us to see Redman get into the zone; ideas at a certain point during his set just started pouring out of him as he ventured on to the floor of the club, away from the stage area as if to free up the music. It was grand.

In another satisfying instance of bearing witness to the next generation of musicians, in June of 2003—thirty-nine years after seeing him at the Both/And—I saw Dewey Redman at San Francisco's Herbst Theatre along with his thirty-four year old son Joshua and the renown bassist Charlie Haden. For me, Joshua represents the exhilarating promise of the future. He is a great tenor saxophonist in his own right, and has been active and influential in the burgeoning S.F. Jazz scene and also in New York. Although he lives in New York, many of his activities are associated with the S.F Jazz Center that includes educational outreach thanks in large part to its director of education, Rebeca Mauleón, and outstanding musical projects with other like-minded—and equally talented—Bay Area musicians. That would include bassist/composer Cory Combs, who has taught several highly-informative classes at the Center, and whose comments grace the back cover of this book. When you see and hear any of them talk about their commitment to music, and listen to them play, you are utterly convinced that Jazz is in very capable hands. It is undeniably evident that they are all very stand-up and highly educated people who are determined to bring dignity to their musical accomplishments, without sacrificing the adventurous attitude that real innovation requires. And very much a part of this exemplary mind-set is what they've absorbed from John Coltrane. In the Ken Burns documentary on Jazz, when Joshua Redman talks about Coltrane, he says: "He raised the standard of what it means to be a dedicated musician." I am of the opinion that in regard to Coltrane's influence on succeeding generations as represented by Joshua Redman, his imprint can be seen in their eyes when they talk about him. It is a reality both undeniably-evident and indelible.

From an interview by Nat Hentoff for his liner notes to the album *Coltrane Live at the Village Vanguard*, recorded in November, 1961, Coltrane is quoted saying: "I like the feeling of a club, especially one with an intimate atmosphere like the Vanguard. It's important to have that real contact with an audience because that's what we're trying to do—communicate." Hentoff, talking about the live performance of "Chasin' the Trane," says "It is possible, therefore, to experience vicariously that rare contemporary phenomenon—a man going-for-broke. And in public no less. If you can open yourself emotionally to so relentless a self-exploration, you can gain considerable insight into the marrow of the Jazz experience and into Coltrane's own indomitably resourceful musicianship throughout the whirlpool of a blues." And here is what Coltrane was thinking, during the time of that interview, with regard to future plans: "I've already been looking into those approaches to music—as in India—in which particular sounds and scales are intended to produce specific emotional meanings. I've got to keep probing. There's so much more to do." And again, from a blurb by Amiri Baraka found on the album *Ascension*, regarding Coltrane's relentless search for something new, "Trane is now a scope of feeling. A more fixed traveler, whose wildest onslaughts are georgous artifacts not even deaf people should miss." And from those *Live at Birdland* liner notes, Baraka's last two sentences: "If you can hear, this music will make you think of a lot of weird and wonderful things. You might even become one of them."

From the same episode of *Ken Burns Jazz* in which Joshua Redman comments on Coltrane, Gary Giddins talks about the impact of hearing the sixteen minute solo on "Chasin' the Trane," about which Nat Hentoff gave praise. With regard to the extended solo, Giddins observes: "...the idea here was the effusiveness—it wasn't like a solo where every note was as if in a poem; this wasn't a poem, it was a very long novel..." whose effect was "...overwhelming."

The "overwhelming effect" that Gary Giddins talked about of the long solos Coltrane and the band stretched out, were not unlike, I would contend, the word-play throughout James Joyce's *Ulysses*—particularly the fifty-six pages without punctuation in Molly Bloom's soliloquy found at the end of the book. There are reasonable comparisons between techniques used by James Joyce and Coltrane, and I believe that Coltrane is for Jazz what Joyce was for literature. They use every element of their respective mediums not just in superfluous helter-skelter compilations of words or arrangements of notes as if cut-and-pasted out of archaic repositories, but language keenly used after long-developed understanding and familiarity. I want to say that they were entitled to use esoteric measures because of the studious investment each had made. Their command of their respective languages was so all-encompassing and masterful, that it justified their detailed use of vocabulary in ways that were highly unique.

In Declan Kiberd's *Ulysses and Us,* he observes that essayist, literary and art critic Walter Pater contended that "...all the arts aspire to the condition of music, and Joyce wished to see how close he could bring language to pure melody." Kiberd points out that when Ulysses was written, "...the Irish had become English-speaking only in the previous two generations. Their discovery of the expressive potentials of English still had the freshness and excitement of surprise." Kiberd then adds, echoing Thomas Reid, that "The early experience of any foreign language is mainly musical, a matter of pure sound, before meaning supervenes," and, "…with only a smattering of the new language…they had to improvise."

From an article in the *SF Chronicle* about the SF Jazz Poetry Festival, poet Jack Foley is quoted saying, "Jazz, it seems to me, is less about the soloist—however talented—than it is about the complex interweaving of various sounds and voices. The late free Jazz saxophonist Glenn Spearman thought of music as being like James Joyce's 'Finnegans Wake,' an expression of the constantly changing interpenetration of everything with everything."

The constant struggle to survive, carve out a measure of freedom, and rise above the depressing pace of its arrival is spelled out in Joyce's revealing and penetrating portrait of life in Dublin. Coltrane's "stream of consciousness" expressions convey similarly the sharp eye of a careful observer in complex, nuanced, and complete fashion. Each of their unique perspectives compelled them incessantly to strive for something transcendent through art and they succeeded in extraordinarily dramatic fashion.

In thinking about these things I can't escape commenting that in the same year, 1963, in which "Walk Right In" by the Rooftop Singers became so popular, the John Coltrane Quartet was performing and recording incredibly advanced forays into virtuosic group improvisation of which, unfortunately, the vast majority of Americans were unaware. It seems such a shame to have to say that.

In his concluding comments from his notes on the Jazz Icons DVD, Ashley Kahn says of Coltrane, "His philosophy was all-inclusive and universal, and he saw his music as one activity among many, one part of a life-consuming drive to turn thought and positive intention into an influential sound." Coltrane's own thoughts from 1965 then follow: "Once you become aware of this force for unity in life, you can't ever forget it. It becomes part of everything you do. My goal of meditating on this through music, however, remains the same. And that is to uplift people, as much as I can, to inspire them to realize more and more of their capacities for living meaningful lives." This he did.

Sonny Rollins

Thinking about our next magician, the phrase "embarrassment of riches" came to mind. I hesitate to use the phrase because it may convey social situations in which something unfair or undeserved has developed, and that is not the case with Sonny Rollins. He has had a long and successful career as a Jazz musician, no small feat in itself, has received several prestigious awards in the U.S. and internationally, has proven to be one of the most resourceful improvisers in Jazz, and is greatly admired as a man and musician by his peers. His striking physical presence adds significantly to his impressive and credentialed persona. Well over six feet tall, he has a penetrating gaze that when seen makes one think, "I need to be doing more with my life." That striking face, however, is connected to a thoughtful mind and a warm heart. Like many artists who are never content with where they've been, that state-of-mind was reflected in his constantly-changing physical appearance as he continuously reinvented himself and his music and lived, in a real way, multiple lives.

In interviews, Rollins is a delight, always giving wise and in-depth responses while maintaining a clear line of ideas, departing from but never abandoning the thematic center—just as he does when he's taking a solo. There exists a long list of musicians who know Rollins and have played with him over years that marvel at his accomplishment through which he continues to amaze when it comes to scaling the heights during those moments of group interplay when the music really starts to go places that are beautifully unique.

Rollins is known for his relentless pursuit of those heights and when, upon study, you realize the extent to which he has—as much as anyone—seemingly exhausted every theme and variation idea possible in improvisation, he comes up with yet another wrinkle in the way a melody might be extrapolated. I've heard Elvin Jones talk about how Sonny "...can take some little jingle...," never intended for enlargement, and "...turn it into this wonderful thing." For me, Rollins represents the closest thing humanity has produced to an inexhaustible fount, a condition achieved by the fact that he has always been in search of what he called "the golden chord."

Sonny's long-time bass player Bob Cranshaw (they've played together for over fifty years) talked in an interview about them playing one night when the entire band was really "on," with Sonny leading the way, yet again, on the path of discovery. Cranshaw, thinking back on that occasion offered a speculation regarding Sonny's mindset in the moment: "Oh, so you guys really want to play tonight? OK." Cranshaw went on to say, "I was right with him, and told myself, this is the night I stay with him, and it felt like I could, then he intensified things..." and the effect was of Sonny pulling away from the pack.

When I was in high school, a friend loaned me a book that was a collection of writings on Jazz. One essay described what I think was a festival situation that brought various artists together on stage and it turned into what they used to call "cutting sessions" in which the musicians traded bars and tried to out-do one another. To the best of my recollection, it went something like this: Baritone saxophonist Gerry Mulligan was one of the participants, and after going back and forth for a while in this musical manner with Rollins, Mulligan gave up, strolled off the stage and lay down in some grass nearby. A concerned person on the scene came over and asked "Are you ok?"—"I'm fine," he said, "just let me listen to the music."

Born in 1930, Sonny Rollins was a product of the Harlem Renaissance, and more. His parents were from St. Thomas in the Virgin Island's where, according to Sonny's older sister Gloria, education was of paramount importance, and where in his family, one was expected to learn an instrument. They came to New York thinking there would be more educational opportunities. Sonny also had an older brother, who according to Gloria was a very good violinist, and Gloria herself learned piano. She said some uproar was caused when Sonny expressed a desire to play the not-very-classical saxophone, but being the youngest child, they allowed him (thank goodness) to get away with it.

At the early age of nineteen, he had already played with piano legend Bud Powell, and in 1951, at twenty-one, was asked by Miles Davis to join his band. His notoriety spread quickly, making him a main attraction at clubs everywhere, and he was embraced by the critics as well. By 1959, his career was still going strong, but he decided to take a sabbatical from performing to do more study and hone his already impressive technique.

George Avakian was an important and influential producer known for his long tenure with Columbia. He was responsible for many important re-issues on Columbia, accomplishing this while attending Yale in 1940, and later started a course in Jazz history at Columbia University in 1946. He produced the first one-hundred long-playing discs of popular music and Jazz for Columbia Records, including the first live performance LP of the Benny Goodman Orchestra at Carnegie Hall, and in doing so, brought instant viability to the live-recording format. I am just this moment learning that the Goodman concert was the first live-performance recording on Columbia. The impression made from hearing that first live album certainly had lasting influence on the way I collected records because, ever since then, I've been partial to live albums, and that Carnegie Hall recording stands as a grand beginning to a great idea.

Avakian wrote the liner notes to *The Bridge*, Sonny's first recording after his hiatus, and in talking about Sonny's break from performing, said this: "In the musical world, the shock of Sonny's retirement came in the fact that he had achieved the kind of stature, critical acclaim and public acceptance that musicians dream of and so seldom attain. It was like a pitcher on a pennant-winning team announcing, after he had had a twenty-game [winning] season, that he was quitting for a while to learn how to pitch."

Rollins had made the commitment to serious practice and did not want to waste the time he, at considerable risk, had set aside for that purpose. A problem arose because he would not subject neighbors in his apartment building to the disturbance constant practice would bring about. In Avakian's liner notes, he quotes Rollins who said: "For instance, there was this pregnant girl in a neighboring apartment. I couldn't subject her to all that sound—and of course I couldn't do myself any good by inhibiting my practicing. I didn't know what prenatal effects would result in the baby; but do you know he's a beautiful, happy child." So he walked to the Williamsburg Bridge, very near the apartment, using the pedestrian walkway where "everyday" he practiced, practiced, practiced. The fine altoist Jackie McLean would eventually join him for some of those practice sessions and talked about it on *Jazz Profiles*, saying Sonny would sprint for a while, then follow it up with pull-ups grabbing the bridge framing to use as a bar. Then while still winded, he'd pick up the horn and play to increase his lung power, the seriousness of which was further demonstrated during this time as he had also stopped smoking.

Two years after he dropped out of the music scene, the February 1962 completion of *The Bridge* marked his return to the musical fold. Jazz lovers were eager to find out how Rollins' stylistic makeover would be demonstrated, and he did not disappoint.

The recording is an extraordinary piece of work. All of the musicians involved make solid contributions, and I especially like the guitar playing of Jim Hall, whose presence probably came as a surprise to many. There were plenty of Jazz guitarists, but guitar as a regular fixture in Jazz combos was seldom the case. Trumpet, sax, piano, bass, and drums—that's what one mostly saw, with perhaps one more reed instrument, or trombone—but a quartet with sax and guitar, not so much. Consequently, this was a pretty big moment in Jazz history for guitar as well, because the album was so eagerly anticipated and was instantly a classic.

On the *Jazz Profiles* radio program when Rollins was the musician featured, examples of his playing throughout his career was done chronologically, so one got a comprehensive feel for his music and a demonstration of his development over time. As good as he was before his release of *The Bridge*, when one listens to all that he does on that album in terms of conception and execution compared to the earlier examples presented, the increase in his abilities is very tangible. Still, even with the serious approach required for the rigorous regimen he subjected himself to, in order to increase his skills, he remained down-to-earth and playful enough to include a quote from Maceo Parker's sax solo on James Brown's "Night Train," smack-dab in the middle of "The Bridge," the most complex piece from this very significant and statement-making album. And if you talk to anyone familiar with his work, they will tell you that he is hands-down the best user of quotes to ever play a note of Jazz. He has the ability to mix in quotes in surprising places then cleverly return to the theme, and he sometimes doubles or triples up quotes; spicing up the main text with little excursions.

Using the example of Michael Jordan again, suppose he walked into a gym after having been transported back to the 1930s, and suppose he proceeds, during a five-on-five half-court college practice session back then, to go to the unused end of the court and reenact his 1988 slam-dunk-contest-winning effort, of which there is a famous photograph which shows him in full flight after taking off from the free-throw line before throwing it down. Had those players from that time witnessed such a thing, they would have recoiled amid various levels of terror. Jordan's dunk can be looked at as the shedding off of the dross which conventional thought imposes, and in doing so, he seems to defy gravity. If you desire another example of a human exceeding assumed limitations, by all means check out Sonny Rollins, whose high-flying alchemy, like Jordan's, has been historically preserved.

Should we have to defend our lives upon a throne of judgement, "woe betide" those of us not having the proper response regarding our music collection, because I suspect we'll all be questioned on this: **"What? No Sonny Rollins?"** The powers that be will not appreciate our sin of omission concerning a favored and esteemed avatar responsible for dispatching a lifetime of sublime and heavenly sounds.

I've seen Sonny on several occasions, each of them uniquely significant. The first time was at the Greek Theater at the Berkeley Jazz Festival in 1969. The festival, the initial planning of which involved our friend Ralph J. Gleason, had been an annual affair begun in 1967 that always featured great lineups. Sadly it is no more. Others on the bill that day that I recall were: Singer Abbey Lincoln with her husband and great drummer Max Roach, The Cannonball Adderley Quintet performing its surprise hit "Mercy, Mercy," Albert King, who of the three famous blues musicians named King (B.B., Freddie, and Albert are not related), I thought Albert was the best singer of the lot, and the big left-hander with the flying-V was no slouch on the guitar either. And finally, I remember the Edwin Hawkins Singers who also had a surprise gospel hit, "Oh Happy Day," which drew quite a lively response from the crowd that day. That 1969 performance featured Sonny all by himself, the first time he had done such a thing. He stalked the stage, covering its wide expanse left and right, owning, as they say, every inch of it, in a great demonstration of performance control and virtuosity.

The next time I saw him, a decade later, was on May 26, 1979 at another Berkeley Jazz Festival. The significance here is that it was and remains the greatest concert we ever witnessed. There were so many gifted musicians involved that day, that it made the lineup appear to be too good to be true. What looked great on paper and fired the imagination with expectation was superseded that marvelous day in every instance by the musicians and their performances, in real time, under the proscenium arch of the Greek Theater. It featured, in order of appearance, a good local band whose name I can't recall, The Pat Metheny Group, Sonny Rollins, and Weather Report. I had been impressed by Metheny when I heard him on the radio for the first time just a few months prior to the concert. The band's very good first album, *Pat Metheny*

Group, with Lyle Mays, Mark Egan, and Dan Gottlieb, was recorded in January of 1978, so when I saw them at this concert in 1979, their careers were really starting to take off. They played several of the songs off their album that day, and those compositions and the manner in which they were delivered sounded very fresh. Metheny was only twenty-four at the time, and I know that he and his bandmates were thrilled to be part of such an impressive line-up because Pat said as much from the stage giving a special nod to Jaco Pastorius, with whom Metheny had worked, and after whom one of his compositions was named. Pastorius, with Weather Report, would appear later that day. As you can imagine, it was a very inspired performance.

Helping to make the day special was the fact that Sylvia and I were young ourselves, thirty-one and thirty-two respectively; five years into a very happy marriage, and enjoying a free day with each other as our children stayed with their grandparents. Typical for the annual festival usually happening in the month of May, we found ourselves under beautiful spring-blue skies with thousands of other like-minded music lovers, and I especially enjoyed (and still do) the vibe at the Greek. I took a photo from one of those afternoons showing Sylvia in a tube-top against the backdrop of the Greek Theater's stone tiers, an idyllic vision of beauty with the nicest smile you've ever seen; long brown hair curling over her right shoulder, all the way behind on the left. So nice. We followed our time-tested plan for such outings: a smuggled bota-bag of wine in the bottom of Sylvia's purse (Sylvia having come up with the ingenious plan of putting crinkled up Kleenex with that "used look" on top so as to discourage probing fingers at security check points), a Togo's deli-sandwich picked up on our way out of town, and some kind of dessert goodie. What a great day it turned out to be.

After the Pat Metheny Group's strong performance, Sonny Rollins came out. When Sonny began playing, he wasted no time getting into a groove. It was irresistibly good. It just kept coming, non-stop ideas that explored every rhythmic emphasis you could imagine. It was vintage Sonny: incredible improvisation supported by his great band and showing Sonny's ever-flexible attitude, as he used, on this amazing day, electronic instruments like the newer bands with whom he shared the stage.

Weather Report was on top of the Jazz world in 1979. It's leader, keyboardist Joe Zawinul, I had seen ten years earlier at my first Berkeley Jazz Festival when he was still a member of the Cannonball Adderly Quintet who topped the bill that day. Now he presided over an all-star cast of extremely talented musicians: Wayne Shorter on tenor and soprano sax, Jaco Pastorius on electric bass, and Peter Erskine on drums. Augmenting what these musicians had to offer was an elaborate sound system which took nearly an hour to assemble. Adding to the special quality of the proceedings that day was the wise decision to play through the Greek Theater's healthy PA system, while technicians worked, Ravel's "Bolero." When Bolero reached its dramatic conclusion, it was the only time I ever heard thunderous applause during an intermission; people were primed for more, and they got it. Weather Report came to the stage amid a rousing reception. They were awesome, and the sound system that took so long to assemble (Oh, my goodness!) penetrated to the marrow. Zawinul's keyboard work spread to every square foot of the Greek Theater, past the sloping grassy hill, and to the UC Berkeley campus beyond. The wait had been worth it. What a day. And note the ticket price!

On another occasion in January of 2010, I with my friend Phil Wharton saw Rollins again. Phil and his closest friend Dennis Meehan had provided me with early declarations of the beauty and value of Jazz, and as I heard more and more examples from their collections, it was like being given admission to a special club. These things happened during our junior year in high school, and after graduation everyone went separate ways. I lost track of both of them. A chance meeting by mutual friends and their conversation led to my learning that Phil was living on a houseboat in Sausalito, and had been for a long while; Dennis was living in San Francisco. It's true, what they say, that you can't go home again, but I thought an effort to head that way might be worthwhile. What better way to revisit our Jazz upbringing than to go see Sonny Rollins? It's a little much to expect every time out the kind the fire he has brought to so many of his performances throughout his long career, and that is true for any performer regardless of age; at seventy-nine, the age he was when we saw him, it was a miracle that he was still performing at all. With a final nod to yesteryear, we stopped by City Lights Bookstore before heading back to Sausalito.

It had been forty-six years earlier when the three of us had first ventured out of Napa in Dennis' '51 Ford to the Trois Couleur in Berkeley, a small club that allowed minors. We saw, with the exception of Monk Montgomery (Wes Montgomery's bass-playing brother), combos of little-known musicians, but we were delighted to be part of the scene. I remember an occasion in which very few people were in the club one evening. After a tenor sax solo, the three of us burst into enthusiastic applause at an inappropriate level, and the musician, with embarrassment, nodded thanks to us. Yes, we were naively eager, a minor transgression I forgive myself because I remember comments about Eric Dolphy from Charles Mingus after Dolphy's death June 29, 1964. They were included in the liner notes for Dolphy's farewell album *Last Date*. Mingus, talking about what a great spirit Eric Dolphy was, said: "I went through a time at a club we were playing in for a long while when I stopped taking solos. I was dragged because people weren't listening. He kept after me to solo again. 'Man,' he'd say, 'You've *got* to play. There are *some* people out there listening. Somebody cares. ' " We were those people; then and for the rest of our lives.

A Magical Moment

Two extraordinary figures from the first half of the 19th Century were Frederic Chopin and George Sand. One was an incredible musician, the other an incredible writer. Chopin was a child prodigy whose "poetic genius was based on a professional technique that was without equal in his generation," according to musician and author Charles Rosen. George Sand took the male pseudonym because women authors were not duly recognized and because it would be an easier author-name to recall than the one provided by her family: Amantine Lucile Aurore Dupin. With great courage, Sand achieved a degree of independence that few of her contemporaries had, and was remarkably ahead of her time in this regard. Her writings dealt with inequalities among social classes, and in 1960s lingo, we would have said of her that "she tells it like it is."

From the textbook compilation, *Literature of the Western World* by Wilkie and Hurt, there is a biography prefacing her short story *The Marquise*, in which we learn that Sand, "...published, on her own, the novel *Indiana*...an impassioned protest, in the name of human dignity and free love, against the spiritual crippling of human beings, especially women, in institutionalized marriage." As regards the ill-treatment of women by men, Sand was as much annoyed by its acceptance as she was by its perpetration. In the penetrating and intense story, the Marquise is a young bride to an older man, and "At sixteen and a half I was already a widow." Understandably soured by the experience, she has no desire to return quickly to marriage. Sand cuts to the chase concerning the pressure to marry so prevalent in her time, as demonstrated by the Marquise's cadre of friends who have collectively failed as match-makers: "As long as these women believed that I was on the way to being converted by their maxims...they stood by me. But when, finally, they saw that I was incorruptible, that I had reached the age of twenty without anything coming of their efforts, they recoiled from me in horror."

The autobiographical voice comes through as Sand too, had had an early marriage at age eighteen. She had two children, left the marriage after nine years, obtained legal separation four years later, and had had many well-known relationships during that time. I mention all this about Sand because it is needed for what lies ahead.

Chopin and Sand met, and after a bit of sizing up, the pair found themselves caught up in a torrid love affair. Talking about the untypical extent to which she had fallen, Sand said, "I must say I was confused and amazed at the effect this little creature had on me....I have still not recovered from my astonishment, and if I were a proud person I should be feeling humiliated at having been carried away..." If intelligence is the great aphrodisiac, there's no shame in falling for one of the Romantic era's brightest lights whose beautiful compositions are the very essence of romance, and his music is frequently used in film as soundtrack for beautiful moments in nature or the thrilling embrace of lovers.

There are many explosive components that make theirs a truly remarkable pairing. He was twenty-seven and she was thirty-four, perhaps an ideal time during which great sex and its attendant boost to one's well-being comes easily, and Sand, in particular, was uniquely prepared psychologically for its maximum enjoyment; Chopin had to have been equally enamored. "Enamored," seemed a good word choice, so when I checked its definition to, with surety, validate its appropriateness, I found the following examples for its use: "to be enamored of a certain lady; a brilliant woman with whom he became enamored." Yes, I smiled to myself, this word fits just fine.

Although brief, it was one of the world's most perfect storms in romance history in which the blending of two souls and bodies, one life absorbed in music, the other absorbed in the beauty of words, become equally absorbed by one another. It seems a puny understatement to say of them that they had chemistry; they had that and more. Music was an essential ingredient in this intoxicating blend of elements that brought them together, and when the relationship was at its intense peak, Sand wrote a play. They were utterly beside themselves in love and this state of elation comes through, explodes really, in *The Seven Strings of the Lyre*. From *Music, Mysticism, and Magic*, Joscelyn Godwin talking about the play, tells us in his introduction: "The Spirit of the Lyre has been plausibly interpreted as the genius of Chopin; the twin themes of the power of music and the even greater power of love certainly reflect George Sand's brief period of fulfilment before the lovers' unfortunate trip to Majorca," when Chopin's always fragile health worsened under wintry conditions for which they were not properly clad.

The play, never intended for performance, but rather to be read, had been strongly discouraged by her publisher Francois Buloz, who, according to Godwin, found the work "…far too mystical…" Well, it certainly was that but I think the troubling notion uppermost in his mind was, rather, that it was far too sexual. Godwin adds that the sentiments revealed in the play were "…not of the earthly realm which she knew and described so well, but of the world of pure imagination." To me, what Sand wrote was poetry inspired by the physical world and by real experiences in that world that are possible—with the right attitude—for everyone. Here are three striking excerpts revealing the splendor of their shared love, the power of which produced an afterglow of cosmic proportion that brought about an all-consuming warm bath of synesthesia that easily allows and is part of the outpouring of her words in this eroticized state of grace. George Sand writes:

Make of yourself a surface so limpid that the ray of the infinite can pass through you and embrace you, and reduce your being to dust, so as to assimilate you to him and dissolve you in divine fluid in his burning breast, ever devouring, ever fecund.

May your ears hear and your eyes see! All is harmony, sound and color. Seven tones and seven colors intertwine and move around you in eternal nuptials. There is no silent color. The universe is a lyre. There is no invisible sound. The universe is a prism.

Color is the manifestation of beauty; sound is the manifestation of glory. Beauty is sung incessantly on all the strings of the infinite Lyre; harmony is incessantly vivified by all the rays of the infinite Sun. All the voices and all the rays of the Infinite tremble and vibrate incessantly before the glory and beauty of the Eternal!

- George Sand (*The Seven Strings of the Lyre*) -

Epilogue

In the first year of my retirement in 2010, I purchased season tickets to the Golden State Warriors. We began going to games in Steph Curry's second season. Talk about a gift that kept on giving. We've been privileged to witness, on another type of stage, countless displays of amazing five-man improvisation, skill, and artistry from the talent-rich Warriors. Simply the best basketball I've ever witnessed. We shared tickets with another couple until the end of the 2017-18 season and have thoroughly enjoyed going to the games; in other activities we continue to check off concert and travel excursions from our bucket list.

We are not, however, always on the go and draw great satisfaction from quiet time in our home, keeping our minds occupied, one way or another, mostly by having our heads buried in the pages of a book. I want to take this opportunity to sound a traditionalist-note on behalf of good old paper books. I lobby to encourage the recognition of the solid entertainment value of this low-tech and relatively low-cost entity. A family without a personal computer is a neglected circumstance, and libraries offer the use of computers and more. Wonderful books, anything one can think of, can still be gotten for free at your library or purchased cheaply at library book sales. The (oh-so) user-friendly book page is the monitor equivalent that travels easily, need not be plugged in, charged, nor fed batteries, and they never announce to its user that they are buffering. Books, for the most part, do not require heavy lifting or athletic ability and there are neither dress-code nor social-skills requirements for their use. Books are on duty 24-7-365. Of the person having a generous and honest spirit, we say of them that they are "an open book." Books wait patiently, without complaint, for our fickle attention, and will magically sustain themselves unless left to the elements. Books may inform us about the birds and the bees while not having the power of reproduction themselves, yet they teem, a situation which I hope doesn't end anytime soon, as their preservation, like the libraries which house them, is of the utmost importance.

At a book sale at the Benicia Public Library, for instance, I came across a volume so thin as to be nearly invisible between its neighbors of wider width on the shelf. If I can't see a title on a book's edge, I pull it out to see if it might be intriguing. One never knows. Out of the general respect I have for books, I always suspect a penalty from the book gods if they see that someone was too lazy to check carefully. Not only was this volume thin, it was in tatters. Had I not rescued it at this sale, I think its next stop would have been the dumpster. So just what was the title of this valuable find requiring an extra moment of probing to discover?—*The Music Lover*, by Henry Van Dyke. I sampled a few of the pages and saw quickly that it was a keeper.

Adding to its charm, which I did not see until a bit later, was an inscription on a blank page in the front of the book from its original buyer dated 1907, the year of its publication, presenting the book as a gift. It reads:

> To Mrs. Johns—a lover of all good things—from her friend, F.S.B.
>
> Christmas,
1907.

The book, 6-1/2 x 9 inches and only a ¼-inch thick, was even smaller than those dimensions suggested, because on its twenty-seven (in total) pages, the print area was only 2-3/4 x 3-3/4 inches inside large margins all around. In terms of content however, it went far beyond the boundaries and number of its pages.

For a maximum appreciation of the concert experience by any lover of music, I think there is an ideal spot in whatever venue one is in. The inclination is to want to get as close as one can, but for me, it is possible to get too close. As mentioned earlier, John

Dewey cited the painter Delacroix who talked about a painting's "…magical accord." If one is in a gallery looking at a great painting, that "magical accord" is not available to the viewer if they are too far away or too close. Similarly, the stirring group cohesion in moments of intense musical unity can be lessened because of the focus on individualism physical closeness imposes.

Having these things in mind, after having gone to many concerts at The Napa Opera House/City Winery (now called JaM Cellars) and experiencing the reconfigured seating arrangement, I found that my favorite seat in the house when it was available was in the balcony, centrally-located, just left of the mixing board in the front row of seats closest to the rail. Therefore, something way beyond amusement happened that day in the library when I opened Henry Van Dyke's book and read the first and second sentences.

> The Lover of Music had come to his favorite seat. It was in the front row of the balcony, just where the curve reaches its outermost point, and, like a rounded headland, meets the unbroken flow of the long-rolling, invisible waves of rhythmical sound.

The book continued in that manner, one descriptive gem after another, without a wasted word. Describing his experience, and continuing with the "headland" analogy, the narrator says, "There was nothing between him and the orchestra. He looked over the railing of the gallery…straight across the gulf in which the mass of the audience…seemed to be submerged, to the brilliant island of the stage."

Talking about the collection of influences in the lives of each musician, that as a company of human beings, contributed to the performance overall, the narrator says: "Here was the wonderful hidden system of communication, more magical than any mechanism, just because it left room, along each separate channel, for the coming in of those slight, incalculable elements of personal emotion which lend the touch of life to rhythm and tone."

I learned from a Wikipedia entry that Henry Van Dyke graduated from Princeton in 1873. He was an author, an educator, and a clergyman who served effectively although inexperienced as an ambassador, during the outbreak of World War I, as Minister to the Netherlands and Luxembourg, and helped to "maintain the rights of Americans in Europe." He was friends with Helen Keller who said of him, "Dr. Van Dyke is the kind of a friend to have when one is up against a difficult problem. He will take trouble, days and nights of trouble, if it is for somebody else or for some cause he is interested in."

And the most delightful fact coming from this original and multi-leveled gift that fate allows me to hold in my hands, is that "Time Is," one of Mr. Van Dyke's well-known poems, was the inspiration for a song bearing the same title by the group It's a Beautiful Day, from their eponymous 1969 debut album. They were the same group that was on the opening bill in the last phase of the Dream Bowl's existence, February 7, 1969. And what was the price of the book that let me in on these life-affirming connections? A mere twenty-five cents.

In remarks in *Sports Illustrated* by Alexander Wolff honoring Nelson Mandela after his December 5, 2013 death, he tells us that Mandela was an "amateur heavyweight" boxer, an activity for which one needed to be tough, something I thought was still detectable even in his aging face, something certainly needed to withstand the abuses of twenty-seven years of imprisonment. Wolff said, "Mandela loved the meritocracy of athletic endeavor—how, as he said in a 2000 speech, '[sport] laughs in the face of all types of discrimination.'" The same can be said of music.

Challenges remain, however, for anyone hoping to make a living as a musician. It was pointed out by percussionist and educator John Santos, who taught a six-class series *Jazz Latino* that

I attended in San Francisco, that a typical ITunes purchase for a single is ninety-nine cents which is less than the two dollars my sisters and I paid for 45s in the 1950s; not a healthy trend for musicians. It's hard to say how things will turn out because the radical changes in the industry have been fast and far-reaching. However, I think there are good things that are happening. As David Byrne points out in *How Music Works*, a band can send out a video on-line at very little cost which does not mount, no matter the quantity.

Drummer, educator, and bandleader Tommy Igoe, in an article about him in the Sunday Datebook of the *SF Chronicle*, commented on recording studios saying, "There are always going to be a few top-end studios, but there's only a fraction of what there used to be. There are so many great rooms that closed; it's heartbreaking. They've been replaced by people who are making music ad hoc in their own place. If you want to make a living playing music and be kind of like a gun for hire, you have to have a recording studio in your place." I share Igoe's sentiments, agreeing that it is sad to know that these "rooms" are dying off, but he touched on alternative activities that are not necessarily bad.

Currently, for all intents and purposes, the record deal is a thing of the past, and groups are forced therefore to put more effort into live performance; at the same time, groups are more able to make their own recordings since studio-quality does not require actually being in one. When I learn about a band I have not yet heard, I'll search on-line for a video. These days, if you're in a band, the making of a video is as fundamental as buying an instrument, so I've seen, for example, recordings from a kitchen, in a cave, in a parking garage, Bart Davenport singing "Clara" on the roof of the Uptown Nightclub, Oakland, and in Alan Stone's mother's living room where he and his band did a great version of his song "Unaware." As far as quality is concerned, all of those recordings are good, and four out of the five were excellent. Each place, with the exception of the rooftop location, was chosen, I'm convinced, because they had surprisingly great acoustics, probably discovered on the fly, and the relative ease of being able to record almost anywhere and take advantage of these sonic sweet spots is certainly a good thing. If Alan Lomax was alive today, he would not have to traipse off to remote locations to do "field recordings," because he would look around and see that it was being done for him. Presently, it is much easier to make a high-quality recording without a crippling outlay of cash. Bands still need a space in which to record, but as we've seen, options increase with less expensive gear that transports easily. The positive upshot in all this is that more artists will have an opportunity to be heard, not just those able to afford the use of a famous studio. These developments strike me as being an essential realization of the notion of "a level playing field." And with an opinion that I sense is the prevailing one for musicians operating under current industry conditions, Madeline Tasquin, a multi-talented singer/songwriter, said in a *SF Chronicle* interview that "Any energy I might spend on complaining about the music industry is energy that could otherwise be spent creating a new industry, a new song, a successful turnout for an inspiring local band. Keep evolving. Shut up and create." The feeling I have that there are lots of dedicated artists operating with such an attitude is backed up by evidence I've seen and heard searching for these various videos. There is great music being made, but you have to look for it, as I don't believe it will be delivered very often through popular outlets.

I said earlier, that after that entrancing moment listening to Coltrane, I didn't talk about it. I did however, leave in the margin of page in a 1964 *down beat* magazine, as a benchmark reminder of personal importance, a communication using but one word: "Swept."

As regards the encouraging power of music, I'm always on the lookout for compelling sentiment that talks about such experiences, and I've come across a number of them from unexpected sources. In a documentary about ice-skater Peggy

Fleming, I was reminded that she was the only U.S.A. Gold Medal winner in the 1968 Winter Olympics. I was not a huge fan of the Winter Olympics, preferring the track and field events of the Summer Olympics, but I watched those skating routines when they happened and still think of them as some of the most graceful ever to have been performed. It didn't hurt that she was beautiful and she seemed to be beautiful on the inside as well, a very captivating person. However, it was still a tremendous athletic challenge which she executed with perfection. Can you imagine the pressure though, on this twenty year-old representing her country, because despite years of preparation, one slip on the most-slippery of surfaces, and you're out. She said in regard to that huge moment in her life poised there in the silence waiting to begin, that as she glided on to the ice beginning her routine: "The music took my hand."

Ran Ortner is a painter who does huge paintings of swirling ocean water that appear strikingly real and whose waves leap with such exuberance off each canvas, that I can imagine viewers checking the exhibit floor for overflow. In an interview in *The Sun* magazine discussing the elements of passion and intellect that activate artistic creation, Ortner had this to say:

> I don't oppose the emphasis on intellect and on concept—in fact, I like it very much—but I do feel the passions are underrepresented. Humans are deeply emotional beings. We don't rationalize our way into love; we fall. We don't rationalize our way into the richest experiences; we get swept away.

And in a similar fashion, Jerry Garcia talked about the danger of "getting caught up," in the development of technique to an inappropriate degree, and concluded his insightful fifty-three minute Youtube interview ("The History of Rock and Roll") with this comment: "Music—it's emotional in nature, it communicates emotionally. That's one of the things it does really well, and I think that if you don't [brief pause] if that isn't the sense of what you're doing, then I don't know what it is."

So I say go out as soon as you can to witness and enjoy the emotion that's communicated in music. Opportunities to do this are all around. Local musicians need support. All musicians need support. Even maintaining an attitude as exemplary as the one stated by Madeline Tasquin above, such persons need more than our respect; they need our money if we've got it to give.

It's always true that today is the first day of the rest of your life. A great musical adventure, one especially designed for you and never too late to construct, is out there waiting. The experience is as near at hand—as your I-Phone if you have one; your local library if you don't. The apps now available that are specifically designed for music listening have staggeringly vast data-bases. Live music is probably happening tonight in your own town or a venue not far away. By all means, go for it!

And as for the "beautiful things…that crack your heart wide open…" of which Donna Tartt wrote; music delivers such things at a very generous rate. It's a trite consideration, I know, but it truly does seem just like yesterday when I headed out to the Dream Bowl to see the Dead. I can no longer do many of the enjoyable things permitted by youth, but I can say with complete honesty that the ability to enjoy music has not diminished one bit, if anything it's been increased; a very encouraging aspect of aging and a practical consideration when faced as we are with ever greater limits on our ability to move around. In a review in the *San Francisco Chronicle* of Michael Cunningham's *The Snow Queen*, Heller McAlpin comments: "At the heart of Cunningham's novels is a quest for not just meaning in life, but transcendence, even in the face of middle-age ennui and coming to terms with unfulfilled expectations." Transcendent moments abound in music and are beneficial in helping us deal with the "ennui," that is an inevitable part of the aging process. The carver of miniatures sees close, the sailor sees far. Even as our hearing begins to fail, this can be a time to retrain our listening skills to be more discriminating. And here's the best thing: finding those shining musical treasures does not involve the toil of prospecting. Those nuggets are all around on top of the ground needing, simply, to be picked up. There exists an ongoing source of talented donors working hard to dispense a steady stream of precious material, and we still have archives stockpiled with admirable efforts from all those musicians that have come before. How fortunate we are!

The Dream Bowl is no more, but rather than fret about its demise, we can honor it by celebrating its history and better yet by honoring current music venues so as to ensure that history does not repeat itself.

I remain thankful, however, that I finally got to go inside the Dream Bowl, a building that for a long period I had seen only from a distance and my being there satisfied the curiosity I once had as a young boy, while at the same time it increased my hunger to discover all the other stories that were part of its incredible history. And once inside, as a young man, the compelling impact of the music of Santana and the Grateful Dead helped begin another stage of wonder and adventure that has greatly enriched my life and continues to do so each and every day.

Acknowledgements

First and foremost, I'd like to thank my mother MaryEllen Simmons and my stepfather George Simmons whose generosity and support were always there, long before I started this project. Thanks to my wife Sylvia, the most caring person I know, for tons of computer expertise, unrelenting support, meticulous proofreading, and countless hours compiling copyright information. Thanks to son Michael for his thoughtful contribution from his musician's perspective. Thanks to daughter Christine who provided much-needed help setting up my laptop, which included finding very cool music-themed screen savers which were inspirational each time I booted up. Thanks to daughter Carol who is always brimming with fresh ideas and enthusiasm. Thanks to daughter Jennie whose genuine interest in the book and eagerness to see it completed, helped keep me energized.

Special thanks go to my sisters Paula Amen-Schmitt and Lynda Castell-Blanch, the first two people to see the manuscript. I was buoyed up considerably by Lynda's insightful comments. Paula constantly helped with all manner of useful information and suggestions, both practical and spiritual in nature. With her keen writer-and-poet's eye, I always wrote with the knowledge that she would see it, and I tried therefore to get it right. Without Paula, I don't meet Sandy Callahan. Without Lynda, I don't meet John Hannaford. Thanks to Napa historian and educator Lauren Coodley, author of several books, and with whom Paula shares a long and dear friendship, along with collaborative efforts on various books. Lauren offered both encouragement and helpful advice. Thanks to the author of *The Adventures of a Squeezebox Kid*, Ray Guadagni from Napa, whose friendship and swapped stories, shared on the book-writing trail, made the adventure more enjoyable. He also made possible our introduction to publisher Mary Catharine Nelson from Ideas into Books: Westview® who helped in many ways to bring the book to its final form. She worked extremely hard and saved me from committing stylistic and grammatical sins, improving the book immeasurably. Thanks to good friend and musician Doug Strobel for his interest, encouragement, and the much-appreciated kind words, carefully crafted, in his blurb for the book. Thanks to Cory Combs from the SF Jazz Center who took time from a very active life to write a very considerate blurb for the book. It meant a lot.

Various friends in Napa helped me with important details of the city's history: Peggy and Jerry Aaron, Bob Jenkins, Dan Oliveres, and Bill Kroplin. Thanks to them, and also to Don Townsend who patiently provided very useful information on several topics. Special thanks to Jeff Green for the photo on the back cover, his gift of the Coltrane DVD talked about in the book, and his enthusiasm regarding this book and everything and everyone he touches. Thanks to Larry Otis for providing first-hand information on what a "revue" looks like. Thanks to Don Kleid for loaning the book *Louie Louie* to Jeff who lent it to me. Thanks to Mike Soon for allowing me one last look at this historic place in which so many feelings had been generated and stories made. Thanks also to Don Kleid and his parents Alfred and Alna for graciously hosting an annual 4th of July get-together for the class of '65. Thanks to Joe and Debbie Cabral for their annual summer BBQ, both of which provide an over-flowing melting pot of oral history from which I was able to glean anecdotal gems that brightened the story. A special thanks to John Hannaford for telling us of his unique experiences at the Dream Bowl and elsewhere. The Traverso family, son Gene and his mother Genevive deserve thanks for giving me details that were important in getting the book started.

Thanks to Guido and Rosey Colla, the first people I interviewed, who kick-started the book and led me to important connections, and to Sandy and Bill Callahan who were absolutely essential in fleshing out the Dream Bowl's final chapter.

From Vallejo, thanks go to Babe Pallotta, care-giver Debbie who led me to Louise Birch, Richard Bean, and Kathy Rosengren whose help, in every instance, was crucially important. From Benicia, thanks to the shining spirit of Kiki Chiotti. Thanks to Raymond Sweeney who provided so much for the Country and Western years. Thanks to radio personalities David Gans and Gary Lambert, who filled in important details I would never have been able to ascertain on my own.

I needed lots of help getting copyright approval which is a complicated and costly endeavor. I got that help from people in offices who, I sensed, went out of their way to help me complete all that was required, so thanks to all of them. A special shout out to Lawrence Wong from Penguin Random House who handled quickly a slew of permissions requests.

More often than not, though, individual authors and publishers allowed me free permission to use quoted material, and I was delighted to receive prompt and encouraging emails from critic and author Greil Marcus, and Psychotherapist Francis Weller okaying the use of their material.

And lastly, closer to home, thanks to our cat Rocky. On those occasions, and there were plenty of them, when I was staring out our sliding glass doors from my writing table, struggling for the next idea, I'd feel Rocky rubbing his head against my right leg. It's hard to quantify just how great those little moments felt, and how helpful they were.

WORKS CITED

BOOKS

Ackerman, Diane. *A Natural History of the Senses*. Vintage Books, a division of Random House, Inc., 1990, p. 177.

Aklyer, Frank and Ed Enright, editors. *DownBeat – The Great Jazz Interviews: A 75th Anniversary Anthology*. "Critics in the Doghouse: Basie Examines Basie" by Count Basie as told to Dave Dexter Jr., July 1939, Hal Leonard Books, 2009, p. 16.

Austerlitz, Paul. Excerpt from *Jazz Consciousness: Music, Race, and Humanity*. © 2005 b Paul Austerlitz. Published by Wesleyan University Press. Used by permission.

Basie, Count, as told to Albert Murray. *Good Morning Blues*. Random House, Inc. Copyright © 1985 by Albert Murray and Count Basie Enterprises, Inc.

Brooks, Michael. "Glenn Cornick: From Jethro Tull to Wild Turkey." *Rock Guitarists: From the pages of Guitar Player Magazine*, Guitar Player Books, 1974, p. 49.

Byrne, David. *How Music Works*. McSweeney's, 2012, pp. 32+.

Campbell, Joseph, in conversation with Michael Toms. *An Open Life*. Larson Publications, 1988, p. 24.

Cash, Johnny with Patrick Carr. *CASH: THE AUTOBIOGRAPHY*. Copyright (c) 1997 by John R. Cash. Courtesy of HarperCollins Publishers.

Chandra, Vikram. *Geek Sublime: The Beauty of Code, the Code of Beauty*. Graywolf Press, 2014, pp. 87-88.

Davis, Miles with Quincy Troupe. *Miles: An Autobiography*. Copyright © 1989 by Miles Davis. Reprinted with the permission of Simon and Schuster, Inc. All rights reserved.

Dawidoff, Nicholas. *In the Country of Country: A Journey to the Roots of American Music*. Vintage Books, a division of Random House, Inc., 1998, pp. 172+.

Dewey, John. Excerpt(s) from *Art as Experience*. Copyright © 1934 by John Dewey; copyright renewed © 1961 by The Center for Dewey Studies. Used by permission of G. P. Putnam's Sons, an imprint of Penguin Publishing Group, a division of Penguin Random House LLC. All rights reserved.

Doctorow, E. L. *City of God.* A Plume Book, published by the Penguin Group, 2001, p. 139.

Feather, Leonard. *The Book of Jazz: A Guide to the Entire Field.* Paperback Library, Inc., 1961, p. 176.

Garcia, Jerry, Charles Reich and Jann Wenner. *Garcia: A Signpost to New Space.* Straight Arrow Books, 1972, p. 16.

Giddins, Gary. *Weather Bird: Jazz at the Dawn of Its Second Century.* By permission of Oxford University Press. 2004, pp. 132-133.

Gleason, Ralph. *Celebrating the Duke.* Copyright and re-print permission by Toby Gleason.

Godwin, Joscelyn (Editor). *Music, Mysticism and Magic: A Sourcebook.* Penguin Group (USA) Inc., 1986, pp. 51+.

Grant, Marshall, with Chris Zar. *I Was There When It Happened: My Life With Johnny Cash.* Cumberland House Publishing, Inc., 2006, pp. 33+.

Haas, Charlie. *The Enthusiast: A Novel.* Copyright © 2009 by Charlie Haas. Courtesy of HarperCollins Publishers. "P.S. Insights, Interviews & More…", p. 8.

Hall, Douglas Kent, from interviews by Sue C. Clark. *The Superstars In Their Own Words.* Music Sales Corporation, 1970, pp. 5+.

Hampton, Lionel, with James Haskins. *Hamp: An Autobiography.* Warner Books, Inc., 1989.

Hart, Mickey, Jay Stevens and Fredric Lieberman. *Drumming at the Edge of Magic: A Journey into the Spirit of Percussion.* HarperCollins, 1990, pp. 102+.

Hilburn, Robert. *Johnny Cash: The Life.* Little Brown and Company, 2013, pp. 547+.

Hofstadter, Douglas. *Gödel, Escher, Bach: An Eternal Golden Braid.* Basic Books, Inc., 1979, p. 246.

Homer. *The Iliad of Homer.* Trans. Richard Lattimore. The University of Chicago Press, 1951, pp. 387+.

Jung, C. G. *The Spirit in Man, Art, and Literature.* Reproduced with permission of PRINCETON UNIVERSITY PRESS in the format Book via Copyright Clearance Center.

Kahn, Ashley. Excerpt(s) from *A Love Supreme: The Making of John Coltrane's Masterpiece.* Copyright © 2002 by Ashley Kahn. Used by permission of Viking Books, an imprint of Penguin Publishing

Group, a division of Penguin Random House LLC. All rights reserved.

Kiberd, Declan. *Ulysses and Us: The Art of Everyday Life in Joyce's Masterpiece.* W. W. Norton & Company, Inc., 2010, pp. 168-169.

Krause, Bernie. *The Great Animal Orchestra: Finding the Origins of Music in the World's Wild Places.* Little, Brown and Company, a division of Hachette Book Group, Inc., 2012: pp. 10+.

Kreutzmann, Bill, and Benjy Eisen. *My Three Decades of Drumming, Dreams, and Drugs with the Grateful Dead* © 2015 by Bill Kreutzmann and Benjy Eisen. Reprinted by permission of St. Martin's Press. All rights reserved. p. 77.

LaFaro-Fernández, Helene. *Jade Visions: The Life and Music of Scott LaFaro.* University of North Texas Press, 2009, p. 133.

Levitin, Daniel. Excerpt(s) from *This is Your Brain on Music: The Science of a Human Obsession.* Copyright © 2006 by Daniel J. Levitin. Used by permission of Dutton, an imprint of Penguin Publishing Group, a division of Penguin Random House LLC. All rights reserved.

Lund, Midge, with Kiki Chiotti. *The Musicians: A Chronicle of* *Vallejo's Bands, 1920-1949.* Printed by Rick Foley, The Copy Shop, Benicia, CA. 1988, pp. 38+.

Mannes, Elena. *The Power of Music: Pioneering Discoveries in the New Science of Song.* Bloomsbury Publishing Inc., 2011, p. 94.

Marcus, Greil (Editor). *Stranded: Rock and Roll for a Desert Island.* Prologue: "The Sea's Endless, Awful Rhythm & Me Without Even a Dirty Picture" by Nick Tosches. Da Capo Press, Inc., 1996, pp. xxi+.

Marsh, Dave. *Louie Louie.* Hyperion, 1993, pp. 57+.

Meyer, Marvin, translator. *The Secret Teachings of Jesus: Four Gnostic Gospels.* Random House, Inc., Gospel of Thomas, Saying 112.

Meyers, Brian. *To Be The Play.* Fishergate Publishing Company, Inc., 1978, pp. 21+.

Molendijk, Arie. *Friedrich Max Müller and the Sacred Books of the East.* By permission of Oxford University Press. 2016, p. 70.

Plato. *The Republic.* Trans. Benjamin Jowett. Dover Publications, Inc., 2000, p. 73.

Ratliff, Ben. Excerpts from "Two Concepts Going" from

Michael Amen

COLTRANE. Copyright © 2007 by Ben Ratliff. Reprinted by permission of Farrar, Straus and Giroux. p. 129+.

Reid, Thomas. *An Inquiry into the Human Mind on the Principles of Common Sense*. Edited by Derek Brookes. Reproduced with permission of Pennsylvania State University Press in the format Book via Copyright Clearance Center, 2000, pp. 14+.

Richardson, Peter. *A Cultural History of the Grateful Dead: No Simple Highway*. St. Martin's Press, 2015, p. 86.

Ross, Alex. Excerpt from "Doctor Faust: *Schoenberg, Debussy, and Atonality*" from "Part I: 1900-1933 from THE REST IS NOISE. Copyright © 2007 by Alex Ross. Reprinted by permission of Farrar, Straus and Giroux. pp. 45+.

Sacks, Oliver. *Musicophilia: Tales of Music and the Brain*. Alfred A. Knopf, a division of Random House, 2007, p. 251.

Schopenhauer, Arthur. *The World as Will and Representation – Volume 1*. Dover Publications, Inc., 1969, pp. 256+.

Smith, Adam. *Powers of Mind*. Random House, Inc., 1975, p. 232.

Stricklin, Al, with Jon McConal. *My Years with Bob Wills*. The Naylor Company, 1976, pp. 20+.

Tartt, Donna. *The Goldfinch*. Little, Brown and Company, Hachette Book Group, 2013, p. 757.

Taylor, Thomas. *Iamblichus' Life of Pythagoras*. Published by Inner Traditions International and Bear & Company, ©1986. All rights reserved.
http://www.Innertraditions.com
Reprinted with permission of the publisher.

Van Dyke, Henry. *The Music Lover*. Moffat, Yard & Company, 1907, pp. 1+.

Wein, George, with Nate Chinen. *Myself Among Others: A Life in Music*. Copyright © 2003. Reprinted by permission of Da Capo Press, an imprint of Perseus Books, LLC, a subsidiary of Hatchette Book Group, Inc., pp. 356-357.

Weller, Francis. *The Wild Edge of Sorrow: Rituals of Renewal and the Sacred Work of Grief*. North Atlantic Books, 2015.

Wilkie, Brian and James Hurt. *Literature of the Western World, Volume II: Neoclassicism Through The Modern Period*. Macmillan Publishing Company, 1992, pp. 891+.

Wingell, Richard. *Writing about Music: An Introductory Guide.* Prentice-Hall, Inc., 1997, p. 17.

DVDs

John Coltrane: Live in '60, '61 & '65. DVD booklet insert comments by Ashley Kahn. Reelin' In The Years® Productions LLC, 2007, p. 17+.

Eat That Question: Frank Zappa In His Own Words. Directed by Thorsten Schütte, Sony Picture Classics, 2016.

"Episode Four – The True Welcome." *Jazz – A Film by Ken Burns*, directed by Ken Burns, PBS Distribution, Florentine Films, 2000.

"Episode Five – Swing: Pure Pleasure." *Jazz – A Film by Ken Burns*, directed by Ken Burns, PBS Distribution, Florentine Films, 2000.

"Episode Nine – The Adventure." *Jazz – A Film by Ken Burns*, directed by Ken Burns, PBS Distribution, Florentine Films, 2000.

The Grateful Dead: Anthem to Beauty. Directed by Jeremy Marre, Eagle Rock Entertainment, Ltd., 2005.

The Making of the Dark Side of the Moon. Directed by Matthew

Longfellow, Eagle Vision, a division of Eagle Rock Entertainment, Ltd., 2003.

ELECTRONIC SOURCES (WEB PUBLICATIONS & VIDEOS)

"About Us." *Caltest Analytical Laboratory*, par. 1, www.caltestlabs.com/AboutUs.aspx.

"Bob Wills." *Wikipedia, The Free Encyclopedia.* 1.5 – Swing era, par. 2, en.wikipedia.org/wiki/Bob_Wills.

Flippo, Chet. "Ray Charles Should Be in Country Music Hall of Fame: Why? Because He Belongs There." *CMT News: NASHVILLE SKYLINE*, 26 Aug. 2004, par. 4, www.cmt.com/news/1490588/nashville-skyline-ray-charles-should-be-in-country-music-hall-of-fame/.

"Frédéric Chopin." *Wikipedia, The Free Encyclopedia*, par. 1+,

en.wikipedia.net.ru/wiki/Fr%C3%A9d%C3%A9ric_Chopin#George_Sand.

Freeman, Doug. "Dirty Laundry: Hey, you got soul in my country." *The Austin Chronicle*, 18 September 2008, Daily Music, pars. 1-2,

285

Michael Amen

www.austinchronicle.com/daily/
music/2008-09-18/675161/.

Greene, Andy. "Rolling Stone at
50: Interviewing Bob Dylan."
Rolling Stone, 17 February 2017,
Music News, par. 3,
https://www.rollingstone.com/
music/music-news/rolling-
stone-at-50-interviewing-bob-
dylan-193285/.

"Henry van Dyke, Jr." *Wikipedia,*
The Free Encyclopedia. 1-
Biography, pars. 4+,
en.wikipedia.org/wiki/Henry_va
n_Dyke,_Jr.

"Jerry Garcia Interview 'The
History of Rock 'N' Roll'",
YouTube,
www.youtube.com/watch?v=N
VkkbJ_KI2Y.

"Jerry Garcia The Last
Interview." *YouTube*,
www.youtube.com/watch?v=wu
V-DDreOq4.

Kesey, Ken. AZ QUOTES.
www.azquotes.com/quote/1117
367.

Kesey, Ken. AZ QUOTES.
www.azquotes.com/quote/3663
05.

Key, Jerry. "The Key Brothers."
A Rockabilly Hall of Fame®
Presentation. pars. 3-6,
www.rockabillyhall.com/KeyBro
thers.html.

"KROW Becomes KABL
Monday, May 11, 1959."
California Historical Radio Society:
Bay Area Radio Museum, pars. 6+,
bayarearadio.org/audio/kabl/kro
w-becomes-kabl_may-
1959.shtml.

Metzger, John. "Traveling So
Many Roads with Bob
Matthews." *The Music Box,* vol.
12, #7, July 2005, pars. 2+,
www.musicbox-
online.com/bobm-
int.html#axzz4mj8t6MAl.

"Modern Sounds in Country and
Western Music." *Wikipedia, The*
Free Encyclopedia. 3-Recording,
par. 3,
en.wikipedia.org/wiki/Modern_
Sounds_in_Country_and_Wester
n_Music.

"Pink Floyd Clare Torry "The
Great Gig in the Sky" interview."
YouTube,
m.youtube.com/watch?v=mIW7
xZSlZoM.

"Sitting on Top of the World."
Wikipedia, The Free Encyclopedia,
par. 1,
en.wikipedia.org/wiki/Sitting_on
_Top_of_the_World.

INTERVIEWS

Personal Interviews: Richard
Bean, Louise Birch, Randy
Callahan, Sandy Callahan, Kiki
Chiotti, Guido Colla, Rosey
Colla, John Hannaford, Larry

Otis, Kathy Rosengren, Raymond Sweeney, Gene Traverso, Genevive Traverso

Cranshaw, Bob. Interview by Nancy Wilson. *Jazz Profiles*, KCSM.

Gimble, Johnny. Radio interview.

Moore, Tiny. Radio interview.

Perkins, Carl. Interview by Terry Gross. *Fresh Air*, KQED.

Silver, Horace. Interview by Nancy Wilson. *Jazz Profiles*, KCSM.

Waldron, Mal. Interview by Art Sato. *In Your Ear*, KPFA.

Weir, Bob. Interviews by David Gans (2). *Deadhead Hour*, KPFA.

JOURNALS

Gleason, Ralph J. "Like a Rolling Stone." *American Scholar Journal*. Autumn 1967.

Hanley, Ryan Patrick. "Rousseau's Virtue Epistemology." *Journal of the History of Philosophy*. The Johns Hopkins University Press, 50.2 (April 2012): p. 243.

Meriwether, Nicholas (Editor). *First Fusion – A New Renaissance*. A Commemorative Journal Celebrating the Debut of First Fusion: A New Renaissance. A Benefit for the Marin Symphony Orchestra featuring Bob Weir and Giancarlo Aquilanti, May 7, 2011.

LINER NOTES

Bob Wills and His Texas Playboys. *For The Last Time*. United Artists Records, Inc., 1974. Liner notes by Charles R. Townsend.

Cash, Johnny. *American IV: The Man Comes Around*. American Recordings, 2002. Liner notes by Johnny Cash.

Chan, Charlie, et al. *Jazz at Massey Hall*. Fantasy Records, 1962. Liner notes by Grover Sales, Jr.

Coltrane, John. *A Love Supreme*. MCA Records, Inc., 1995 (Re-release date). Liner notes by John Coltrane.

Coltrane, John. *Ascension*. Impulse!, a product of ABC-Paramount Records, Inc., 1965. Quotation on back cover by Leroi Jones.

Coltrane, John. *Coltrane Live at Birdland*. Impulse Records, a product of ABC Paramount Records, Inc., 1964. Liner notes by Leroi Jones.

Coltrane, John. *Coltrane "Live" At The Village Vanguard*. ABC Paramount – Impulse Records, Stereo A-10, 1961. Liner notes by Nat Hentoff.

Coltrane, John. *Standard Coltrane*. Prestige Records Inc., 1962. Liner notes by Robert Levin.

Dolphy, Eric. *Last Date*. Limelight Records, 1964. Liner notes by Nat Hentoff.

Goodman, Benny, et al. *The Famous 1938 Carnegie Hall Jazz Concert*. Sony Music Entertainment Inc., 1999 (Re-release date). Liner notes by Irving Kolodin.

Grateful Dead. *Cornell 5/8/77*. Rhino Entertainment Company, a Warner Music Group Company, 2017. Liner notes by Nicholas G. Meriwether.

Grateful Dead. *Skull and Roses*. Warner Bros. Records, 2001 (Re-release date). Liner notes by Paul Nichols & Hale Milgrim.

Rollins, Sonny. *The Bridge*. RCA Victor Studios, 1962. Liner notes by George Avakian.

Zappa, Frank. *Jazz From Hell*. Rykodisc, 1986. Liner notes.

LYRICS & RECORDINGS

Anderson, Ian. "My God." Words and Music by Ian Anderson. Copyright © 1971 Chrysalis Music Ltd. Copyright renewed. All Rights Administered by BMG Rights Management (US) LLC. All Rights Reserved. Used by Permission. Reprinted by Permission of Hal Leonard LLC.

Cash, Johnny. "Big River." Words and Music by John R. Cash. © 1958 (Renewed 1986) HOUSE OF CASH, INC. (BMI). All Rights Administered by BMG RIGHTS MANAGEMENT (US) LLC. All Rights Reserved. Used by Permission. Reprinted by Permission of Hal Leonard LLC.

The Drifters. "Save The Last Dance For Me." Lyrics by Doc Pomus, music by Mort Shuman, Single, Atlantic Records, 1960.

Grateful Dead. "Help on the Way." Words by Robert Hunter. Music by Jerry Garcia. Copyright © 1975 ICE NINE PUBLISHING CO., INC. Copyright Renewed. All Rights Administered by UNIVERSAL MUSIC CORP. All Rights Reserved. Used by Permission. Reprinted by Permission of Hal Leonard LLC.

Grateful Dead. "New Potato Caboose." Words and Music by

Philip Lesh and Robert M. Peterson. Copyright © 1968 ICE NINE PUBLISHING CO., INC. Copyright Renewed. All Rights Administered by UNIVERSAL MUSIC CORP. All Rights Reserved. Used by Permission. Reprinted by Permission of Hal Leonard LLC.

Grateful Dead. "Scarlet Begonias." Words by Robert Hunter. Music by Jerry Garcia. Copyright © 1974 ICE NINE PUBLISHING CO., INC. Copyright Renewed. All Rights Administered by UNIVERSAL MUSIC CORP. All Rights Reserved. Used by Permission. Reprinted by Permission of Hal Leonard LLC.

Grateful Dead. "Wharf Rat." Words by Robert Hunter. Music by Jerry Garcia. Copyright © 1971 ICE NINE PUBLISHING CO., INC. Copyright Renewed. All Rights Administered by UNIVERSAL MUSIC CORP. All Rights Reserved. Used by Permission. Reprinted by Permission of Hal Leonard LLC.

Pomus, Doc and Mort Shuman. "Save The Last Dance For Me." Words and Music by Doc Pomus and Mort Shuman. © 1960 (Renewed) Pomus Songs Inc. and Mort Shuman Songs LLP. All Rights for Pomus Songs Inc. Administered by Spirit One Music. All Rights Reserved. Used by Permission. Reprinted by Permission of Hal Leonard LLC.

Weir, Bob. Introduction to "Truckin'. *Grateful Dead - Europe '72*, Warner Bros. Records, 1972.

"Where or When" (from "BABES IN ARMS"). Words by LORENZ HART. Music by RICHARD RODGERS. © 1937 (Renewed) WB MUSIC CORP. and WILLIAMSON MUSIC CO. All Rights Reserved. Used by Permission of ALFRED PUBLISHING, LLC.

PERIODICALS

"101 Objects that Made America: America in the World." *Smithsonian.* Volume 44, Number 7, November 2013. Copyright 2013 Smithsonian Institution. Reprinted with permission from Smithsonian Enterprises. All rights reserved. Reproduction in any medium is strictly prohibited without permission from Smithsonian Institution.

Cohen, Rich. "Remembering the unmatched straight talk of The Sports Writers on TV." *Sports Illustrated*, 28 Apr. 2014, p. 53.

Conrad, Ariane. "Water, Water Everywhere: Ran Ortner's Love Affair With The Sea." *The Sun*, Issue 438, The Sun Publishing Company, Inc., June 2012, p. 9.

"Contributors." *The Sun*, Issue 458, The Sun Publishing Company, Inc., February 2014, p. 0.

Davis, Lynn. "And So On." *The Sun*, Issue 454, The Sun Publishing Company, Inc., October 2013, p. 22.

DuShane, Tony. "Madeline Tasquin is a creative tour de force." *San Francisco Chronicle* by Hearst Corporation. 12 November 2014. Reproduced with permission of Hearst Corporation in the format Book via Copyright Clearance Center.

Feather, Leonard. "Buddy Rich: Blindfold Test." *down beat*, Vol. 34, No. 8, Maher Publications, 20 Apr. 1967, p. 44.

Haas, Charlie. "New Life for the Grateful Dead." *New West*, Vol. 4, No. 25, New York Magazine Company, Inc., 17 Dec. 1979.

Hamlin, Jesse. "Benny Goodman's music still swings." *San Francisco Chronicle* by Hearst Corporation. 26 May 2009. Reproduced with permission of Hearst Corporation in the format Book via Copyright Clearance Center.

Hilburn, Robert. "Johnny Cash." *Rolling Stone*, Issue 129, Wenner Media, LLC, 1 Mar. 1973, pars. 6+.

Hildebrand, Lee. "Tommy Igoe sheds 'big band' albatross." *San Francisco Chronicle* by Hearst Corporation. Sunday Datebook for July 12-19, 2014, p. 29.

Reproduced with permission of Hearst Corporation in the format Book via Copyright Clearance Center.

Hunter, Pam. "Memories of the Dream Bowl: A great musical era relived–." *Napa Register*, February 24, 1973, pp. 1-D+.

Jones, Chad. "'Sea of Reeds': Josh Kornbluth talks, plays music." *San Francisco Chronicle* by Hearst Corporation. 1 January 2014. Reproduced with permission of Hearst Corporation in the format Book via Copyright Clearance Center.

Karp, Evan. "SFJazz Poetry Festival spotlights U.S. ethnicities." *San Francisco Chronicle* by Hearst Corporation. 2 April 2014. Reproduced with permission of Hearst Corporation in the format Book via Copyright Clearance Center.

McAlpin, Heller. "'The Snow Queen,' by Michael Cunningham review." *San Francisco Chronicle* by Hearst Corporation. 6 June 2014. Reproduced with permission of Hearst Corporation in the format Book via Copyright Clearance Center.

O'Donohue, John. "The Question Holds The Lantern." *The Sun*, Issue 407, The Sun Publishing Company, Inc., Nov. 2009, p. 37.

Powell, Caleb. "High Plains Drifter: Poe Ballantine on Writing, Madness, and His Journey From Vagabond to Family Man." *The Sun*, Issue 458, The Sun Publishing Company, Inc., February 2014, p. 12.

Schneckloth, Tim. "Merle Haggard Country Jazz Messiah." *down beat*, Vol. 47, No. 5, Maher Publications, May 1980, pp. 17+.

Sievert, Jon. "Jerry Garcia." *Guitar Player*, GPI Publications, Oct. 1978, pp. 118+.

Wilner, Paul. "Jazz 101: An improvisational history." *San Francisco Chronicle* by Hearst Corporation. 13 January 2013, Special Commemorative Section: SFJAZZ CENTER, pp. L4+. Reproduced with permission of Hearst Corporation in the format Book via Copyright Clearance Center.

Wolff, Alexander. "Leading Off - IN REMEMBRANCE: Nelson Mandela 1918—2013." *Sports Illustrated*, 16 Dec. 2013.

RADIO SHOWS

Introduction of the Gyoto Monks by Houston Smith on a KPFA Special Presentation.

Travus T. Hipp on KSAN.

"Mary Travers & Friend" interview with Frank Zappa on nationally syndicated radio show.

TV SHOWS

"Benny Goodman: Adventures in the Kingdom of Swing." *American Masters*, KQED, 29 Dec. 2000.

"Mel Brooks: Make A Noise." *American Masters*, KQED, 20 May 2013.

"The Other One: The Long Strange Trip of Bob Weir." A Netflix documentary, Next Entertainment, 2014.

"West Pole." KQED, August 16, 1968

UNPUBLISHED WRITINGS

Lambert, Gary. Email to Mike Amen, January 13, 2012.

Papenburg, Michael. "Rising Above – improvisation in music."

IMAGES

Coffee mug with Dream Bowl poster courtesy of Dennis Loren at "Cahoots Graffix™ and Posters."

CPSIA information can be obtained
at www.ICGtesting.com
Printed in the USA
FSHW020117031119
63627FS

9 781628 801248